Library
Research
Skills
Handbook

Myrtle S. Bolner
Doris B. Dantin
Ruth C. Murray
Louisiana State University

 KENDALL/HUNT PUBLISHING COMPANY
2460 Kerper Boulevard P.O. Box 539 Dubuque, Iowa 52004-0539

Library Research Skills Handbook is dedicated to the many students at Louisiana State University who have taken the Library Research Methods and Materials course at Louisiana State University. They have been our inspiration for developing this handbook.

Formerly entitled *Books, Libraries, and Research*

Copyright © 1991 by Kendall/Hunt Publishing Company

ISBN 0-8403-6466-0

Printed in the United States of America
10 9 8 7 6 5 4 3

Contents

7 GUIDE TO BIOGRAPHICAL SOURCES   188

8 FINDING AND USING INDEXES AND ABSTRACTS   204

9 GUIDE TO GOVERNMENT PUBLICATIONS   262

INTRODUCTION TO ONLINE DATABASES 284

PREPARING THE RESEARCH PAPER 300

Preface

After Alice stepped through the Looking Glass and retrieved the King and Queen from the burning embers in the fireplace, she heard the King say: " 'The *horror* of that moment, . . . I shall never, *never* forget it!' 'You will though,' the Queen said, 'if you don't make a memorandum of it.' "[1] And so it is with learning facts in college. Psychological findings confirm the Queen's insight: college graduates forget 90% of the facts they have learned in college within five years unless they are reintroduced to them in a meaningful way. We live in an information age in which we are constantly being bombarded by various information media. It is ironic, therefore, that one of the concerns of educators is that individuals are becoming information illiterates. The concern is not that students "forget" facts, but that today's adults do not know how to locate, evaluate, and use information. It is in this context that acquiring information skills becomes such an important element of the college student's education.

Information is not confined within the walls of libraries; it encompasses a variety of systems and services: schools, books, newspapers, magazines, television, electronic databases. However, libraries have always been a key link in the information chain. They serve as immense reservoirs for knowledge and information, collecting, organizing, and making accessible humankind's accumulated learning about the universe and its inhabitants. Information in libraries can enlighten us as to the physical environment, the political and social order, the scientific and technical accomplishments, and, indeed, all aspects of life. Libraries have made it possible for humans to preserve and locate those elements of the past which contribute to the future growth and development of civilization. Viewed in that light, it is clear that learning library skills is an essential part of the education process.

In order to use the library's riches to their fullest the user must have access to the library's contents, "learn the library's language," learn how information is organized, and have some ability to use that knowledge. In other words, the user must become *library literate*. It is our aim to provide a handbook that will serve a threefold purpose: (1) make library users aware of the different kinds of information that is available in libraries, (2) provide them with a guide to the means of accessing information, and (3) help them to evaluate and use information productively. The authors recognize that along with basic retrieval skills the user must acquire what is the most important ingredient for the effective use of the library—the ability to analyze and use information critically. Critical thinking in the context of library research involves a certain attitude and disposition on the part of the information user, a willingness to challenge the propositions and assertions encountered as one taps the library's resources. Most importantly, critical thinking calls for the testing of values and beliefs in the light of knowledge and evidence discovered in the course of an information search.

The book discusses the ways information is organized in libraries and the principal tools for accessing information—library catalogs, reference books, indexes, government publications, and online databases. The authors have suggested many titles of reference books, indexes, and electronic databases on a variety of subjects. The more frequently used sources are described in some detail while others are simply listed.

An earlier version of this book was published under the title *Books, Libraries, and Research*. This new version and new title reflect a change in authorship as well as a change to reflect new technologies in information storage and retrieval. The authors are grateful to Mary G. Hauer for her contributions to the earlier

---

1. Lewis Carroll, *Alice in Wonderland and Through the Looking Glass* (Cleveland: World Syndicate, n.d.) 124, Ch. 1.

work, and particularly for suggesting the format and arrangement of the first edition of *Books, Libraries and Research*.

We wish to thank the staff of the Louisiana State University Libraries, and in particular the Library Instruction staff for suggestions. Special thanks are due Denise Sokolowski, Librarian, University of Maryland, European Division, for her many excellent suggestions and continuing interest in the book.

Introduction

The student will find that library research skills are essential to achieving success in the courses of the college curriculum and that the library is, in effect, an extension of the classroom. Yet, many students lack the skills necessary to use the information resources which their college or university provides. One of the best ways to acquire library research skills is through specific instruction, and many institutions provide formal courses designed to familiarize students with library resources and research techniques. In other instances, librarians and instructors cooperate to design library research strategies that support classroom instruction.

This handbook is arranged so that it may be used either in a step-by-step progression as in a formal course or as a reference book by library users with specific research needs. The first chapter provides a brief introduction to the evolution of libraries and information storage and retrieval. Chapters 2 and 3 provide an overall view of library services and materials. The organization of materials in libraries is discussed in Chapter 4. Chapter 5 is devoted to an explanation of retrieving library materials through the library catalog. Chapters 6 through 10 concentrate on specific information sources: reference books, biographical sources, indexes, government publications, and online databases. Chapter 11 provides a systematic guide to planning, researching, writing, and documenting a research paper. Included are a number of clear models for documenting research and examples of note and bibliographic form. The forms recommended are based on the *MLA Handbook for Writers of Research Papers* (3rd ed. New York: MLA, 1988). The questions and exercises at the ends of the chapters are designed to provide a review of the material covered in the chapter and to reinforce learning by giving students hands on experience with the library resources essential to successful research. Some chapters contain several exercises. It is expected that the instructor will choose those exercises which they think are most appropriate for their students.

The authors have chosen to use the topic, "artificial intelligence," to illustrate the many facets of information retrieval. Where that topic was not appropriate to the sources under discussion, other subject headings were used.

The authors' use of the term paper concept is based on their experience in teaching library research methods at Louisiana State University. The student selects, or is assigned, a topic which serves as the framework for the project. Other steps are the formulation of a thesis statement, preparation of a working outline, gathering information, evaluating the relevance and worth of the information, and compiling and documenting the information. The final product varies: it may be a brief research paper or an annotated bibliography. The worksheets located at the end of the book are used to record the information that the student gathers on the topic. The worksheets serve the same purpose as note cards which are traditionally used to record information for a research topic. Additionally, the worksheets provide space for the student to record his/her research methodology. This serves to make students aware of the process used to locate appropriate materials which can be a helpful aid in the future.

The concept of using a research paper to provide students with an opportunity to collect, organize, evaluate, and use information is the methodology which the authors have found to be effective in teaching research skills. Once students have mastered this technique they should be able to vary their research activity according to subsequent demands, regardless of the topic involved.

College and university libraries vary from simple collections of mostly paper materials located in a single room to very large and complex collections located in multiple buildings and in information networks beyond the library. Similarly, the format of library materials ranges from the familiar paper format of books and magazines to highly technical information sources in a variety of formats. Elementary library research for information in paper format is often baffling; when one adds retrieval of information stored in electronic format, the task seems almost overwhelming. In this book students are introduced to information in a variety of formats, for example both the card catalog and the online catalog are discussed in great detail. Students will recognize that advances in electronics and communications will continue to change the way that information is stored and retrieved. It is expected that the foundations acquired in using this handbook will enable students to progress to more complex information systems as these evolve.

Development
of Books and Libraries

Figure 1.1. Clay tablet, c2350 B.C., found at Jokha in ancient Babylonia. A temple tablet somewhat larger than the average, it is a list of produce supplied to the temple.

A PREVIEW

This chapter traces the development of information storage and retrieval from the stone age to the electronic age. Information storage and retrieval has progressed from crude writings on cave walls to highly technical electronic systems such as online databases and CD-ROMs. An objective of this chapter is to show the development of books and libraries as part of the large picture of the evolution of information storage and retrieval.

As high technology invades the sphere of information storage and retrieval, it is difficult to imagine that information storage actually began with primitive images crudely engraved on cave walls. A great span of time separates the fossil print carved indelibly in rock and the laser disk systems that are now almost as common as printed books. Yet, both reflect the human need to receive and process information. The quest that led our primitive ancestors to transform grunts and gestures into speech also led to the development of highly technical ways of preserving and communicating knowledge. In today's highly mechanized society we identify information processing with the computer, but information processing actually encompasses all of the ways that humans create, select, store, and transmit knowledge.

Information processing began with the oral tradition. Long before human beings could write they communicated by means of the spoken word. Culture, traditions, and historical accounts passed from generation to generation in stories, folklore, songs, and poetry. The limitations of an oral means of communication unassisted by technology are self-evident. Speech can only be preserved by repetition. Not only is the possibility for distortion great, but only those in close proximity can receive the information. Writing, considered by many to be the greatest human accomplishment, developed because of the need to record and preserve information uninhibited by limitations of memory and distance.

DEVELOPMENT OF WRITING

Writing began with pictures depicting the spoken word and culminated in the alphabet, a system for communicating through written words. We know about our ancestors because that information was preserved in the form of pictures on cave walls. Approximately 40,000 years elapsed between the crude cave wall drawings and the development of the approximately 50 alphabets presently in use. There were three distinct stages in the evolution of writing: (1) *pictographic*, (2) *ideographic*, and (3) *phonetic*. In the pictographic stage simple pictures of objects were drawn mostly on natural surfaces such as cave walls. Ideographs were drawings representing an idea. For example, a drawing of an eye with tears dropping from it represented sorrow. In the phonetic stage symbols came to represent linguistic elements. Phonetic writing has passed through three distinct stages: (1) *word symbol*, with a single symbol representing a word; (2) *syllabic*, with a symbol representing each syllable; and (3) *alphabetic*, with a single symbol representing a single sound. It is difficult to identify the dates of each stage which led to the development of the alphabet, especially since some cultures such as the Chinese still use an ideographic form of writing. The Indian tribes of North America used pictographic and ideographic forms of writing until recent times.

The Sumerians who lived in southern Mesopotamia were the first to develop a system of writing that was pre-alphabetic. The writing was done on clay tablets using a stylus which produced a wedge-shaped impression. This style of writing, *cuneiform*, began about 5000 B.C. From the Sumerians, writing spread to neighboring cultures with each culture borrowing symbols from the other. The Babylonians and Assyrians in turn adapted and advanced cuneiform writing.

The Egyptians developed a system of writing known as *hieroglyphic* about 4000 B.C. Like early cuneiform, early hieroglyphic writing was ideographic. Phonetic writing using hieroglyphics dates from about 3000 B.C. As writing spread to other cultures it was simplified. The Phoenicians, prompted by trade and travel, borrowed from the Egyptians and Assyrians to devise a system of writing using 20 to 30 characters. The Greeks, refining the system of the Phoenicians, were the first to develop a system of vowel sounds. The Roman alphabet, the parent of the English alphabet, came to us by way of Etruria (modern Italy) and Greece. The Romans reduced the alphabet to a manageable 23 letters. The Roman alphabet spread over Europe, and, except for the addition of three letters and changes in the form of script, it has remained unchanged.

DEVELOPMENT OF BOOKS AND LIBRARIES

Information processing includes not only writing but the storing of information. Without written records, we would have very little knowledge of the past and nothing on which to base the future. Throughout history knowledge has been accumulated, organized, and transmitted in libraries. The word library comes from the word *liber*, meaning book, or collection of books. The libraries of today, are not merely collections of books; rather they are collections of information. In like manner, the first "libraries" were not collections of books. As we have seen, information was recorded on natural forms—cave walls, bones, pieces of bark. Later small clay tablets and larger pieces of stone were used as recording devices. Information storage began with the writing that was preserved on cave walls. A more systematic way of collecting and preserving information was developed when clay tablets were put into organized collections. These collections of clay tablets were actually the first "libraries." (See Figure 1.1.)

While the people of Mesopotamia, the Sumerians, the Babylonians, and the Assyrians were writing on clay, the ancient Egyptians were writing on papyrus. Papyrus was made from the reed-like papyrus plant which grew along the Nile

River. The stems were pressed into sheets which were joined end to end to form a scroll. Papyrus was extremely perishable, so we have little of it extant today. The oldest papyrus discovered by archaeologists is dated circa 2500 B.C. Papyrus was widely used in the countries bordering the Mediterranean Sea, most notably Egypt, Greece, and Rome, from about 500 B.C. to 300 A.D. The great libraries of ancient Egypt, Greece, and Rome consisted of papyrus rolls. The greatest collection of scrolls in the ancient world was in Alexandria, Egypt. The collection numbered about 700,000 scrolls and was reputed to have included a copy of every scroll in existence. No one knows the fate of the library, but speculation is that it was destroyed by Christians around 391 A.D. in their campaign against pagan literature.

A refined form of animal skin, parchment, is thought to have been invented at Pergamum (which is now Turkey) circa 197–159 B.C. The library at Pergamum was built in order to compete with the library at Alexandria. In retaliation the Egyptians placed an embargo on papyrus and cut off the supply of writing material to the inhabitants of Pergamum. The people, forced to find a substitute for papyrus materials, invented parchment. Made from sheepskin pressed into thin sheets, parchment sheets could not be joined together to form scrolls like papyrus. At first the sheets were rolled like papyrus, but later they were folded over so that they resembled folded note cards. These were used extensively by the Greeks and Romans until about 300 A.D. when the codex gained widespread use among the early Christians. The codex was made of vellum or parchment leaves stitched together and covered with thin boards held together with leather thongs in much the same manner as the modern book. By 400 A.D. the codex had replaced the papyrus roll.

The Greeks are credited with establishing the first public libraries in Athens about 500 B.C. The period was marked by a high level of culture and a great interest in education and learning. The library was established to provide the public with literature. Aristotle founded a library at his Lyceum which contained the most extensive collection in Greece. After the Roman invasion of Greece, what remained of the collection was taken to Rome in 88 B.C.

Rome had no libraries during its first 500 years. Roman soldiers brought back scrolls taken from Greek libraries, but most of the scrolls ended up in the homes of the wealthy. Rome's first public library was built about 33 B.C. There were 26 public libraries in Rome in 476 A.D. when the Vandals destroyed all signs of Roman learning and culture and plunged Rome into the Dark Ages. Little remains of all the great papyrus libraries of ancient Greece, Egypt, and Rome.

THE MIDDLE AGES

The fall of the Roman Empire was followed by a decline in educational and artistic activity which lasted until the late 1400s. Very little learning took place and classical culture and literature were preserved mainly in the monasteries of the Roman Catholic Church. Monasteries were founded in Italy following the fall of Rome. Most of the monasteries contained a *scriptorium*, a room where the monks laboriously copied by hand whatever ancient manuscripts they could collect—religious tracts, the Bible, Latin grammars, and a few secular books.

Beginning with the sixth century A.D., the copying of manuscripts had become a highly developed art form which lasted until the 1400s and the invention of printing. Copying had evolved from a laborious task to a delicate art which reached its full glory in illuminated manuscripts. Illumination consisted of embellishing the beautifully lettered script with designs of magnificent color and artistry.

MODERN LIBRARIES

The first modern European universities appeared about 1100 as the Dark Ages were ending. There was at this time a renewed interest in classical learning accompanied by an increased demand for books. This demand for reading material resulted in two events which changed civilization—the use of paper as a writing material and the invention of the printing press.

Paper had been invented by the Chinese about 105 A.D., but it was a thousand years before this great invention reached Europe. Paper was used in Baghdad in about 800 and in Spain in the 1100s. The introduction of paper in Europe coincided with the increased demand for books which accompanied the beginning of the Renaissance in the late 1400s.

For centuries books were written slowly and laboriously by hand. It took months and even years to hand-copy a book. Consequently, books were available only to a few privileged scholars. The increased demand for books during the Renaissance caused an awareness of the need to produce books more quickly. A form of hand-printing had been developed in China about 1,000 years before, but it is doubtful that people in the West were aware of it. The first printed books in the West were hand-printed from letters carved into wooden blocks. This was a difficult and time-consuming process and was no improvement over the hand-copying method of producing manuscripts.

The invention of a movable type printing press about 1457 revolutionized book publishing. A German printer, Johann Gutenberg, is generally given credit for the invention that was to make a monumental contribution to the intellectual development of humankind. The Gutenberg Bible was the first book printed on movable type. About 200 copies of the *Gutenberg Bible* were printed, 40 or 50 of which are still in existence. What was truly innovative about Gutenberg's press was that once a book had been printed the same type could be reassembled and used again for printing other books. Within a few years printing spread throughout Europe, and the number of books being produced increased tremendously. By the end of the fifteenth century more than 30,000 different books had been printed. Printing brought about extraordinary changes in books and libraries. Books became available to virtually everyone. They were placed on open shelves in libraries where they were easily accessible. Libraries began to resemble the libraries of today.

The 1600s and 1700s are known as the "Golden Age of Libraries." Many of the great libraries of Europe were founded during this period. The British Museum (1759) which is now part of the British Library and the Bibliotheque Nationale of France (1789) are among the world's greatest libraries.

Libraries in the United States date back to the founding of the Harvard University Library in 1638. Subscription libraries were established beginning in 1731, making books available to the public. The first subscription library, the Library Company of Philadelphia, was established by Benjamin Franklin. Subscribers paid dues which entitled them to borrow the books free of charge. Other subscription libraries spread throughout the colonies. Congress established the Library of Congress in 1800 for the purpose of providing reference service to the United States Congress. In 1812 the original library was destroyed by fire, so in 1815 Congress purchased the personal library of Thomas Jefferson. Today the Library of Congress is the largest library in the United States and serves as the national library. Two copies of each book copyrighted in the United States are kept in the Library of Congress. In addition, the Library acquires books from all over the world. The collection contains over 83 million books, periodicals, films, tapes, manuscripts, recordings, microforms, optical disks, and computer-stored records. Approximately one and a half million items are added to the collection annually.

Libraries in the United States have been closely associated with the ideal of free schooling for everyone. The first tax-supported library in the United States was established in Peterborough, New Hampshire, in 1833. The idea of public libraries spread rapidly and received its greatest impetus in the late 1800s when Andrew Carnegie donated millions of dollars for the construction of free public libraries. His generous gift helped build more than 2,500 libraries in the United States and other English-speaking countries, but more than that it helped to foster the notion that libraries were a necessary public service. Since that time the number of libraries of all types have grown; it is inconceivable that any community in the United States would be without library service.

ELECTRONIC LIBRARIES

During the last half of the twentieth century a new concept of the role of libraries emerged. We no longer think of libraries as storehouses for books. Rather, the emphasis has been on libraries as the purveyors of information. Libraries have played a leading role in the scientific advancement that has brought about so much change and progress in the world today. They serve as information centers, disseminating information for immediate use and application. In turn, the application of scientific and technological advancements to the library has enhanced its performance as an information center. Just as the printing press changed the course of history, so also has electronics brought drastic changes to information processing. Almost every library function has been affected by advances in electronics. The advent of the computer, coupled with advances in telecommunications, changed information handling in ways never before dreamed of in the days of Johann Gutenberg. The computer is able to store an unlimited amount of information and, at the same time, provide access points in ways never before possible with traditional library sources. Advances in telecommunications in which text and images are transmitted over telephone wires and printed at receiving stations have revolutionized the publishing and dissemination of information.

The use of computers to automate library services began in the 1960s when libraries used computers for routine functions such as circulation and record keeping. The most significant event in library automation occurred in 1965 when the Library of Congress began creating catalog records in MARC (machine readable catalog) language. MARC records can be stored on magnetic tapes and retrieved with the use of computers, thus, replacing the traditional card catalog. This automated catalog is called an *online catalog* or an OPAC (online public access catalog). Catalog records in MARC format became available to libraries throughout the country through library networks. The first library network to offer automated services to member libraries was OCLC (Online Computer Library Center) which began in 1968. Linked by telephone to the network computer center, libraries participating in the OCLC shared cataloging project share cataloging records, thus saving on the costs and human resources needed to catalog each individual work for the first time. Additionally, the records can be transferred to tapes and added to local systems. In 1981, the Library of Congress discontinued its card catalog, prompting many libraries in the United States also to change from card catalogs to online catalogs.

At the same time that libraries were moving toward shared resources and online catalogs, advances were made in other areas of information storage and retrieval. Beginning in the 1970s, online databases produced by commercial vendors and transmitted via telephone wires became available to libraries. (See Chapter 10.) Since their introduction, the number of databases available online has grown from less than a hundred to thousands. Online databases consist of both bibliographic and textual data. They are now available from government and non-profit sources as well as from the commercial vendors.

The use of microcomputers in libraries has been widespread since the beginning of the 1980s when librarians began to create in-house databases and store them on floppy disks or transfer them to tapes stored on a mainframe computer. Microcomputers are now used in libraries to assist with many routine functions such as scheduling and maintaining statistics.

The advent of laser disk technology around 1980 added another dimension to the electronic library. Optical disks are created with a laser used to burn pits in the light-sensitive surface of a plastic coated disk. The disk is then "read" by a beam of light and converted to data or images by a computer. This technology provides extremely high density storage as well as a potentially effective way of preserving material. The first laser disks were large 12 inch disks with enormous storage capacity. Expensive equipment is required to create and playback these disks. In the mid-1980s the Library of Congress instituted a project to preserve much of its archival collection on large 12 inch optical disks, but it was not practical for smaller libraries to contemplate this type of technology. CD-ROM (Compact Disk-Read Only Memory) was introduced shortly after the larger laser disks between 1984 and 1987. CD-ROM is a type of optical disk that provides tremendous storage capabilities, but is small in size. Each disk measures 4.75 inches in diameter and is able to hold as many as 250,000 printed pages (about 300 books) or the contents of 1200 floppy disks. It requires standard microcomputer hardware and software and is relatively inexpensive to produce.

As we can see computerized information storage and retrieval have increasingly become a part of library services. Today's library no longer features simply printed matter and quiet study areas. The electronic library is now a reality. Information in electronic format can now be found in almost every library. Online databases now number in the thousands; there are hundreds of indexes and reference works available on CD-ROM; services in libraries such as circulation and inter-library loan are now automated; online catalogs are now widely available; and electronic publishing, in which materials such as journal articles are available only electronically, is gradually coming into being.

If the changes in information processing of the last half of the twentieth century continue at that same rate over the next decade, we are likely to continue to see drastic changes in libraries. Some are predicting a totally electronic library in which all materials and services are in electronic format. They envision a "paperless society" in which printed books and magazines will be replaced by CD-ROMs and online databases. Others are predicting that library buildings as we know them will no longer exist, and information will be transmitted to individuals via telephone or other electronic device. Probably neither of these scenarios will be entirely realized. It is unlikely that libraries will get rid of the books in their collections, nor is it likely in the near future that publishers will cease to publish books in paper format. It is likely that advances in automation will continue to occur, and that we will see more and more publications in electronic format and that more services will be automated. Regardless of how futuristic a library looks, it will continue to serve the basic human need for information. The materials of the past, both distant and recent, will still be present, augmented by the services which are continually being developed to facilitate their use. Library users will be expected to become more information literate in order to take full advantage of the services made possible by technological progress.

REVIEW QUESTIONS
CHAPTER 1

1. What is information processing? What does information processing encompass?

2. Why was writing developed?

3. What were the three stages in the evolution of writing?

4. What are the stages in the development of the English alphabet?

5. Name other forms of writing material used before the development of paper.

6. What effect did Johann Gutenberg's invention of movable type have on civilization?

7. Name three persons who contributed to the development of libraries in the United States. Describe the contributions of each.

8. How has the perception of the role of libraries changed in the last half of the twentieth century.

9. Describe three developments in library services as a result of electronic technology.

10. What is an electronic library? Describe how a typical academic library might look in ten years.

11. What services are automated in your library? Name any publications in your library in electronic format.

Introduction
to Academic Libraries

2

A PREVIEW

The bewilderment of using an academic library is lessened if the library user knows something of how materials are organized in libraries and which services are available. Although library arrangements and services vary from library to library, there are many elements which are common to all libraries. This chapter describes typical ways in which libraries organize their materials and the kinds of services which they provide.

The phrase "heart of the university" is frequently used to describe the role of the library in institutions of higher learning. It is difficult to imagine a college or university without a library. Libraries have always been a part of higher education in America. When John Harvard founded Harvard University in 1638, he saw to it that a library was established as part of the University. In his will, Harvard left the University his own private collection of 400 volumes which formed the core collection of the library. As other academic institutions opened, they, too, established libraries. These early libraries were small, open only a few hours a day, and had policies that severely limited access. Academic libraries today in no way resemble these early institutions. Not only has there been phenomenal growth in the size of collections, but also great strides have been made to improve library services. Hours of service have increased and physical facilities have improved. It is the mark of a good university to have a large library—one which will meet the research and instructional needs of the faculty as well as the needs of the graduate and undergraduate student. The amount of information being made available grows daily, and the university, as no other institution, has an obligation to make this information accessible to students, faculty, and others interested in research. In fulfilling their missions, college and university libraries in the second half of the twentieth century have had to confront major challenges: they must keep up with the enormous proliferation of information; they must take advantage of technological innovations in an attempt to provide users access to all this information; they must deal with unprecedented increases in the student population; and they must do all these things in the context of a wide diversity of needs among the faculty and students within the university.

One of the first things students should learn in college is how to use the library. To do this they must become familiar with its services and materials. Many students are introduced to libraries in elementary or high school, or perhaps they are familiar with their public library. They will find, however, that the college or university library is more complex; it is often larger than the library with which they may be familiar, it probably provides a greater variety of services, and it may use a different scheme for classifying its materials.

The college and university library provides a place where students and faculty can read, study, and conduct research. It strives to maintain as complete a collection of books, periodicals, and other information-related materials as possible, but it is frequently hampered in this effort by financial constraints and by the destructive acts of those it seeks to serve. Mutilation and theft of library materials by library patrons are major problems in college and university libraries. All such acts ultimately result in a decrease in the materials available and a lessening of services. It is incumbent on library users to share the responsibility of preserving library materials by seeing to it that such destructive acts do not occur.

Librarians are constantly studying library arrangements and services in order to improve access to library materials. While there is some uniformity of arrangement among college and university libraries, there are also many variations. Differences in arrangement among libraries is governed by a number of factors: size of the institution, educational mission, and availability of resources. Some schools have separate libraries for undergraduates; other schools have only one central library; many universities have a central library as well as branch libraries which serve various colleges or departments within the university.

ARRANGEMENT OF LIBRARY MATERIALS

In addition to locating library facilities on campus for maximum use, librarians are also concerned with arranging materials within the library. This chapter gives an overview of the arrangement of library materials and the various functions and services commonly found in college and university libraries. It is imperative for students to know what services are available and where library materials are located if they are to take advantage of its services and resources.

One approach to library arrangement is the *divisional plan*, in which all the books, periodicals, pamphlets, reference tools, and reserve books in a field of knowledge are placed together in the same area. The books are usually in "open" stacks, where patrons are free to choose their own material. Typical divisions are Humanities, Sciences, and Social Sciences. Each division has its own reference librarians and staff assistants. Some libraries with the divisional plan of arrangement usually have other departments for handling special materials such as government documents, newspapers, microforms, rare books, audio-visual materials, and archives. Some have separate rooms for reserved books; others have reserved book sections in each division.

Most libraries, however, use an arrangement generally known as the *traditional plan*, in which materials are arranged by function or by service provided. Typically, all the books are shelved together in one large stack area, one reference department provides reference service for all subject fields, periodicals are located in one place, and microforms are located together in one area.

The functions and services discussed below are common to many college and university libraries.

Stacks

Books which circulate are arranged by call number on rows of shelves called *stacks*. Some libraries have "closed" stacks to which only library staff and those with special permission have access. Patrons present a "call slip" to a library attendant who gets the material. Having closed stacks reduces the loss of library material by theft and mutilation. It also reduces the number of books which are out of order in the stacks. In most libraries, however, books are shelved in "open" stacks where patrons are free to browse and select materials for themselves. Browsing is helpful in locating materials which the user might not have discovered in the library catalog. Some libraries have a combination of the two systems—the general stack areas are "open" while special collections are "closed." In some college and university libraries, stacks are open to faculty and graduate students, but closed to undergraduates.

The Library Catalog

The key to locating materials in the library is the catalog. When a library receives a book it is sent to the Catalog Department where it is assigned a call number which determines where it will be located in the library. A record, called a *catalog record*, is then made that includes call number, author's name, title, publication information, and a note giving the size of the book and other descriptive information such as availability of maps, illustrations, and/or bibliographies. Subject headings are assigned in order to help the library user locate the book by its subject. The catalog record is then placed in the library's catalog where it is available to library users. There are several different types of library catalogs. The one with which most users are familiar is the *card catalog* in which the cards for each book are inserted alphabetically in file drawers. Some libraries have their catalog records in books, called *book catalogs*; others have *COM (Computer Output Microform) catalogs*, which are lists on microfiche that are generated from computer tapes; other libraries have their catalog records on CD-ROM (Compact Disk-Read Only Memory). Still other libraries have *online catalogs* where the catalog records are stored on computer tapes and made available via computer terminals. The advantage of an online catalog is that it enables users to search by author, title, subject, or keyword very quickly. It may also give the circulation status of a book. A complete discussion of the library catalog can be found in Chapter 5.

Reference Department

Perhaps the single most useful collection in any library is the reference collection. This collection consists of encyclopedias, dictionaries, almanacs, handbooks, manuals, indexes, etc. which are frequently used for finding information. It also contains reference tools in other formats such as CD-ROM. The reference department typically has open shelves which are systematically arranged, although some materials such as indexes are shelved on separate index tables to facilitate their use. Highly used reference books may also be shelved in a special area near the librarian's desk. Reference librarians familiar with this collection are available to help patrons find information in the reference department. As a rule, reference materials do not circulate and must be used in the reference department.

Reserve Book Department

A necessary collection in the college and university library is the reserve book collection. Professors request that books which are needed for classes be placed together in the reserve book area. In order to insure their availability to students who will be using them for assigned reading, the materials on reserve circulate for a limited time, usually two hours or overnight.

Periodical Department

In most libraries periodicals (magazines and journals) are shelved together in one area for convenience of use. Other libraries have found that it is more desirable to have only the current periodicals in one area with the bound volumes of periodicals in a separate area or in the stacks with other books.

Newspaper Room

Current newspapers may be housed with other periodical literature or they may be kept in a separate area. Newspapers are kept for a limited period of time because they are printed on paper which does not last. Many libraries subscribe to both a paper copy and a microfilm copy of the newspaper; they then house current newspapers and microform together since the older issues of newspapers are preserved on microfilm.

Microform Department

Today much of the information stored in libraries is on microform—a photographic reproduction of printed matter in a greatly reduced form. Microform materials include microfilm, microfiche, microcards, and microprints. These materials are not readable with the naked eye and require the use of special equipment or readers. For some time libraries have stored back issues of newspapers on microfilm, but in recent years there has been a trend toward increased use of microform storage for other types of materials. Periodicals, government documents, theses, dissertations, manuscripts, and, in fact, all forms of printed matter are now being copied on microform in order to save printing costs and library storage space.

Audio/Visual Department

Audio/visual materials consist of recordings, cassette tapes, video tapes, compact disks, films, and slides. These are usually kept in special areas which are designed to accommodate these types of materials. There one finds booths where it is possible to listen to music or view tapes without disturbing others.

Government Publications Department

Many university libraries serve as depositories for state, local, national, and international documents. These publications are usually shelved separately in a special area. Some libraries locate state and local government documents in the documents room with national and international documents, but it is also quite common to house these materials in a distinct ''state'' room designed to preserve, in all forms, materials dealing with the particular state. Documents housed in special areas are usually arranged by classification systems designed especially for those systems. For example, U.S. Government documents are usually shelved by the Superintendent of Documents system. (See Chapter 9.)

Archives and Manuscripts

Records and documents such as letters, manuscripts, diaries, personal journals, photographs, and other materials which are of historical value are preserved in an archives department. These areas are staffed by archivists who are specifically trained in methods of acquisition and preservation of historical materials.

Rare Books Department

University librarians, like most book collectors, pride themselves in assembling books which are valuable because of their artistic and/or unique qualities or because they are old and no longer available. Such books need protection and care in handling. They are shelved in specially designed areas and are not allowed to circulate.

Special Collections

In fulfilling its research mission, a university library frequently has a number of highly specialized collections. The advantage of such collections is that they support the university's effort to become a center for research in particular subject fields. Examples of such collections might be Black history, women's studies, or Asian studies.

Branch Libraries

Branch libraries consist of subject collections such as agriculture, business, chemistry, engineering, music, law, or architecture in libraries located away from the central library. These are conveniently located in buildings which serve the needs of students and faculty in a particular discipline.

LIBRARY SERVICES

As more and more materials accumulate in libraries, the task of accessing stored information becomes more complex. While the introduction of computer technology into information handling has resulted in more efficient and faster methods of storing and retrieving information, it has not done away with basic library services. It is still necessary for library users to become familiar with all the library services, regardless of whether or not these are automated, in order to use the library effectively. The services outlined below are representative of services offered in most academic libraries.

Circulation Desk

Books and other materials are usually checked out from a centrally located desk which handles all matters dealing with the lending of library materials. In most libraries the circulation desk is located near the entrance or the exit of the library. Information regarding lending policies, fines, schedules, etc. is available at the circulation desk. Many of the tasks such as checking books out and in, verifying circulation status, and sending out overdue and recall notices, once performed manually at the circulation desk, are now automated.

Reference Librarians

An important and indispensable resource in any library is the librarian. In order to acquire, maintain, and disseminate the vast amount of information which is stored in libraries, trained personnel are needed. Most libraries require that its professional librarians have a Master's degree or the equivalent from an

American Library Association (ALA) accredited institution. Persons trained in librarianship or information sciences perform a variety of services: administrative, technical, and public. Administrators are concerned with the overall operation of the library and with the budget, staff, and physical plant. Technical service librarians work in the cataloging department, the preparations department, the acquisitions department, the collection development, the serials department, or other departments whose primary mission is the acquisition, preparation, and maintenance of library materials. Public service librarians are those who serve the patron directly. Not everyone who works in a library is a librarian. Support staff such as clerks, paraprofessionals, and technicians help to maintain the library's services.

Library patrons are more familiar with public service librarians because these are the individuals with whom they come into contact when seeking assistance. Reference librarians are available to answer questions about the collection, to help with search strategy, and generally to help locate and sort out information. A student seeking assistance with a research project will find that the librarian is better able to help if the student has some knowledge of basic library sources and services. When reference librarians are approached for assistance with a question that involves research, they conduct an informal reference interview to determine the purpose of the research, the type of information desired (e.g., statistical, historical, etc.), specific questions to be answered, limitations (e.g., date, geographical, etc.), and extent and findings of preliminary research. It is important for students to learn to ask the appropriate questions during the reference interview. For example, a student might ask where the books on computers are located when he/she really wants to know about computer crimes among government workers. It is beneficial for the student to conduct a preliminary search, such as searching the catalog, browsing, or looking up material in reference books, before approaching the reference desk for help. This enables the student to focus on the type of information needed to deal with various aspects of the topic and then ask specific questions. It also gives the librarian a starting point from which to proceed in directing the student to appropriate sources.

Online Search Services

Most libraries now offer online or computer assisted searching as part of their reference services. The search is carried out by means of a computer which is located in the library and linked by telephone to a computer data center in a distant location. The computer data center, usually called the vendor, provides access to information that is stored in machine readable form and which can be searched as a unit. These units of information, known as databases, contain either the full-text or bibliographic citations to periodical and newspaper articles, books, government publications, patents, conference proceedings, dissertations, research reports, statistical sources, directories, and the like. Much of the information that is stored in databases is available in printed form in the library. The patron should consult the librarian for advice on whether to use printed indexes and abstracts or online databases for a specific search. Reference librarians trained in search techniques usually conduct the searches, although some libraries allow patrons to conduct their own online searching. The library usually charges a fee for online searching in order to recover the cost charged by vendors. A more detailed discussion of online searching, along with a selected list of databases, can be found in Chapter 10.

Interlibrary Loan

Most public and institutional libraries subscribe to the Interlibrary Loan Code adopted by the American Library Association in 1968. It is designed to permit libraries to cooperate in exchanging materials. The rising cost of library operations and acquisitions have forced more and more libraries to seek cooperation with other institutions in order to serve their patrons. Libraries lend each other books and other materials which are unavailable at the local library. The loans are for limited periods, and the costs of borrowing material (postage, handling, and duplication) are generally borne by the patron. If a lending library does not circulate an item, it may send photocopies. Patrons borrowing books are required to fill out forms giving accurate and complete information on the item they would like to borrow. This usually includes the author, title, publication information and a reference showing where the citation was found. Interlibrary loan is for specific titles only and not for subject requests such as "all the works on the Cold War."

Library Cooperatives

A practice which is prevalent among libraries today is that of forming a cooperative for the purpose of making holdings and services available to cooperative members and their patrons on a reciprocal basis. These groups are known by various names: library networks, information centers, consortia, or library systems. Some groups share general printed materials while others share specialized materials such as periodicals, films, slides, and other audio-visual material.

Regional library systems, in which libraries in a geographical area share resources, are widespread throughout the United States. There are also national library networks in which members from different libraries all over the country cooperate to share resources. OCLC (Online Computer Library Center) is a national network with a diversity of services ranging from shared cataloging to bibliographic searching. Members of OCLC may use its services to handle requests for interlibrary loan material, to catalog materials, and to help identify and locate library materials. Some libraries contract to use the computer resources of OCLC, such as its shared cataloging service, but are not full participating members. Some regional networks serve as brokers for OCLC services to its member libraries. SOLINET (Southeastern Library Network) serves as the regional network for libraries in the Southeast. WLN (Western Library Network) is a major library network serving libraries in the Northwest. RLG (Research Libraries Group) is a consortium made up of a number of large research libraries in the United States which cooperate to share resources. In addition to shared cataloging, RLG also provides interlibrary loan services and serves as a bibliographic reference tool. Its online union catalog, called RLIN, lists the holdings of member libraries and may be searched by author, title, subject, or keyword.

REVIEW QUESTIONS
CHAPTER 2

1. What are the differences between the *traditional* and the *divisional* plans of library arrangement? Which type does your library have?

2. What are the differences between open and closed stacks in a library? What are the advantages and disadvantages of each? Describe the stack arrangement in your library.

3. What purpose does the reserve book department serve in the library?

4. What is the function of an audio/visual room in a library? Name the different types of audio/visual materials found in your library.

5. What kinds of materials are found in an archives department?

6. Why is the reference librarian an important resource in the library?

7. What service does an interlibrary loan department perform for the library patron?

8. What are branch libraries? What are the branch libraries on your campus?

9. Why is it advantageous for a library to belong to a cooperative network such as OCLC or RLG?

10. What is online searching?

11. Which of the library services discussed in this chapter does your library provide?

LIBRARY TOUR EXERCISE

Take a tour of your library and complete the exercise below. Write NA for any items that are not applicable for your library.

1. Look in the online catalog and locate a book on child abuse and give the following information:

   a. Complete call number: _____

   b. Title of the book: _____

   _____

   c. Classification system: _____

   d. Where in the library is the book located? _____

   _____

2. Look in the card catalog and locate a book on heraldry and give the following information:

   a. Complete call number: _____

   b. Title of the book: _____

   _____

   c. Classification system: _____

   d. Where in the library is the book located? _____

   _____

3. Locate any reference book from the reference department and give the following information:

   a. Title of the book: _____

   _____

   b. Call number: _____

   c. Where in the reference department is it located? (e.g., reference stacks, ready reference, index tables) _____

4. Locate a book that has been assigned as reading for a course and give the following information:

   a. Title of the book: _____

   _____

   b. Course name and number for which the book is assigned: _____

   c. In which department or area is the book located? _____

5. Locate the latest copy of *Time Magazine* and give the following information:

   a. Call number: _____

   b. Date of the issue: _____

   c. Volume no.: _____

d. Title of one article from the issue: _____

e. Inclusive pages of the article: _____

f. Where in the library is it located? _____

6. Locate a copy of *Time Magazine* that is five years old and give the following information:

a. Call number: _____

b. Date of the issue: _____

c. Volume no.: _____

d. Title of one article from the issue: _____

_____

e. Inclusive pages of the article: _____

f. Where in the library is it located? _____

7. Locate a recent issue of a newspaper from a city near your hometown and give the following information:

a. Title of the newspaper: _____

b. Date of the issue which you located: _____

c. Call number: _____

d. In which department or area is it located? _____

8. Locate a U.S. government document and give the following information:

a. Title of the document: _____

b. Call number: _____

c. In which department or area is it located? _____

9. Locate a recording of a musical work and give the following information:

a. Title of the recording: _____

b. Call number: _____

c. In which department or area is it located? _____

10. Locate a videotape of *one* of the following:
Wizard of Oz, Cyrano de Bergerac, Romeo and Juliet, West Side Story, Death of a Salesman, Our Town. Give the following information:

a. Title of the videotape: _____

b. Call number: _____

c. In which department or area is it located? _____

Understanding
Library Materials

3

A PREVIEW

The information sources in libraries have become so complex that one can hardly keep pace with them. It is essential, however, that library users have a basic understanding of the formats of the more commonly used materials. In this chapter the parts of the book are analyzed in detail. Other information sources are treated with sufficient detail to provide the researcher with an understanding of basic library materials.

As computerized information becomes more and more prevalent in libraries, it becomes increasingly necessary for users to become "library literate." It is no longer sufficient to think of the library as a collection of books, one must be aware of all the materials in a library and how these are used. Over the past two decades we have witnessed a revolution, not only in the amount of information being produced, but also in the kinds of media used to record and store information. Today even the smallest library has been affected by automation. Some people think that the new technologies will make information retrieval easier; others believe that information retrieval has become more complicated as a result of new technologies. There are truisms in both of these viewpoints. Information retrieval is facilitated by new technologies, but it is necessary to know what sources are available and how to use them in order to make effective use of them. At the same time, one must realize that computers have not replaced books in libraries. The traditional word preserved on paper is still the most extensive of the information purveyors, but other forms are becoming increasingly popular. Photography, magnetic recordings, video tapes, laser disks, online databases, and electronic catalogs, are being used with increasing frequency to advance the means by which information is stored and retrieved. Understanding the format of the various library materials is necessary in order to make full use of all the sources available in a library. This chapter will explain in detail the book's format and give descriptions of other library materials both in printed and nonprinted formats.

BOOKS

A book consists of written or printed pages fastened together at one edge and covered with a protective cover. The first printed books consisted only of the cover and the text of the work. There were no title or introductory pages as in

KEY TERMS

Information Storage and
    Retrieval
Book Format
Serials
Theses and Dissertations
Archives
Vertical Files
A-V (Audio-Visual Materials)
Electronic Information
Online Catalog
Online Database
CD-ROM

modern books. The *colophon*, or inscription at the end of the text, was usually the only extraneous material found in the book. It described the type, paper, and binding used and frequently included the printer's emblem or distinctive mark. As printing evolved, publishers developed a uniform way to arrange the contents of books which greatly enhanced their usability. These common features are discussed below. (Some books may not have all the different parts described, and the order of their appearance may vary.)

Book Cover

The cover of the book holds the pages of the book together and protects them. The edge of the cover where the pages are bound together is called the spine. On the spine are ordinarily printed the short-title of the book, the author's name, the publisher, and, in the case of library books, the call number. The front of the cover is often decorated. It may also give the author's name and the short-title of the book. The *end papers* are those sheets attached to the inside of the front and back covers. Sometimes the end papers contain illustrative or informational material such as maps, tables, charts, etc.

Preliminary Pages

The preliminary pages precede the text of the book and usually describe its contents. The reader should examine these pages before proceeding to the text. The preface, introduction, or table of contents located among the preliminary pages may be useful for determining whether a book is suitable for the reader's purpose; sometimes explanations in the preliminary pages help the reader understand the text which follows. The preliminary pages are usually numbered with small Roman numerals in order to distinguish them from the text or the main body of the work. The following items are found in the preliminary pages:

1. The *flyleaves* are blank pages next to the end papers.
2. The *half-title* page gives the short-title of the book and the name of the series if the book is one of a series.
3. The *frontispiece* is an illustration or portrait which faces the title page.
4. The *title page* is the first significant page in the book. It is always on the right, or *recto*, of the leaf. The left side of a leaf is known as the *verso*.

    The following information can be found on the *recto* of the title page:

    Title. The full name of the book, including the *subtitle* or *descriptive title*.

    Author. The author's name and sometimes a list of credentials such as degrees, academic position, and, occasionally, the names of other works.

    Editor, Compiler, Illustrator, or *Translator*. The name of anyone other than the author who made a significant contribution to the book.

    Edition. Given if the book is other than a first edition. All copies of a book printed from one set of type make up an edition. *Reprints* are copies of the same edition printed at a later time. When any changes are made, it is a *revised edition* or a *new edition*.

    Imprint. The place of publication, the publisher, and the date of publication. These are usually found at the bottom of the title page although the publication date is sometimes omitted from the title page. The publication date identifies when a book was published and made available to the public.

Colophon. The publisher's distinctive mark or emblem is sometimes found on the title page. (The statement describing the type, paper, etc. may appear on the *verso* of the title page or at the end of the book.)

The *verso* of the title page contains the following information:

Copyright. The copyright grants legal rights to an author or publisher to sell, distribute, or reproduce a literary or artistic work. A small *c* before a date identifies it as the copyright date.

Printing history. A list of different editions and printings of the work. The publication date is occasionally found on the *verso* with the printing history rather than on the *recto* of the title page. Sometimes one finds a copy of the catalog card on the *verso* of the title page.

5. The *dedication* page gives a brief announcement in which the author dedicates the book to a person, a group, or a cause.
6. The *table of contents* lists in order the chapters or parts of the book and gives the pages on which they begin. Some books include a brief summary of each chapter in the table of contents.
7. The *list of illustrations* gives the pages on which illustrative material can be found.
8. The *preface* or *foreword* gives the author's purpose in writing the book and acknowledges those persons who have helped in its preparation.
9. The *introduction* describes the subject and gives a preliminary statement leading into the main contents of the book.

Text and Notes

The main body of printed matter is the text of the book. It is usually divided into chapters or separate parts and includes explanatory material and identification of reference sources in the form of notes at the bottoms of the pages (footnotes) or at the ends of chapters (endnotes).

Auxiliary Material

1. *Glossary.* A list with definitions of the technical terms or unusual words used in the text.
2. *Appendix.* Supplementary materials such as tables, maps, questionnaires, or case studies.
3. *Notes.* If they are not included with the text, notes are placed at the end of the book.
4. *Bibliography.* A list of all books, articles, and other materials the author used in writing the book. It may also include other sources which are relevant to the subject.
5. *Index.* An alphabetical list of the subjects discussed in the book, along with the corresponding page numbers. Some books also include a separate name and/or author index.

SERIALS

A *serial* is a publication which is issued on a continuing basis at regularly stated intervals. The publication frequency varies: some serials are published each day (daily); others, once a week (weekly), every two weeks (biweekly), once a month (monthly), every two months (bimonthly), twice a year (semiannually), or once a year (annually). Serials include periodicals, newspapers, annuals and yearbooks, and the proceedings, transactions, memoirs, etc. of societies and associations.

Periodicals include *magazines* and *journals* which are issued at regular intervals, usually weekly, biweekly, monthly, bimonthly, or quarterly. Magazines contain popular reading, while journals are more scholarly. Periodicals are numbered consecutively and given volume designations so that several issues make up a volume. In many libraries, when a complete volume of a periodical has been accumulated, the issues are bound together in hard covers. These bound volumes may be shelved with other books by classification number, or they may be shelved in a separate periodical area. Some libraries acquire the current copies of periodicals in paper and the back issues on microform. Libraries often preserve newspapers on microfilm because the paper on which they are originally printed does not last long. Usually, the paper copies of newspapers are kept only until the microfilm copies arrive. Annuals and yearbooks are treated much as other book materials and shelved in the general collection or in the reference collection. The proceedings, transactions, memoirs, etc. of a society or association are usually shelved in the stacks unless they are acquired on microform.

The serial titles owned by a library are usually listed in the library's catalog but may also appear in a separate serials list, which identifies those titles and issues which have been received in the library. This list is kept in the serials room, in the reference room, and/or at the catalog.

THESES AND DISSERTATIONS

A *dissertation* is research that is conducted and written in partial fulfillment of the requirements for the doctoral degree at a university. A *thesis* is a research project completed in partial fulfillment of the requirements for the master's degree. At least one copy of the original of all the dissertations and theses written at a university are usually kept in the university library. Many libraries acquire microfilm copies of the theses and dissertations in order to preserve the original. Libraries may acquire dissertations and theses from other universities on microfilm.

ARCHIVES

Archives consist of both unpublished and published materials that have special historical value, such as the public and private papers of notable persons or the records of an institution. The format of archival materials varies: for example, archives might include original manuscripts, letters, photographs, diaries, legal records, books, etc. (See Figure 3.1.) The materials found in archives may be likened to the items one frequently finds in the attics of old family homes: birth and marriage certificates, letters, newspaper clippings, etc., which tell that family's story. Archives require special care and handling, and it is not unusual to find that access is limited to only serious researchers. Archival material may also be put on microform in order to preserve the original from overuse. Librarians are also looking at new technologies which will solve the problems of preserving old and valuable material. In 1985, the Library of Congress began a pilot program in which copies of archival material are being stored on optical disks. (See Figure 3.5.)

Figure 3.1. A fascimile of a manuscript from the National Archives.

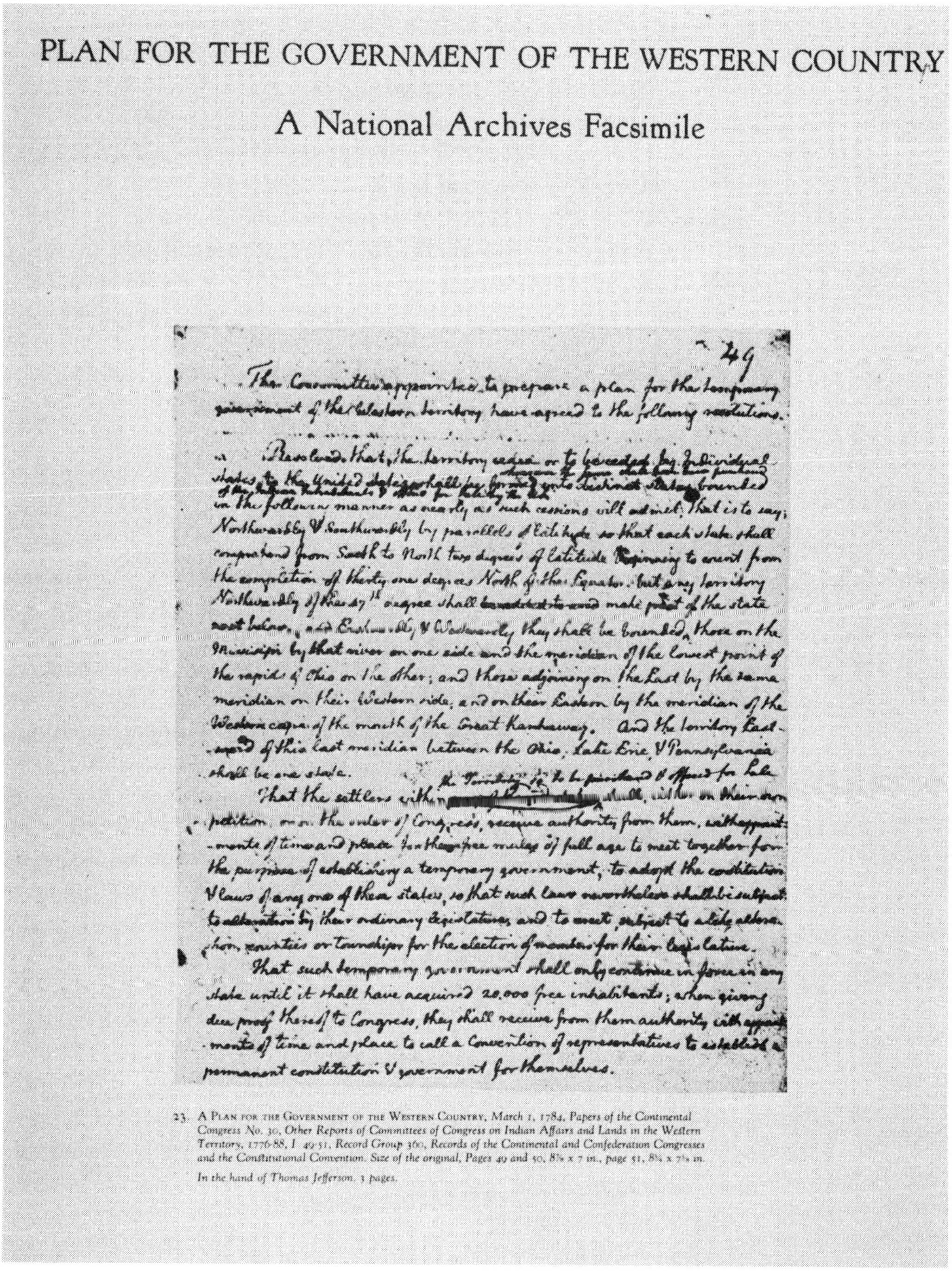

PLAN FOR THE GOVERNMENT OF THE WESTERN COUNTRY

A National Archives Facsimile

49

The Committee appointed to prepare a plan for the temporary government of the Western territory have agreed to the following resolutions.

Resolved, that the territory ceded or to be ceded by Individual states to the United states shall be formed into distinct states bounded in the following manner as nearly as such cessions will admit, that is to say; Northwardly & Southwardly by parallels of latitude so that each state shall comprehend from South to North two degrees of latitude beginning to count from the completion of thirty one degrees North of the Equator. but any territory Northwardly of the 47th degree shall make part of the state next below. and Eastwardly & Westwardly they shall be bounded, those on the Missisipi by that river on one side and the meridian of the lowest point of the rapids of Ohio on the other; and those adjoining on the East by the same meridian on their Western side, and on their Eastern by the meridian of the Western cape of the mouth of the Great Kanhaway. And the territory Eastward of this last meridian between the Ohio, Lake Erie, & Pennsylvania shall be one state.

That the settlers within the territory so to be purchased & offered for sale shall, either on their own petition, or on the order of Congress, receive authority from them, with appointments of time and place for their free males of full age to meet together for the purpose of establishing a temporary government, to adopt the constitution & laws of any one of these states, so that such laws nevertheless shall be subject to alteration by their ordinary legislature, and to erect, subject to a like alteration, counties or townships for the election of members for their legislature.

That such temporary government shall only continue in force in any state until it shall have acquired 20,000 free inhabitants; when giving due proof thereof to Congress, they shall receive from them authority with appointments of time and place to call a Convention of representatives to establish a permanent constitution & government for themselves.

23. A Plan for the Government of the Western Country, *March 1, 1784, Papers of the Continental Congress No. 30, Other Reports of Committees of Congress on Indian Affairs and Lands in the Western Territory, 1776-88, I 49-51, Record Group 360, Records of the Continental and Confederation Congresses and the Constitutional Convention. Size of the original, Pages 49 and 50, 8⅞ x 7 in., page 51, 8¾ x 7⅛ in.*

In the hand of Thomas Jefferson. 3 pages.

VERTICAL FILE

The vertical file consists of pamphlets, brochures, newspaper and magazine clippings, pictures, maps, and other materials which are not suitable for cataloging and shelving along with the regular book collection. Vertical file materials are usually placed in manila folders and stored alphabetically by subjects in filing cabinets. The material placed in the vertical file is ephemeral in nature—that is, it has little, if any, historical value and will soon be out-of-date. Therefore, the vertical file must be weeded from time to time to get rid of dated material. Vertical file material is useful for providing up-to-date information. Additionally, much of the information kept in the vertical file might never appear in any other published form. Some libraries maintain a separate index of vertical file material.

A-V (AUDIO-VISUAL) MATERIALS

Audio-visual materials include audio, video, and microform formats. A-V materials require special equipment for their use and are usually housed in separate areas of the library. (See Chapter 2.)

Audio materials include records, audio cassettes, and reel-to-reel tapes. The audio materials in most libraries include musical as well as spoken records. *Video* materials include microforms, video-cassettes, slides, and synchronized slide-tapes. *Microforms* are printed materials which are reduced in size by photographic means and can only be read with special readers. (See Figures 3.2 and 3.3.) There are several types of these photographically reduced materials: *microfilm* is print which is reproduced on a roll of 35 or 16 mm film; *microfiche* is a flat sheet of film, usually measuring four by six inches, on which separate pages of text are reproduced; *microprint* is the reproduction in positive form of a microphotograph. (See Figure 3.4.) Microprint is printed on opaque paper, unlike microfilm and microfiche, which are printed or reproduced on film. *Microcard* is a form of microprint, but its reduction is greater. Microprints and microcards are no longer being distributed because of the difficulty in reproducing them on paper. Acquiring materials in microform permits libraries to save valuable space and perhaps to acquire material not available any other way. For instance, the census records containing the names of persons are available from the National Archives and Records Administration only on microfilm. While it is more likely that newspapers and periodicals are acquired in microform format, it is not unusual to find books, especially out-of-print ones, on microfiche or microfilm.

ELECTRONIC INFORMATION SOURCES

Technology has had a major impact on the types of information sources found in libraries. More and more information is in electronic format which utilizes computers for information storage and retrieval. The sources of electronic information common to many libraries are: (1) *online catalogs*; (2) *library networks*; (3) *online databases*; (4) *in-house databases*; and (5) *optical disks*. Information is now being stored on magnetic tapes, hard disks, floppy disks, and CD-ROM. (See Figure 3.5.) In addition, libraries are linked to online databases via telecommunications networks. The kind of information available in electronic format includes bibliographic information such as descriptions of books, periodical articles, and other literary works; raw data (e.g., statistics, census data, voting records); the full text of periodicals, books, and reports; and illustrative material such as maps and photographs.

The *online catalog* is the most widespread of electronic library sources. Known as the OPAC (Online Public Access Catalog), it contains the catalog records of the materials in the library in much the same way as a card catalog. The records are stored on magnetic tapes and retrieved at computer terminals located both inside and outside the library. For example, students might have access to the online catalog from their dormitory rooms, or professors, from their office or home computers. (Details on the OPAC can be found in Chapter 5.)

Many libraries belong to *networks* which are linked together via telecommunications facilities for the purpose of sharing resources. Such services as inter-library loan, cooperative cataloging, and bibliographic reference services are available to members of the network. Members share cataloging records and agree to lend one another materials.

The term "online database" is used to describe information which is stored in a computer and retrieved by other computers through telephone lines and communications networks. *Online databases* came into being during the early 1970s when private companies began to market them to users. These early databases consisted mainly of bibliographic type information such as that found in printed indexes and catalogs. Although online databases were expensive to access, they proved to be a tremendously effective way to find information. Initially only a handful of online databases were available, but that changed quickly in response to the demands of users. There are now thousands of online databases, providing nearly every type of information: bibliographic, full text, raw data, and illustrative materials. Although commercial vendors are still the major producers of online databases, government agencies and professional and scholarly organizations also produce and disseminate online databases. The costs of accessing online databases varies, but in general, the benefits of online databases outweigh the costs. (See Chapter 10 for a fuller discussion of online databases.)

Libraries with microcomputers create *in-house databases* which can be stored on hard disks, floppy disks, or magnetic tapes. The kinds of information created may consist of community information, campus announcements, job listings, local statistics, research in progress, and vertical file type material.

Optical disk technology has given rise to CD-ROM. These small (4.75 inches) plastic coated disks hold an enormous amount of data. One disk is equal in contents to approximately 250,000 printed pages, or about 300 books. The information stored on CD-ROM cannot be erased or altered, although it can be transferred to another utility such as a floppy disk or magnetic tape. CD-ROM requires a microcomputer with appropriate software and a disk player to run the program. There are hundreds of CD-ROM databases available. These include indexes, census data, corporation records, encyclopedias, government document collections, statistics, compilations of maps, journal backfiles, and other literary works.

The equipment used to store and access information in electronic format consists of microcomputers, computer terminals, and laser disk players. Telecommunications equipment is required for online databases, online catalogs, and library networking. In addition, software (computer programs) are necessary to run the various programs.

Figure 3.2.
Microfilm reader.

Figure 3.3.
Microfiche reader.

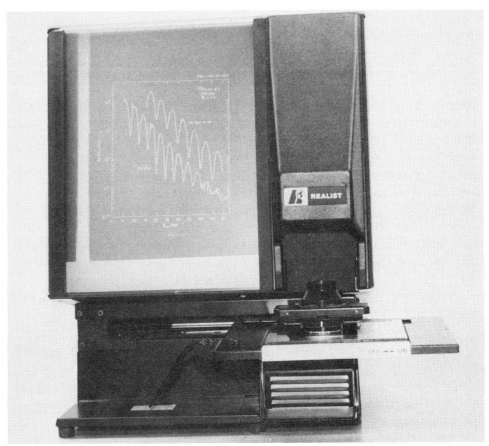

Figure 3.4. Microform material; clockwise: microfilm, microcard, microfiche, and microprint.

Figure 3.5. Information in electronic format; clockwise: magnetic tape, compact disks, floppy disks.

The format of computer-generated material is different, at least in appearance although not in content, from traditional library sources. Computer technology is developing and changing at such a fast pace that it is not possible to predict what the format of electronic information will look like even in the very near future. Library users must become familiar with computers and with the kinds of information available in electronic format if they are to keep pace with the library's resources.

REVIEW QUESTIONS
CHAPTER 3

1. Why is it important to read the preliminary pages in a book before proceeding to the text?

2. What is the difference between the copyright date and the publishing date of a book? Where are the copyright date and publishing history usually found?

3. Name the items that are included in the imprint of a book.

4. What different purposes do the table of contents and the index serve?

5. What is the difference between the preface and the introduction?

6. What is the purpose of the bibliography in a book?

7. Serials include what kinds of publications?

8. What is the difference between a thesis and a dissertation?

9. What kinds of materials are included in audio-visual collections?

10. Name the forms of electronic information common to many libraries.

11. Which of the library materials discussed in this chapter are found in your library?

PARTS OF A BOOK EXERCISE

Using the library catalog, select a book on a topic that interests you and examine its contents. Give the following information:

1. What topic or heading did you use to find this book in the library catalog?

2. Give the following about the book. If you do not find some of these items, write NA (not applicable) in the blank.
   a. Call number.

   b. Author's or authors' name(s). (If the book has editor instead of author, write ''ed'' after the name.)

   c. Full title.

   d. Place of publication. (Give first one listed.)

   e. Publisher.

   f. Edition (if given).

   g. Date of latest copyright and publishing date.

   h. Does the author state the purpose of the book? If so, state briefly what it is.

i. Is there an introduction? Identify two points made in the introduction.

j. Does the book have a table of contents?

k. Is there a list of maps or illustrations? Give pages.

l. Does it have a bibliography? Give pages.

m. Does the book have an appendix? If so, what does it contain?

n. Does the book contain an index? How many pages make up the index. What is its purpose?

o. Is there a glossary in the book? What is its purpose?

p. Does the book have a colophon? Where is it located?

3. Make a bibliographic citation for your book. Forms are shown in the textbook in Chapter 11.

How Library
Materials Are Classified

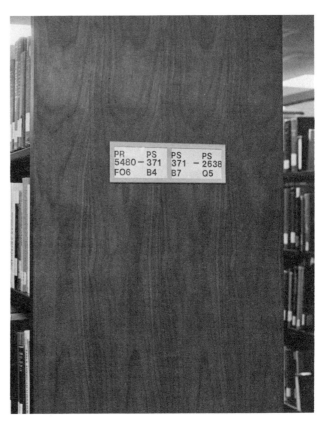

A PREVIEW

Because libraries contain such a wide variety of materials, it has been necessary to group like materials together in order to provide access. This rationale has resulted in the development of uniform classification systems for library materials. This chapter surveys the major classification schemes used by libraries and introduces the library user to the effective use of these systems.

Ever since there has been any kind of written record, attempts have been made to classify materials in some fashion. The purpose of any classification system is to bring together comparable materials so that they can be found easily and so that the library will have some logical arrangement. In addition, library patrons should be able to browse the shelves in a given subject classification number or letter and find materials on that subject grouped together. Early libraries sometimes arranged materials by author, color, or even size. The Library of Congress was originally arranged by size, but this became impractical when the library began to grow very rapidly. Modern libraries have stack areas in which materials are arranged by subject, but often these may be grouped according to format such as microform, electronic format, serials, and audio visual.

The two most commonly used classification systems in American libraries are the *Dewey Decimal Classification System* (commonly called Dewey or DC) and the *Library of Congress Classification System* (referred to as LC). Most public libraries use the Dewey system while colleges and universities use either system. Some older universities, such as Harvard University, originally developed their own system of classification and later combined it with either Dewey Decimal or Library of Congress. Other universities, such as Massachusetts Institute of Technology, changed classification systems from Dewey to LC but did not reclassify the materials in Dewey making it necessary for library patrons to learn to use both systems. Still other libraries, such as Louisiana State University, have reclassified or are in the process of reclassifying their entire collection into the Library of Congress system.

The Library of Congress system is better adapted for large research libraries than the Dewey Decimal system since it has a broader classification base and therefore provides more room for expansion as new subjects are added to the fields of knowledge. The Dewey Decimal system has half as many classes in its base, and it is much more difficult to adapt it to new subjects without getting into very long and unwieldy call numbers.

KEY TERMS

Classification System
Dewey Decimal Classification System
Library of Congress Classification System
Superintendent of Documents Classification System (SuDocs)
Shelf List
Call Numbers

Books which are written on one particular subject can be classified easily under that subject. However, this is not always possible since many books deal with more than one subject. Books are classified under the largest subject covered or under what the catalogers feel is the most important subject for their particular library. Catalogers are specially trained librarians who prepare bibliographic descriptions, assign call numbers, and determine appropriate subject headings for materials being added to the library's collection. The call numbers and subject headings are selected so that the materials being cataloged will be compatible with similar existing materials in the collection. MARC (Machine Readable Cataloging) records which are produced by the Library of Congress and marketed by various vendors include suggested Library of Congress call numbers, Dewey Decimal classification numbers, and subject headings as part of the record. Libraries purchasing these records can choose to use these suggested numbers and subject headings or create their own.

There is more variation among libraries using the Dewey system than the Library of Congress since the latter is a broader and more precise system. Subjects covered in the book which are not reflected in the call number selected by the cataloger are brought out by means of subject headings. For example, the book noted on page 80 by John A. Moyne, *Understanding Language: Man or Machine,* is classified under P37, the Library of Congress Classification number for general philology and linguistics, but the subject headings on the catalog card indicate that the book covers *psycholinguistics; linguistics—data processing; comprehension; artificial intelligence; grammar, comparative* and *general;* and *formal languages.* Subject headings will be discussed in more detail in Chapter 5.

Libraries which have extensive collections of materials published by the United States government often use the *Superintendent of Documents* or SuDocs System to classify their government-generated publications. This classification system was devised by the Superintendent of Documents to organize the thousands of publications issued each year into a systematic scheme. The SuDocs system is based on an issuing agency classification rather than on a subject classification as is the case with both Dewey and LC. The classification number only indirectly reflects the subject matter of the book or periodical. For example, a book on foreign affairs might be classified in "S" because it was published by the Department of State, not because of its subject matter.

In addition to the three major systems discussed above, libraries may also use other systems for classifying smaller special collections such as state documents, United Nations documents, or archives.

For most library users it is not necessary to learn all the details of the classification systems. In order to make effective use of the library's resources, however, the researcher needs to know which classification systems are being used and to understand the basic principles on which each classification system rests. It is also helpful to identify relevant numbers or letters/numbers in the particular field in which he/she is working. This will enable the researcher to browse the shelves to see what is available.

Some libraries have a public *shelf list* which can be used to determine the holdings of the library in a particular classification. A *shelf list* is a listing by call number on cards or on computer print-out sheets, or in a computer database of all the catalogued and classified materials owned by the library. Because the shelf list duplicates the shelf order arrangement of materials, it is useful in determining what the library owns in a particular classification. When a shelf list is available, it should be consulted since it accounts for books that might be checked out or may not be on the shelves for other reasons. This does not eliminate the need to use the library catalog.

DEWEY DECIMAL CLASSIFICATION SYSTEM

The Dewey Decimal Classification system was originated by Melvil Dewey in the latter part of the 19th century. His was not the first classification system but was one of the first based on the decimal system. The system divides all knowledge into ten different classes. These ten primary classes are further subdivided by several sets of subclasses. Within the subclasses, the cataloger is able to show even smaller subdivisions by means of decimals. The Second Summary of the Dewey Decimal Classification System is reproduced on the following pages.

SECOND SUMMARY OF THE
DEWEY DECIMAL CLASSIFICATION SYSTEM[1]

The Hundred Divisions

000 Generalities

010 Bibliography

020 Library & information sciences

030 General encyclopedic works

040 [unassigned]

050 General serials & their indexes

060 General organizations & museology

070 News media, journalism, publishing

080 General collections

090 Manuscripts & rare books

100 Philosophy & psychology

110 Metaphysics

120 Epistemology, causation, humankind

130 Paranormal phenomena

140 Specific philosophical schools

150 Psychology

160 Logic

170 Ethics (Moral philosophy)

180 Ancient, medieval, Oriental philosophy

190 Modern Western philosophy

200 Religion

210 Natural theology

---

1. Reproduced from Edition 12 of the *Dewey Decimal Classification*, published in 1990, by permission of Forest Press OCLC Online Computer Library Center, owner of copyright.

220 Bible
230 Christian theology
240 Christian moral & devotional theology
250 Christian orders & Local church
260 Christian social theology
270 Christian church history
280 Christian denominations & sects
290 Other & comparative religions

300 Social sciences

310 General Statistics
320 Political science
330 Economics
340 Law
350 Public administration
360 Social services; association
370 Education
380 Commerce, communication, transport
390 Customs, etiquette, folklore

400 Language

410 Linguistics
420 English & Old English
430 Germanic languages German
440 Romance languages French
450 Italian, Romanian, Rhaeto-Romanic
460 Spanish & Portuguese languages
470 Italic languages Latin
480 Hellenic languages Classical Greek
490 Other languages

500 Natural sciences & mathematics

510 Mathematics
520 Astronomy & allied sciences
530 Physics
540 Chemistry & allied sciences
550 Earth Sciences
560 Paleontology Paleozoology
570 Life sciences
580 Botanical sciences
590 Zoological sciences

600 Technology (Applied sciences)

610 Medical sciences Medicine

620 Engineering & allied operations

630 Agriculture

640 Home economics & family living

650 Management & auxiliary services

660 Chemical engineering

670 Manufacturing

680 Manufacture for specific uses

690 Buildings

700 The arts

710 Civic & landscape art

720 Architecture

730 Plastic arts Sculpture

740 Drawing & decorative arts

750 Painting & paintings

760 Graphic arts Printmaking & prints

770 Photography & photographs

780 Music

790 Recreational & performing arts

800 Literature & rhetoric

810 American literature in English

820 English & Old English literatures

830 Literatures of Germanic languages

840 Literatures of Romance languages

850 Italian, Romanian, Rhaeto-Romanic

860 Spanish & Portuguese literatures

870 Italic literatures Latin

880 Hellenic literatures Classical Greek

890 Literatures of other languages

900 Geography & history

910 Geography & travel

920 Biography, genealogy, insignia

930 History of ancient world

940 General history of Europe

950 General history of Asia Far East

960 General history of Africa

970 General history of North America

980 General history of South America

990 General history of other areas

The Dewey Decimal Classification system begins with 000 (Generalities) and continues through 100 (Philosophy and psychology), 300 (Social sciences), 500 (Natural sciences and mathematics), and 900 (Geography and history). Under 900, 940 is general history of Europe, 970 the general history of North America, and 980 the general history of South America. These numbers can be further subdivided.

For example:

970	General history of North America
973	is for the United States
973.2	Colonial period 1607–1775
973.7	Civil War 1861–1865
973.71	Political and economic history (Civil War period)
973.73	Military operations
973.7349	Battle of Gettysburg
973.9	20th century 1901–
973.92	Later 20th century 1953–

The example above illustrates how the addition of each decimal number to the whole number makes the classification more precise. Notice that 973.7 is used for general information on the Civil War, but 973.71 is assigned to books only on the economic and political history of the period. 973.73 is the number for military operations in general, while 973.7349 is for a particular battle of the Civil War. The same principle applies to the Library of Congress Classification system except that both letters and numbers are added to achieve a more precise classification.

LIBRARY OF CONGRESS CLASSIFICATION SYSTEM

The Library of Congress Classification system was designed by the Library of Congress in the latter part of the 19th century solely for its own use. Because it is so comprehensive, it has been adopted by many other large libraries both in the United States and in other parts of the world. Since one condition of copyright is that two copies of the work be presented to the Library of Congress, the Library receives copies of every book copyrighted in the United States. In addition, the Library of Congress acquires numerous other publications from all over the world. Most of these are classified and catalogued by the Library of Congress, and the call numbers are published for the use of anyone wanting to use them. Each book has an individual call number assigned to it, so that there is not as much variation among libraries using this system as with the Dewey Decimal system.

The Library of Congress system, or LC, as it is commonly called, has 21 different classes with numerous subdivisions under each class. Each primary class is designated by a single letter. For example: A is *General works;* B, *Psychology, religion and philosophy;* G, *Geography, anthropology, and recreation;* P, *Language and literature;* and T, *Technology.* The addition of a second letter indicates a smaller subject under the large subject. For example: AE is for *General encyclopedias;* BR, *Christianity;* GC, *Oceanography;* PE, *English language;* PR, *English literature;* and TH, *Building construction.* The K class for law has three letters in some instances. The third letter indicates the state, city, or territory. For example: KFL 0–599 is Louisiana law; KFO 2400–2999, Oregon law; KFN 5000–6199, New York law. Following the first letter or group of letters, each class number has a whole number which indicates a still smaller subdivision. This whole number is often followed by another letter/number combination subdividing the subject even more.

For example:

HF Commerce	HF Commerce	HF Commerce
5686 Accounting	5686 Accounting	5686 Accounting
.D7 Drug stores	.P3 Petroleum industry	.S75 Steel industry

Reproduced on the next several pages is a brief outline of the LC system. Although the system is based on the alphabet, not all of the letters have been used in either the main classes or the subclasses. These letters are reserved for new subjects or for the expansion of older subjects, or in the case of I and O, to avoid confusion with the numbers 1 and 0. Some libraries with very specialized collections sometimes adapt these unused letters to their own use if the existing class proves inadequate.

LIBRARY OF CONGRESS CLASSIFICATION SYSTEM CLASSES AND SUBCLASSES[2]

A General Works

AC	Collections. Series. Collected works
AE	Encyclopedias (General)
AG	Dictionaries and other general reference books
AI	Indexes (General)
AM	Museums (General). Collectors and collecting (General)
AN	Newspapers
AP	Periodicals (General)
AS	Academics and learned societies (General)
AY	Yearbooks. Almanacs. Directories
AZ	History of scholarship and learning. The humanities Popular errors, delusions and superstitions

B Philosophy. Psychology. Religion

B	Philosophy (General)
BC	Logic
BD	Speculative philosophy
BF	Psychology

2. U.S. Library of Congress, Subject Cataloging Division, *LC Classification Outline*, 5th ed. (Washington, D.C.: GPO, 1986).

BH	Aesthetics
BJ	Ethics. Social usages. Etiquette
BL	Religions. Mythology. Rationalism
BM	Judaism
BP	Islam. Bahaism. Theosophy, etc.
BQ	Buddhism
BR	Christianity
BS	The Bible
BT	Doctrinal theology.
BV	Practical theology
BX	Christian denominations

C Auxiliary Sciences of History

C	Auxiliary sciences of history (General)
CB	History of civilization
CC	Archaeology (General)
CD	Diplomatics. Archives. Seals
CE	Technical chronology. Calendar
CJ	Numismatics
CN	Inscriptions. Epigraphy
CR	Heraldry
CS	Genealogy
CT	Biography

D History: General and Old World

D	History (General)
DA	Great Britain
DB	Austria. Liechtenstein. Hungary. Czechoslovakia
DC	France, Andorra, Monaco
DD	Germany
DE	The Mediterranean Region. Greco-Roman World
DF	Greece
DG	Italy
DH	Netherlands. (Low Countries)
DJ	Netherlands (Holland)
DJK	Eastern Europe
DK	Soviet Union
DL	Northern Europe. Scandinavia
DP	Spain. Portugal
DQ	Switzerland
DR	Balkan Peninsula
DS	Asia

DT   Africa

DU   Oceania (South Seas)

DX   Gypsies

E-F History: America

E   11–29   America (General)

    31–46   North America

    51–99   Indians. Indians of North America

    101–135   Discovery of America and early explorations

    151   United States (General)

    184–185.98   Elements in the population

    184.5–185.98   Afro-Americans

    186–199   Colonial history

    201–298   Revolution

    301–453   Revolution to the Civil War

    351–364.9   War of 1812

    401–415.2   War with Mexico

    441–453   Slavery

    456–655   Civil War

    482–489   Confederate States of America

    660–738   Late nineteenth century

    714–735   Spanish-American War

    740–   Twentieth century

F   1–975   United States local history

    1001–1140   British America. Canada

    1201–1392   Mexico

    1401–1419   Latin America (General)

    1421–1577   Central America

    1601–2191   West Indies

    2201–2239   South America (General)

    2251–2291   Colombia

    2301–2349   Venezuela

    2351–2471   Guianas. Guyana. Surinam. French Guiana

    2501–2659   Brazil

    2661–2699   Paraguay

    2701–2799   Uruguay

    2801–3031.5   Argentina

    3051–3285   Chile

    3301–3359   Bolivia

    3401–3619   Peru

    3701–3799   Ecuador

G Geography. Anthropology. Recreation

G	Geography (General) Atlases. Maps
GA	Mathematical geography. Cartography
GB	Physical geography
GC	Oceanography
GF	Human ecology. Anthropogeography
GN	Anthropology
GR	Folklore
GT	Manners and customs (General)
GV	Recreation. Leisure.

H Social Sciences

H	Social sciences (General)
HA	Statistics

Economics

HB	Economic theory. Demography
HC-HD	Economic history and conditions
HE	Transportation and communications
HF	Commerce
HG	Finance
HJ	Public finance

Sociology

HM	Sociology (General and theoretical)
HN	Social history. Social problems. Social reform
HQ	The family. Marriage. Woman
HS	Societies: Secret, benevolent, etc. Clubs
HT	Communities. Classes. Races
HV	Social pathology. Social and public welfare. Criminology
HX	Socialism. Communism. Anarchism

J Political Science

J	General legislative and executive papers
JA	Collections and general works
JC	Political theory. Theory of the state

Constitutional history and administration

JF	General works. Comparative works

Special countries

JK	United States
JL	British America. Latin America
JN	Europe

JQ	Asia. Africa. Australia. Oceania	
JS	Local government	
JV	Colonies and colonization. Emigration and immigration	
JX	International law. International relations	

K Law

K	1–7720	Law (General)
	201–287	Jurisprudence. Philosophy and theory of law
	520–5582	Comparative law. International uniform law
	7000–7720	Conflict of laws

Law of the United Kingdom and Ireland

KD	51–9500	England and Wales
	8850–9312	Local laws of England
	9320–9355	Local laws of Wales
	9400–9500	Wales
KDC	51–990	Scotland
KDE	21–580	Northern Ireland
KDG	26–540	Isle of Man. Channel Islands
KDK	21–1950	Ireland (Eire)
KDZ	0–4999	America. North America
	1100–1199	Organization of American States

Law of Canada

KE	1–9450	Federal law. Common and collective provincial law

Individual provinces and territories

KEA	0–599	Alberta
KEB	0–599	British Columbia
KEM	0–599	Manitoba
KEN	0–599	New Brunswick
	1200–1799	Newfoundland
	5400–5999	Northwest Territories
	7400–7999	Nova Scotia
KEO	0–1199	Ontario
KEP	0–599	Prince Edward Island
KEQ	0–1199	Quebec
KES	0–599	Saskatchewan
KEY	0–599	Yukon Territory
KEZ	0–9999	Individual cities, A-Z

Law of the United States

KF	1–9827	Federal law. Common and collective state law

		Individual states
		Individual states
KFA	0–599	Alabama
	1200–1799	Alaska
	2400–2999	Arizona
	3600–4199	Arkansas
KFC	0–1199	California
	1800–2399	Colorado
	3600–4199	Connecticut
KFD	0–599	Delaware
	1200–1799	District of Columbia
KFF	0–599	Florida
KFG	0–599	Georgia
KFH	0–599	Hawaii
KFI	0–599	Idaho
	1200–1799	Illinois
	3000–3599	Indiana
	4200–4799	Iowa
KFK	0–599	Kansas
	1200–1799	Kentucky
KFL	0–599	Louisiana
KFM	0–599	Maine
	1200–1799	Maryland
	2400–2999	Massachusetts
	4200–4799	Michigan
	5400–5999	Minnesota
	6600–7199	Mississippi
	7800–8399	Missouri
	9000–9599	Montana
KFN	0–599	Nebraska
	600–1199	Nevada
	1200–1799	New Hampshire
	1800–2399	New Jersey
	3600–4199	New Mexico
	5000–6199	New York
	7400–7999	North Carolina
	8600–9199	North Dakota
KFO	0–599	Ohio
	1200–1799	Oklahoma
	2400–2999	Oregon
KFP	0–599	Pennsylvania
KFR	0–599	Rhode Island
KFS	1800–2399	South Carolina

	3000–3599	South Dakota
KFT	0–599	Tennessee
	1200–1799	Texas
KFU	0–599	Utah
KFV	0–599	Vermont
	2400–2999	Virginia
KFW	0–599	Washington
	1200–1799	West Virginia
	2400–2999	Wisconsin
	4200–4799	Wyoming
KFX	0–9999	Individual cities, A-Z
KFZ	1800–2399	Northwest Territory
	8600–9199	Confederate States of America
KG	0–999	Latin America (General)
	3000–3999	Mexico and Central America (General)
KGA	0–9000	Belize
KGB	0–9000	Costa Rica
KGC	0–9000	El Salvador
KGD	0–9990	Guatemala
KGE	0–9990	Honduras
KGF	0–9900	Mexico
KGG	0–9900	Nicaragua
KGH	0–8000	Panama
	9000–9499	Panama Canal Zone
		West Indies. Caribbean area
KGJ	0–999	General
	7000–7499	Anguilla
KGK	0–499	Antigua and Barbuda
	1000–1499	Aruba
KGL	0–499	Bahamas
	1000–1499	Barbados
	2000–2499	Bonaire
	3000–3499	British Leeward Islands
	4000–4499	British Virgin Islands
	5000–5999	British West Indies
	6000–6499	British Windward Islands
KGM	0–499	Cayman Islands
KGN	0–9800	Cuba
KGP	0–499	Curaçao
	2000–2499	Dominica
KGQ	0–9800	Dominican Republic
KGR	0–499	Dutch Leeward Islands (General)

	1000–1499	Dutch West Indies (Netherlands Antilles)
	2000–2499	Dutch Windward Islands (General)
	3000–3499	French West Indies (General)
	4000–4499	Grenada
	5000–5499	Guadeloupe
KGS	0–9000	Haiti
KGT	0–499	Jamaica
	1000–1499	Martinique
	2000–2499	Montserrat
KGU	0–499	Navassa Islands
KGV	0–8200	Puerto Rico
KGW	0–499	Saba
	2000–2499	Saint Christopher (Saint Kitts), Nevis, and Anguilla
	3000–3499	Saint Lucia
	5000–5499	Saint Vincent and the Grenadines
	7000–7499	Sint Eustatius
	8000–8499	Sint Maarten
KGX	0–499	Trinidad and Tobago
KGY	0–499	Turks and Caicos Islands
KGZ	0–499	Virgin Islands of the United States
KH	0–999	South America (General)
KHA	0–9800	Argentina
KHC	0–8200	Bolivia
KHD	0–9900	Brazil
KHF	0–9800	Chile
KHH	0–9900	Colombia
KHK	0–9990	Ecuador
KHL	0–9000	Falkland Islands
KHM	0–9000	French Guiana
KHN	0–9000	Guyana
KHP	0–9700	Paraguay
KHQ	0–980	Peru
KHS	0–9000	Surinam
KHU	0–9800	Uruguay
KHW	0–9900	Venezuela
		Europe
KJ	2–1040	History of Law
	160–1040	Germanic law
KJA	2–3660	Roman law
KJC, KJE		Regional comparative and uniform law

KJG	0–4999	Albania
KJH	0–499	Andorra
KJJ	0–4999	Austria
KJK	0–4999	Belgium
KJM	0–4999	Bulgaria
KJN	0–499	Cyprus
KJP	0–4999	Czechoslovakia
KJR	0–4999	Denmark
KJT	0–4999	Finland
		France
KJV	2–9158	National laws
KJW	51–4360	Individual regions, provinces, departments, etc.
	5201–9600	Individual cities
		Germany
KK	2–9799.3	Germany and West Germany
KKA	7–9796	East Germany
KKB, KKC		Individual states, provinces, and cities
KKE	0–4999	Greece
KKF	0–4999	Hungary
KKG	0–499	Iceland
KKH	0–4999	Italy
KKI	0–499	Liechtenstein
KKK	0–499	Luxembourg
	1000–1499	Malta
KKL	0–499	Monaco
KKM	0–4999	Netherlands
KKN	0–4999	Norway
KKP	0–4999	Poland
KKQ	0–4999	Portugal
KKR	0–4999	Romania
KKS	0–499	San Marino
KKT	0–4999	Spain
KKW	0–4999	Switzerland
KKX	0–4999	Turkey
KKY	04–499	Vatican City
KKZ	0–4999	Yugoslavia

L Education

L	Education (General)
LA	History of education
LB	Theory and practice of education
LC	Special aspects of education
	Individual institutions: universities, colleges, and schools
LD	United States
LE	America, except United States
LF	Europe
LG	Asia. Africa. Oceania
LH	College and school magazines and papers
LJ	Student fraternities and societies, United States
LT	Textbooks

M Music and Books on Music

M	Music
ML	Literature of music
MT	Musical instruction and study

N Fine Arts

N	Visual arts (General)
NA	Architecture
NB	Sculpture
NC	Drawing. Design. Illustration
ND	Painting
NE	Print media
NK	Decorative arts. Applied arts. Decoration and ornament
NX	Arts in general

P Language and Literature

P	Philology and linguistics (General)
PA	Classical languages and literatures
PB	Modern European languages
PC	Romance languages
PD	Germanic languages
PE	English
PF	West Germanic
PG	Slavic, Baltic, Albanian languages and literature
PH	Finno-Ugrian, Basque languages and literatures
PJ	Oriental languages and literatures
PK	Indo-Iranian

PL	Languages and literatures of Eastern Asia, Africa, Oceania
PM	Hyperborean, Indian, and Artificial languages
PN	Literature
PQ	Romance literatures
PR	English literature
PS	American literature
PT	Germanic literatures
PZ	Juvenile belles lettres

Q Science

Q	Science (General)
QA	Mathematics
QB	Astronomy
QC	Physics
QD	Chemistry
QE	Geology
QH	Natural history (General). Biology (General)
QK	Botany
QL	Zoology
QM	Human anatomy
QP	Physiology
QR	Microbiology

R Medicine

R	Medicine (General)
RA	Public aspects of medicine
RB	Pathology
RC	Internal medicine. Practice of medicine
RD	Surgery
RE	Ophthalmology
RF	Otorhinolaryngology
RG	Gynecology and obstetrics
RJ	Pediatrics
RK	Dentistry
RL	Dermatology
RM	Therapeutics. Pharmacology
RS	Pharmacy and materia medica
RT	Nursing
RV	Botanic, Thomsonian, and eclectic medicine
RX	Homeopathy
RZ	Other systems of medicine

S Agriculture

S	Agriculture (General)
SB	Plant culture
SD	Forestry
SF	Animal culture
SH	Aquaculture. Fisheries. Angling
SK	Hunting

T Technology

T	Technology (General)
TA	Engineering (General). Civil engineering (General)
TC	Hydraulic engineering
TD	Environmental technology. Sanitary engineering
TE	Highway engineering. Roads and pavements
TF	Railroad engineering and operation
TG	Bridge engineering
TH	Building construction
TJ	Mechanical engineering and machinery
TK	Electrical engineering. Electronics. Nuclear engineering
TL	Motor vehicles. Aeronautics. Astronautics
TN	Mining engineering. Metallurgy
TP	Chemical technology
TR	Photography
TS	Manufactures
TT	Handicrafts. Arts and crafts
TX	Home economics

U Military Science

U	Military science (General)
UA	Armies: Organization, description, facilities, etc.
UB	Military administration
UC	Maintenance and transportation
UD	Infantry
UE	Cavalry. Armored and mechanized cavalry
UF	Artillery
UG	Military Engineering. Air forces. Air warfare
UH	Other services

V Naval Science

V	Naval science (General)
VA	Navies: Organization, description, facilities, etc.
VB	Naval administration

VC	Naval maintenance
VD	Naval seamen
VE	Marines
VF	Naval ordnance
VG	Minor services of the navies
VK	Navigation. Merchant marine
VM	Naval architecture. Shipbuilding. Marine engineering

Z Bibliography. Library Science

Z	Books in general
4–8	History of books and bookmaking
40–115.5	Writing
116–659	Book industries and trade
662–1000.5	Libraries and library science
1001–8999	Bibliography

SUDOCS CLASSIFICATION SYSTEM

Libraries which serve as depository libraries usually establish separate documents collections arranged by Superintendent of Documents (SuDocs) number. This is the classification system used by the Government Printing Office to assign call numbers to documents before they are sent to depository libraries. Libraries receiving a large number of government publications have found it easier to use the SuDocs classification system rather than to catalog each document in the Library of Congress or Dewey Decimal systems. Libraries receiving only a small percentage of the available documents often integrate the documents in with the general collection. In libraries where documents are housed and classified separately, it is not unusual to find that documents are not listed in the library catalog. This practice is changing, however, with the advent of online catalogs. More and more libraries are including the records for U.S. government documents in the OPAC. However, the online catalog records may include only those materials cataloged since 1976, when the Government Printing Office began cataloging government documents in machine readable form. It is good practice for the library user to determine whether government publications are listed in the library's catalog and the extent to which these are listed. It is also important to be able to distinguish a SuDocs classification number from a Dewey or Library of Congress Classification number. Figure 5.23 is an example of a record of a U.S. government publication in the online catalog.

The SuDocs system is an alphanumeric system based on the agency which issues the publication rather than on subject as in the case of the Dewey or Library of Congress systems. The initial letter or letters designate the government agency, bureau, or department responsible for the publication. Following is an illustration of the arrangement of the SuDocs classification system:

A	Agriculture
AE	Archives and Records
C	Commerce

D	Defense
E	Energy
ED	Education
EP	Environmental Protection
FR	Federal Reserve System
GS	General Services Administration
HE	Health and Human Services
HH	Housing and Urban Development
I	Interior
J	Justice
JU	Judiciary
L	Labor
LC	Library of Congress
NAS	National Aeronautics and Space Agency
Pr	President's Office
S	State Department
SI	Smithsonian Institution
T	Treasury
TD	Transportation
VA	Veterans Administration
Y	Congressional Publications

A sub-agency is assigned the initial letter(s) of the agency of which it is a part plus numbers which identify the specific agency. In some instances, second level agencies are broken down still further. Publications of the Department of Health and Human Services, for instance, are designated with the initial notation HE. The publications of the Secretary of the Department of Health and Human Services are assigned the number HE 1; HE 20. is used for Public Health Services; HE 20.2300 is used for the Center of Disease Control. Publications are then assigned a number based on the series or category grouping of the publication.

For example:

.1	Annual reports
.2	General publications
.3	Bulletins
.4	Circulars
.5	Laws
.6	Regulations
.7	Press releases
.8	Handbooks, manuals, guides
.9	Bibliographies
.10	Directories
.11	Maps and charts

.12 Posters

.13 Forms

.14 Addresses, lectures, etc.

For example:

HE 1.1:yr. is the annual report of the Secretary of Health and Human Services.
HE 20.1:yr. is the annual report of the Public Health Services.

Publications which are part of a series are assigned a number which designates a particular series. Each individual publication in the series is assigned a number or letter/number combination which identifies the individual title, volume, year, or issue number. This number follows a colon. The following example illustrates the elements in a typical SuDocs number:

C 3.134/2:C 83/2/983

C =	Issuing Department—Commerce Department
3 =	Subagency—Bureau of the Census
134/2 =	Series—Statistical Abstract Supplement
C 83/2/983 =	Title and date—*County and City Data Book*, 1983.

CALL NUMBERS

The call number assigned to a book indicates its subject matter, author, or in the case of a book with an editor, the first letters of the title. In turn the call number, either alone or in conjunction with an added location symbol, determines the location of the book on the shelves. For example, a book with the call number BF or BF311 .G339 1985 would be shelved in the stacks, but if the same

311
.G339
1985

call number had "Ref" above it, then the book would be shelved in the reference collection. It is common practice to write call numbers either vertically or horizontally. On a catalog card or on the spine of the book it is usually written vertically for the sake of convenience. On the other hand, call numbers appearing on online catalog or on CD-ROM screens are written horizontally. Either method is considered correct and often depends on the amount of available space. Libraries using the Library of Congress classification system also have the option to place the class number on the top line with the class letter or under the class letter. For example, a call number appearing on the online catalog screen as PN3433.2.H37 1986 might appear on the catalog card or on the spine of the book written either as

PN	*or*	PN3433
3433		.2
.2		.H37
.H37		1986
1986		

Both notation methods are considered correct and is a matter of individual library preference. In a library's collection each book has a distinctive call number so that no two books ever have exactly the same call number. With multivolume sets such as general encyclopedias, each volume has a different volume number making the call number unique to that volume. This is also true of multiple copies of a book. Each book has the same class and book number, but each one has a different copy number, and perhaps location symbol, in its call number.

In both Dewey and LC the call number is composed of the class or classification number and the book number. The class number is the top or first part of the call number and is derived from the subject matter of the book. Generally, every book on the same subject will have the same class number.

The book number, which is also referred to as the Cutter number, stands for the author of the book and sometimes the title. It is called the Cutter number after Charles A. Cutter, who devised a set of tables using the first letter or letters of a name plus a number so that all books with the same class number are together on the shelves, arranged in alphabetical order by the first letter of the author's last name. In the Dewey system, if the author has written several books on the same subject, then the first letter of the title of the book is added to the book number. If different editions of a book are issued, an edition number is added as part of the book number.

For example:

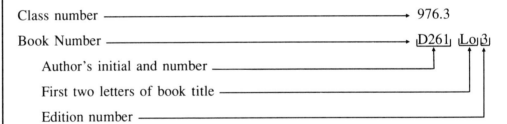

The Library of Congress book numbers follow the same basic pattern. The letter stands for the first letter of the author's last name, but the number varies with the book. If an author writes several books on the same subject, instead of adding a letter standing for the title of the book to the book number, the book number is changed. If there are several editions of the same book, the date of the edition is added to the bottom of the call number.

For example:

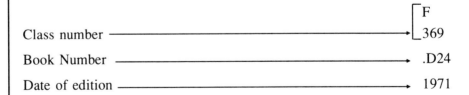

The following illustration demonstrates how several books by the same author are classified in both the Dewey and LC systems. Notice in both examples that the class number remains constant for all of the books since they are all on the same subject. However, in the Dewey system the first part of the book number remains the same, "D261," while the remaining part changes to differentiate among the different titles and different editions of those titles. In the LC system, while the "D" remains constant in all of the book numbers, the number following the "D" changes—D24, D25, D26—for the different titles. Different editions of the same titles are noted by the addition of dates to the call numbers.

In both the Dewey and LC systems, it is necessary to read the numbers/letters in the call numbers sequentially in order to locate books on the shelves or in the shelf list. In Dewey the number before the decimal point is always treated as a whole number or integer while all of the numbers following the decimal point are treated as decimals. Although the decimal point may not appear physically in the call number, the Cutter or book number is nevertheless treated as a decimal.

Library of Congress		**Dewey Decimal**
F 369 .D24 1971	Davis, Edwin Adams Louisiana; a narrative history . . . 1971	976.3 D261Lo3
F 369 .D24 1965	Davis, Edwin Adams Louisiana; a narrative history . . . 1965	976.3 D261Lo2
F 369 .D24 1961	Davis, Edwin Adams Louisiana; a narrative history . . . 1961	976.3 D261Lo
F 369 .D25 1975	Davis, Edwin Adams Louisiana, the Pelican state . . . 1975	976.3 D261L4
F 369 .D25 1969	Davis, Edwin Adams Louisiana, the Pelican state . . . 1969	976.3 D261L3
F 369 .D25	Davis, Edwin Adams Louisiana, the Pelican state . . . 1959	976.3 D261L
F 369 .D26	Davis, Edwin Adams The story of Louisiana . . . 1960	976.3 D261s

For example,

338	would be shelved before	338
A221i		A36

Since both class numbers are the same, "338," the book must then be filed by the second line. The book numbers "A221i" and "A36" are read as ".A221i" and ".A36." Since .A221i is the smaller number it would be shelved first. In the examples below the call numbers all begin with the same number, "338"; therefore, shelving must then proceed to the decimal numbers. Since .908 is smaller than .91, .917, and .94, it would be shelved first. The following call numbers are arranged in correct order as they would stand on the shelf.

338	338	338.908	338.91	338.917	338.94
A221i	A36	F911r	B138e	R896y	R31c

When locating a call number in LC, it is necessary to start with the letter combination and then proceed to the numbers. As with Dewey, the first set of numbers is treated as a whole number. The whole number or integer is followed either by a decimal point and numbers and/or one or more letter/number combinations. These remaining numbers are all treated as decimals.

For example:

PN	would be shelved before	PN
6		6
.S55		.S6

since both .S55 and .S6 are decimals and not whole numbers. In the examples below all of the class letters are the same. Following the class letters "PN" are the numbers 6, 56, 56.3, and 57, which are read as whole numbers and arranged in numerical sequence. The next consideration when reading the call number is the letter/number combination which, in many cases, is followed by a third letter/number combination. All parts of the book numbers are read first alphabetically and then numerically as decimals. In many call numbers, the date of the book is added. When call numbers are exactly the same except for dates, as in the case with multiple editions, the books are arranged in chronological order. Notice in the second and third examples that the call numbers are exactly alike except for the 1967. The call number without the date is shelved before the one with the date. The following call numbers are arranged in correct order as they would stand on the shelf.

PN	PN	PN	PN	PN
6	56	56	56	57
.S55	.H63T5	.H63T5	.3	.A43L5
		1967	.N4J6	
			1971	

The call numbers for documents are usually written horizontally unless there is not space on the spine of the book to write the numbers. In that case, the numbers are written vertically, with the break occurring at a punctuation mark.

For example:

A 13.106/2–2
C 35

Documents with SuDocs call numbers are shelved in alphanumeric sequence. The numbers following periods are whole numbers as are the numbers following slashes or colons. The following SuDocs numbers are in shelf order:

A 2.113:C 35   A 13.92:R 59   A 13.92/2:F 29   A 13.103:163
A 13.106/2–2:11

Many libraries have books housed in areas other than the regular stacks, and these areas are usually indicated by a symbol over the call number. For example, books on the reference shelves often will have the symbols R, Ref, or X. It is necessary to check the library handbook or a chart of symbols to determine their meaning and location.

REVIEW QUESTIONS
CHAPTER 4

1. Which two classification systems are used in most academic libraries in the United States?

2. How many main classes are found in the Dewcy Decimal classification system? How many in the Library of Congress classification system?

3. What does the class or classification number stand for in the call number in either the Dewcy or the LC system?

4. What is the term applied in both systems to the letter/number combination which stands for the author of the book?

5. As more letters and numbers are added to the call number, does it become more precise or less precise? Justify your answer.

6. In both classification systems the number before the decimal point is treated as a whole number. How are the numbers in the book number treated?

7. What is the SuDocs classification system? How does it differ from the Dewey and LC classification systems?

8. Why is it useful for researchers to become familiar with class letters and numbers in their subjects of interest?

9. What is the shelf list?

10. What determines the location of a book in the library's collection? Why are location symbols used in some libraries?

CALL NUMBER EXERCISE

Listed below are two sets of call numbers. For each set, identify the classification system used and arrange each group of numbers within the set in shelf order.

Classification system _____

PS 559 .R87R8	PR 5219 .R26Q3 1856	PR 132 .T8	PQ 3939 .D37E4	PR 5219 .R26L5 1865
HT 393 .L616	HT 393 .L62R323	HT 393 .L62L52	HT 393 .L62R52	HT 393 .L6R52
KFL 112 .A2 1820	KFL 45 .1 .W35	KFL 45 .A212	KFL 211 .Z9L68	KFL 30 .5 .N48A3 1910
TD 525 .L6S4	TD 194 .5 .E58	TD 624 .L8A53	TD 195 .P4U555 1978	TD 525 .L3J48

Classification system _____

261 R51k	261 R6h	261 R13p	261 R13pr	261 R519g
828 M57p	828 M57	828 M57b	828 M5655	828 M152g
973.016 W93	973.7349 Ev26a	973.41 W277	973.8 G767ca	973.8 G767
341.6016 W93	341.7 Am26	341.67 Am35a	341.63 Am14c	341.6016 Am4

Classification system

D301.6:177-19/988
D101.25:3-6625-260-50

D5.350:96943
D103.6/8:IG

D301.6:177-19/989

Y4.Ap6/6:L11/990/pt.2
Y4.Ap6/6: L11/99/0/pt.1

Y3.T25: 2 W53
Y4. Ag8/1:F22/71

Y3 Ad6: 2F31

Al3.13:F39
AE110:9 Sy8

Al3.13: W36/2/989
A13.13:Si9/11/988

Al3.2: Si 3/7

HE20.3038:G28/988
HE23.3002:Ea7

HH1.108/a:N81c
HE20.9408:P27

HH1.2:R26/11

EP1.8:Su7/5
ED1.308:D84

ED1.17:D84
E3.2:Ut3/2

E3.45:988

The Catalog:
Access to Library Information

A PREVIEW

One may think of the library's catalog as a massive index to virtually all the contents of the library. It is the goal of this chapter to describe the library catalog and guide the library user in a systematic way to a mastery of its use. The researcher will be introduced to traditional card catalogs and to the high technology of online catalog systems.

The key to the contents of any library is the catalog; most of the materials owned by a library are listed there. If library users know how to use the library's catalog, they will be able to access those materials. Traditional library catalogs were usually in the form of index cards arranged alphabetically. Catalogs used to find information in today's libraries come in several different formats. These include card, online, COM (Computer Output Microform), CD-ROM (Compact Disk-Read Only Memory) and book catalogs. Many libraries use a combination of several different kinds of catalogs. Some libraries, because of the expense involved, cannot afford to change all of their records when they convert from one catalog system to another; therefore, records for older materials are left in the prior system while current records are entered into the new one. For example, a library changing from a card catalog to an online catalog might leave all of its records for materials cataloged before a certain date in the card catalog and enter only records for materials processed after that date into the new online catalog. It is necessary for the patron to determine which kind or kinds of catalogs the library is using in order to determine what materials are available. This information is generally available in the library's handbook or from a reference librarian.

TYPES OF LIBRARY CATALOGS

Book Catalogs

Early libraries often used *book catalogs* which listed the library's holdings in book form. It was difficult to keep these catalogs up-to-date, and therefore, it was necessary to issue frequent supplements. Because of the ease with which computer-generated materials can be reproduced, some libraries are going back to the book catalog. Usually these are small libraries such as a company library, one affiliated with a research organization, or a library having several branches. With a book catalog, it is rather easy to maintain several catalogs at the same time in different locations. The "updates" are kept in a separate volume until complete revisions are made. Library patrons must consult several different volumes to be sure that they are getting all the references available.

COM Catalogs

A COM catalog (Computer Output Microform) lists the library's holdings on microfiche and may be accessed by author, title, subject, and sometimes by keyword and classification number. The different parts of a microfiche catalog are often color-coded, such as yellow for authors or titles of books, blue for serials, white for subjects, and green for keyword access. The different parts of the catalog are filed in separate files and microfiche readers are placed nearby for ease of use and convenience (see Figure 3.3). Some COM catalogs have microfiche files arranged by classification number. This enables patrons to see what the library owns in a certain classification. For example, to find out what the library has in the LC class, "NC," (the class letter combination for sculpture) one should consult the classified part of the catalog under NC; all of the holdings will be together. The same technique may be used when the library has a public shelf list on cards or call number access on an online catalog.

CD-ROM Catalogs

One of the newer technologies being used in some libraries is the CD-ROM catalog. It is a catalog on compact disk and requires a workstation consisting of a microcomputer with a monitor and compact disk drive. Usually there is a printer attached. The CD-ROM catalog looks and works like an online catalog, but instead of being operated from a mainframe computer, it runs on a microcomputer. The information is in the same machine readable format as the online catalog, and the screens are the same. The only difference is in the type of storage. With an online database, the records are stored on magnetic tape, while records on CD-ROM are stored on a compact disk.

CD-ROM catalogs are not as expensive to install and maintain as an online system, yet they offer the same convenience and ease of use as the online catalog. Searching is performed in the same manner as on an online catalog by author, title, subject, or keyword. With most CD-ROM catalogs it is possible to sort the results of a search by author, title, or call number. Most workstations have printers for printing the search results. CD-ROM catalogs can be set up at separate workstations, each with its own compact disk drive, or they can be arranged in a network to work from one disk drive. Workstations can be clustered in one area or scattered in different areas.

The principal disadvantage of the CD-ROM catalog is that it is not updated as frequently as an online database or a card catalog. The disks are updated by a vendor who must "master" a completely new disk each time information is added. This is usually done only once a month. Thus materials added to the collection will not appear on the system until a new disk is mastered. Some systems have auxiliary cartridges which permit more frequent updates, but even these do not provide continuous additions to the records as is possible with online databases and card catalogs. CD-ROM systems do not have dial-up access capabilities from off-site locations as do many online catalogs.

Card Catalogs

Many libraries have dictionary-type catalogs consisting of multiple drawers containing 3 X 5 cards arranged alphabetically by author, title, subject, and added entries. Added entries consist of cards for such things as editors, compilers, translators, illustrators, arrangers of music, and series. Some dictionary-type catalogs are divided into sections and are referred to as divided catalogs. Divided catalogs may consist of three sections: author, title, and subject or two sections: author/title and subject. The cards in each section are filed alphabetically word-by-word.

Practically every book, with the exception of fiction, has at least three cards in the catalog. These are: the author, or main entry card; the title card; and one or more subject cards. Many books also have several added entry cards for joint authors, editors, compilers, arrangers (music), translators (important in languages, literature, and the sciences), illustrators, or series. The author card is often referred to as the "main entry." Before printed cards were in wide usage, catalog cards were either handwritten or typed, a time-consuming and, therefore, expensive process. To reduce this expense, the complete bibliographic description was placed on the author card; the information on the other cards was abbreviated. If one wanted a full bibliographic description, it was necessary to refer to the author card. Thus, the author card was called the "main entry." With printed cards, except for the top line, all the cards are identical. The author card is still referred to as the "main entry" although its original meaning is no longer valid. Many libraries no longer produce their own catalog cards but instead purchase them from either the Library of Congress or from an online catalog network. Figures 5.1–5.10, 5.13 are examples of cards generated by the Library of Congress; figures 5.11–5.12, 5.14–5.17 were produced by OCLC (Online Computer Library Center), an online processing consortium

Learning to interpret the information on the catalog card is one of the most important and useful skills that the library user can acquire. The catalog card gives the location of each item and provides a full description, including name of the author, complete title, edition, number of pages, size, publisher, place of publication, date of publication, etc. Thus, it is possible to learn a great deal about the item even before it is located in the library. The catalog card also suggests other related subject headings under which additional material can be found.

On the following pages are some of the more common kinds of cards found in the card catalog.

Figure 5.1.   Author card.

```
(1)
  P                 (2)
  37          Moyne, John A.                    (4)
  .M69        (3) Understanding language : man or machine / John A. Moyne.
  1985  (5)      — New York : Plenum Press, c1985.
                          (6)                    (7)
               (8) xvi, 357 p. : ill. ; 24 cm. — (Foundations of computer science) (9)

               (10)  Bibliography: p. 325-345.
                     Includes index.
               (11)  ISBN 0-306-41970-X


                     1. Psycholinguistics.   2. Linguistics—Data processing.   3. Comprehension.
               (12)  4. Artificial intelligence.   5. Grammar, Comparative and general.   6. Formal
                     languages.   I. Title.   II. Series.
               (13)  P37.M69   1985          (14) 401 .9         (15) 85-12341
                                                     (16)  AACR 2   MARC


               (17)  Library of Congress
```

1. Call number for the book. It is always found in the upper left corner of the card. This book is classified in ther Library of Congress Classification system.
2. Author of the book. Some cards have dates after the author's name which indicate the year of birth and sometimes death date. On newer cards this is often omitted because of the high cost of determining such information.
3. Short-title or main title of the book.
4. Subtitle or explanatory title. This is combined with the short-title to form the complete title. The complete title is necessary for bibliographic purposes.
5. Place of publication. Occasionally more than one place is indicated.
6. Publisher of the book. If more than one publisher is given, it usually indicates that the book is a reprint of a foreign publication that has also been published in this country.
7. Copyright date. Sometimes the publication date is given instead of the copyright date. It is written without the small "c" in front of the date. Sometimes both are given. For example: c1985, 1986.
8. Physical description. This includes the number of preliminary pages, number of pages of text, kinds of illustrations, if any, and the height of the book. This book has 16 preliminary pages numbered in small Roman numerals, 357 pages of the text numbered in Arabic numerals, and an unspecified illustration. It is 24 centimeters tall.
9. Series note or series notation. This book is part of the *Foundations of Computer Science* series.
10. This area is reserved for any special notes that the cataloger wants to bring to the attention of the reader. This book has a 20 page bibliography and a 10 page index.
11. International Standard Book Number. Number assigned to book by publisher for identification and ordering purposes.
12. Tracings. The tracings are a record kept by the library of the kinds and number of cards in the card catalog for that particular book. Items indicated by the Arabic numerals are the subject headings These tell the reader the subject matter covered as well as the specific headings to use to find other books on the same subject. The Roman numerals indicate added entry cards such as joint authors, title, illustrators, editors, and sometimes series.
13. Call number assigned by the Library of Congress to this book.
14. Dewey Decimal class number. Since the book number sometimes varies from library to library, only the class number is given. Each library assigns its own book number.
15. Order number used by libraries to order cards for this book from the Library of Congress.
16. Indicates that this is a Machine Readable Cataloging card. This means that the information is available on magnetic tape and is in AACR2 format. AACR2 are cataloging rules which have been prepared by the Anglo-American Cataloging Rules committees for use in American, Canadian, and British libraries.
17. Card produced by the Library of Congress.

The title card (Figure 5.2) is exactly the same as the author card except that the title is typed on the top of the card above the author's name. The title of the book is repeated under the author's name.

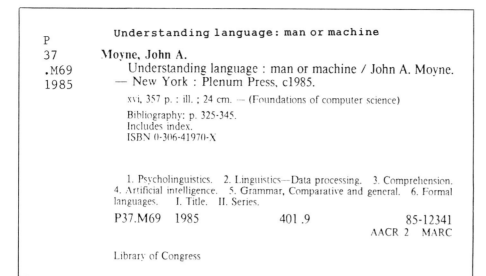

Figure 5.2.   Title card.

Figure 5.2.   Title card.

Figure 5.3.   Subject card.

Subject cards have the subject typed above the author's name in either black capital letters or lower case letters typed in red. This varies from library to library, and some card catalogs will have both. The current practice is to use black capital letters. There are six subject cards in the catalog for the book in Figure 5.3.

Figure 5.4. Cover card for a series.

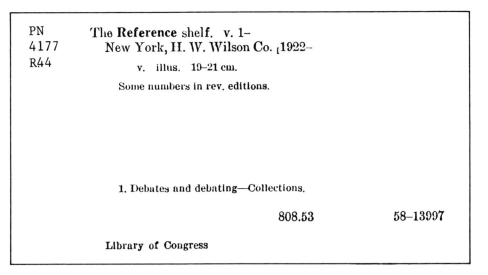

```
PN
4177        The Reference shelf.
R44                                                    (Card 86
            Contents cont'd:
v.57,no.4   The Federal deficit. 1985.
v.57,no.5   Sports in America. 1986.
v.57,no.6   Drugs and American society. 1986.
v.58,no.1   The Star Wars debate. 1986.
v.58,no.2   Vietnam ten years after. 1986.
v.58,no.3   Terrorism. 1986.
```

Figure 5.5. Contents card for a series.

```
PN        The Reference shelf. v. 1–
4177          New York, H. W. Wilson Co. [1922–
R44              v. illus.  19–21 cm.
              Some numbers in rev. editions.




          1. Debates and debating—Collections.

                              808.53              58–13997

          Library of Congress
```

A series is a set of volumes which are published successively and have some connection, such as a common subject, author, or publisher. Books which are part of a series may be located in the card catalog under the name of the series, subject of the series, editor of the series, or the author, title, and subject of each book in the series. Figures 5.4–5.6 illustrate a publisher's series. Figure 5.4 is the title entry or ''cover'' card for the series. The bracket before 1922 indicates that this information was not on the title page of the book and was added by the catalogers. When the series is completed the closing date and the remaining bracket will be added. Figure 5.5 is a partial listing of the individual volumes in the series.

```
PN
4177     The Star Wars debate / edited by Steven Anzovin. — New York
R44        : H.W. Wilson, 1986.
v.58          223 p. ; 19 cm. – (The Reference shelf ; v. 58, no. 1)
no.1          Bibliography: p. 219-223.
              ISBN 0-8242-0723-8 (pbk.)




              1. Strategic Defense Initiative – Addresses, essays, lectures.    I. Anzovin,
           Steven.   II. Series.
           UG743.S72   1986            358 .1754                85-29603
                                                            AACR 2   MARC

           Library of Congress
```

Figure 5.6. Card for an individual title in a series.

```
QA
248      Symposium on Policy Analysis and Information Systems (1980 :
.S97        Duke University)
1980         Fuzzy sets : theory and applications to policy analysis and
           information systems / edited by Paul P. Wang and S. K. Chang.
           — New York : Plenum Press, c1980.
              ix, 412 p. : ill. ; 26 cm.
              Includes bibliographies and index.
              ISBN 0-306-40557-1

              1. Fuzzy sets –Congresses.  2. Policy sciences—Congresses.  3. Social sys-
           tems—Congresses.  4. System analysis—Congresses.   I. Wang, Paul P.  II.
           Chang, S. K. (Shi Kuo), 1944-        III. Title.
           QA248.S97   1980            511.3 22                80-19934
                                                                MARC

           Library of Congress
```

Figure 5.7. Corporate entry or corporate author.

Figure 5.6 is an example of a card for an individual title in a series. The library has chosen to classify this book with the series rather than under the subject matter of the book. The Library of Congress suggested call number for this title in the series is UG 743 .S72 1986, but the call number for the series is PN 4177 .R44. The publisher assigns each book in the series a different volume number or issue number. In the example shown, *The Star Wars Debate*, is volume 58, issue number 1, of *The Reference Shelf* series. The subject matter of the book is reflected in the assigned subject heading—"Strategic Defense Initiative—Addresses, essays, lectures"—rather than in the call number.

A corporate entry or corporate author refers to an organization such as a governmental agency, an association, a company, or other corporate body that issues a publication in its name rather than in the name of the individuals who did the actual writing. The author, or perhaps several joint authors, have done the writing as part of their assigned duties, but the book is the responsibility of the issuing agency and its editor or editors. Some publications from the United States government have both a corporate author and a personal author. (See Figure 5.7)

Figure 5.8. Title entry as main entry.

```
LB
15        The International encyclopedia of education : research and studies
.I569        / editors-in-chief, Torsten Husén, T. Neville Postlethwaite. —
1985         1st ed. — Oxford ; New York : Pergamon Press, 1985.

              10 v. : ill. ; 26 cm.

              Includes bibliographies.
              Vol. 10: Indexes.
              ISBN 0-08-028119-2 (set) : $1750.00


              1. Education—Dictionaries.   2. Education—Research—Dictionaries.   I.
           Husén, Torsten, 1916-      . II. Postlethwaite, T. Neville.
           LB15.I569   1985              370 .3 21              84-20750
                                                            AACR 2   MARC

           Library of Congress
```

Figure 5.9. Entry for an anthology.

```
PN
3433      Hard science fiction / edited by George E. Slusser and Eric S.
.2           Rabkin. — Carbondale : Southern Illinois University Press,
.H37         c1986.
1986          xvi, 284 p. ; 23 cm. — (Alternatives)

              Proceedings of the fifth Eaton Conference on Fantasy and Science Fiction,
           held April 9-10, 1983, at the University of California, Riverside.
              Bibliography: p. 247-272.
              Includes index.
              ISBN 0-8093-1234-4

              1. Science fiction—Congresses.   I. Slusser, George Edgar.   II. Rabkin,
           Eric S.   III. Eaton Conference on Science Fiction and Fantasy Literature (5th
           : 1983 : University of California, Riverside)   IV. Series.
           PN3433.2.H37   1986          809.3 876             84-27644
                                                            AACR 2   MARC

           Library of Congress
```

In the case of books which have an editor rather than an individual author, the title card, not the author card, is usually the main entry. This is true for reference books such as encyclopedias, handbooks, yearbooks, etc. where multiple authors write the separate articles under the direction of one or more editors. (See Figure 5.8).

Figure 5.9 is an example of an anthology or a collection of literary works which are published together under one title. The literature in anthologies may include short stories, poems, essays, plays, or other short literary pieces. Anthologies are usually edited works which are entered under the title in the card catalog. The individual selections within anthologies are not usually listed in the catalog, making it necessary either to examine the book itself or consult an index to literature in collections to determine its contents. Indexes to literature in collections are discussed in Chapter 8. In those cases where the contents of anthologies are listed in the catalog, there is an entry for each individual title and author in the work. The records for essays may also contain subject entries.

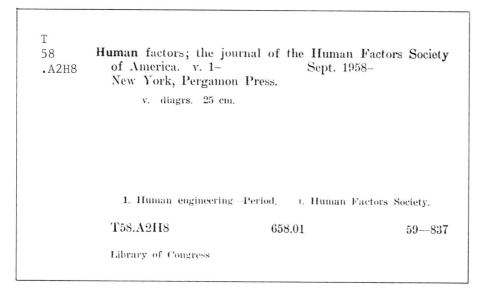

Figure 5.10.   Card for a periodical title.

At the present time it is more usual to find analytics in online catalogs rather than in card catalogs since online catalogs tend to be more comprehensive.

Periodicals are listed in the card catalog by title, subject, and sometimes by the first editor. Periodical cards differ from other cards in the catalog in that they give the title of the magazine as the main entry, followed by volume number and date. In the example shown in Figure 5.10, the date of the first issue of volume 1 is September 1958. The dash after both the volume number and the date indicates that the periodical is still being published. If it were to cease publication, the number of the last volume and the date would be added to the card.

There is one subject heading given for this periodical. Readers interested in finding other periodicals on the subject of "human engineering" should look in the card catalog under the subject heading—HUMAN ENGINEERING—PERIODICALS. They will find a card for *Human Factors* and all the other periodicals that the library owns on this subject.

Most libraries do not list periodical holdings in the library catalog. The usual practice is to have a separate file for periodicals which can be updated easily. A note on the catalog card directs the user to the holdings record. (See Figure 5.10)

Figure 5.11. Microform copy of a newspaper.

```
Film
30          The Washington post [microform]. -- 97th year,
               no. 27 (Jan. 1, 1974)--.
Current          Washington : The Washington Post Co.,
issues           v. : ill. ; 60 cm.
with             Daily.
call no.         Microfilm. New Haven, Conn. :
Newspaper    Research Publications, Inc., 1979-
17           reels ; 35 mm.
                 For holdings see Serial Record.
                 Continues: Washington post and times
            herald.
                    ISSN 0190-8286 = The Washington post

                 I.  Place   ; United States--District
            of Columbia--      Washington.
```

Figure 5.11 shows a record for a newspaper on microfilm. Because newspapers are bulky to store, constitute a fire hazard, and are printed on paper that deteriorates quite rapidly, many libraries acquire microfilm copies of the newspaper. Microfilming gives the library a permanent copy of the newspaper in a format that is easy to store and will last a long time. The date on the card, January 1, 1974, shown in Figure 5.11, is the beginning date of the current title of the newspaper. The former title was *Washington Post* and *Times Herald*. The beginning date indicated on the card does not necessarily mean that the library has microfilm copies of the *Washington Post* dating back to 1974. The note "see Serial Record" indicates that it is necessary to consult the serials acquisition records to determine which issues of the newspaper are owned by the library. To locate the film copy of an issue of this newspaper, it is necessary to know the film number (30) and the date of the issue desired. Usually the film number is the same for all issues of the title. Current issues may be obtained by using the call number "Newspaper 17" and the issue date.

Nonbook Materials

Many libraries have a vast amount of material in nonbook form such as films, microforms, records, reel-to-reel tapes, videotapes, cassettes, and scores. Sometimes the cards for these materials are kept in a separate file, but many times they are interfiled in the card catalog along with all other materials. Since these generally are kept in a separate collection, they usually have a location symbol such as "Film," "LP," "Recording," or "Tape" plus a sequence number instead of a classification number as a means of locating them. The number given with the location symbol is often an accession number. This means that as the materials are received by the library, they are assigned a number indicating their order of receipt. Sometimes a classification number and a location symbol are assigned to nonbook materials.

Recordings of plays or readings from novels or poems are not only entertaining, but also they are useful for research. It is possible to find recordings of great events in history such as the landing on the moon, speeches given by outstanding historical figures such as Sir Winston Churchill, songs of birds recorded in certain areas, or sounds of marine animals recorded in their native environment in college and university libraries. This type of material adds an

```
LP
10993      60 years of country music [ sound
              recording]. -- New York, N.Y. : RCA
              Victor, p1982.
              2 sound discs : 33 1/3 rpm, mono. ;
           12 in.
              RCA Victor: CPL2-4351.
              Various vocalists and ensembles.
              Recorded 1922-1980.
              The 2nd disc in stereo.
              For contents note see main entry
           card.


              1. Country music--United States.
           I. RCA Victor: CPL2-4351.   II. Title:
           Sixty years of country music.
```

Figure 5.12. Card for a recording.

```
M
1247     Kelly, Bryan.
.K24
              March--Washington D. C.  London, Novello [1971]
              score (20 p.) and     parts.  28 cm.  (Novello brass band series)
              Duration : 4 min., 30 sec.




              1. Marches (Band)—Scores and parts.   I. Title.  II. Title:
           Washington D. C.

           M1247.K                                       79-295315

           Library of Congress
```

Figure 5.13. Catalog card for a score.

interesting touch to research projects. The recording noted in Figure 5.12 would be useful to the student studying the history of country music in the United States. Notice that the recording is on two sound discs—one in monaural sound and the other in stereo.

Musical scores frequently are cataloged along with books and other materials. It is possible to locate scores in the card catalog by composer, title, and subject. The main entry in Figure 5.13 is for the composer. In some libraries the scores are shelved together in the stacks by call number, while in other libraries they are housed in separate collections. If they are housed in a separate collection, they usually have a location symbol plus the call number.

Figure 5.14. Thesis on microfilm and in paper copy.

```
378.76       Lee, Anthony, 1951-
L930             Analysis of a chilling system used
1936         for extrusion coating of paper / by
             Anthony Lee. [Baton Rouge : s.n.] ,
Also on      1976.
Film             x, 50 leaves : ill. ; 29 cm.
                 Thesis (M.S. in M.E.)--Louisiana
             State University, Baton Rouge, La.
                 Vita.
                 Bibliography:  leaves 41-42.
                 Abstract.
                 1.  Paper coatings. I. Title
```

Figure 5.15. Microprint card.

```
Micro-
print        Landmarks of science / edited by Sir
25               Harold Hartley and Duane H.D.
             Roller. [New York] : Readex
             Microprint, [1967-75]
                 28,823 cards in 147 boxes; 23 x 15
cm.
             Micro-opaque.
                 "A comprehensive collection of the
             source material in the history of
             science comprising the significant
             contributions to the advancement of
             science and technology."
                 1. Science--Collected works.
             2. Science--History--Sources.
             I. Hartley, Harold, Sir, 1878-
             II. Roller, Duane H. D., 1920-
             III. Readex Microprint Corporation.
```

A thesis is a long treatise or scholarly research paper written in partial fulfillment for the master's degree. The dissertation is similar but represents original work which is written in partial fulfillment of the requirements for the doctoral degree. Theses and dissertations are usually unpublished and, therefore, do not have an imprint except for the date. The thesis in Figure 5.14 is available in its original form shelved by the call number and is also on microfilm. The brackets around ''Baton Rouge: s.n.'' have been placed there because this information does not appear on the title page and was added by the catalogers. The abbreviation ''s.n.'' stands for *sine nominee*, meaning no name of publisher given.

Figure 5.15 is an example of a record for material that has been reproduced on microprint cards. Notice that the physical description lists the number of cards—28,823 in 147 boxes—instead of page numbers. Microprints are 23 × 15 cm. opaque cards containing greatly reduced photographic reproductions of material.

MACHINE INTELLIGENCE

see

ARTIFICIAL INTELLIGENCE

Figure 5.16. Subject cross reference.

ARTIFICIAL INTELLIGENCE

see also Expert systems (Computer science); Machine learning; Question-answering systems.

Figure 5.17. See also reference.

Cross Reference or Directional Cards

The cards that have been discussed so far in this chapter describe books, periodicals, newspapers, and nonbook materials and tell how they can be located. Cross reference cards direct the card catalog user to the proper terminology or to additional sources of information. There are two kinds of cross reference cards—*see* and *see also*. The *see* reference directs the card catalog user from a subject heading or term that is not used to the synonymous term that is used. The *see also* reference card lists related subject headings under which more information can be found.

The *subject cross* reference in Figure 5.16 indicates that MACHINE INTELLIGENCE is not used as a subject heading and that ARTIFICIAL INTELLIGENCE is used instead. The cross reference card is filed in the card catalog in the correct place alphabetically by the first line on the card.

A *name cross reference* is used to direct the card catalog user from the pen name or pseudonym of the author to the author's real name. Some card catalogs have such works entered under both names making the name cross reference card unnecessary. The *see also* card indicates subject headings under which additional information can be found. These are filed after the last card with the same subject heading. For example, there might be five cards in the card catalog with the simple subject heading, ARTIFICIAL INTELLIGENCE. The sixth card would be the one noted in Figure 5.17. The seventh card might be ARTIFICIAL INTELLIGENCE—HISTORY.

Arrangement of the Card Catalog

There are two methods of alphabetizing commonly used in filing—*letter by letter* and *word by word*. Dictionaries use letter-by-letter filing as do some indexes and encyclopedias. Cards in the card catalog are filed word by word. Library users should be aware of differences in the two methods so that they will not miss entries in reference sources. The word-by-word method treats each word in a name, title, or subject heading as a separate unit, while the letter-by-letter method treats all the words in a name, title, or subject heading as if they were one unit. In other words, in the letter-by-letter method all the words in the heading are run together as if they were one word.

For example:

Word by Word	**Letter by Letter**
San Antonio	San Antonio
San Diego	Sanctuary
San Pedro	Sandalwood
Sanctuary	Sand blasting
Sand blasting	Sand, George
Sand, George	San Diego
Sandalwood	San Pedro

Since the card catalog has the cards arranged in alphabetical order, it is necessary to find the section of the catalog that contains the correct part of the alphabet. Each drawer has a label indicating the parts of the alphabet included in that drawer. Usually the drawers are numbered so that they can be returned to their cases in proper order. Within each drawer there are guide cards which indicate the contents of various sections of that drawer. If there is not a guide card with the subject printed across the top, it does not mean that the library does not have books on that topic. Guide cards are used to indicate only some of the subjects found in the drawer. The following filing rules are from *ALA Filing Rules* (Chicago: American Library Association, 1980), 22–38.

Filing Rules

1. All filing is done by the first line on the catalog card.
2. Titles are filed under the first word of the title unless the title begins with a, an, or the. With foreign book titles, the foreign equivalents of the English articles are ignored and are filed by the next word. *Example: The Great Gatsby* is filed under *Great*, and *Les Misérables* is filed under *Misérables*. If the title of a book is not distinctive and begins with terms such as *Collected works of . . .* or *Outline of . . .* , there is no title card. When the title is the same as a standardized subject heading, the subject card substitutes for the title card. This is particularly true with biographies.
3. An author's name or personal name used as a subject is inverted. *Example: Lindbergh, Anne Morrow* not *Anne Morrow Lindbergh.*
4. Several books by the same author are filed first under the author's name and then alphabetically by title. *Example:*

   Colby, Carroll Burleigh. *FBI.* . . .
   Colby, Carroll Burleigh. *Sailing Ships.* . . .
   Colby, Carroll Burleigh. *Wild Bird World.* . . .
5. Several authors with the same last name are filed first by last name and then alphabetically by the first and middle name. If the entire name is the same, then the names are listed chronologically by year of birth. Royalty is listed chronologically by number.

   Example:
   Gillespie, George, 1613–1648.
   Gillespie, George, 1683–1760.
   Gillespie, George Benjamin, 1863–.

   Henry II, King of England, 1133–1189.
   Henry III, King of England, 1207–1272.
   Henry IV, King of England, 1367–1413.

6. Compound personal names are filed as though they are one word. *Example:* Armstrong, Martin D. is filed before Armstrong-Jones, Anthony.
7. Compound proper names are arranged as separate words whether or not they are separated by a hyphen. This includes names beginning with New, Old, West, South, Saint, San, etc. *Example:* New Zealand is filed before Newcastle.
8. Names beginning with M', Mc, and Mac are all filed as written. *Example:* Machine, MacPherson, McCulloch, M'Nulty are arranged in correct order.
9. Abbreviations are filed as written and not as spelled out. *Example: Dr. Schweitzer* not *Doctor Schweitzer, Mr. Roberts* not *Mister Roberts*, and *Mrs. Miniver* not *Mistress Miniver.*
10. Initials, initialisms, and acronyms separated by spaces, dashes, hyphens, diagonal slashes, or periods are regarded as separate words. On the other hand, initials, initialisms, and acronyms which are separated by marks or symbols other than the ones previously listed or which are not separated at all are filed as single words. Thus, initials which are separated by periods are filed before words beginning with the same letter; an acronym which is not separated by periods is filed as a single word. *Example:* C.O.S.P.A.R., cancer, coaching, COBOL (computer program language), coins.
11. Compound words are arranged as one word. *Example:* Silversmith is filed after Silver question.
12. Hyphenated words are arranged as separate words. *Example:* part-time is filed before participant.
13. Modified letters are treated the same as their English equivalents with the modification ignored. *Example:* Muller, C. F. J. is filed before Müller, Erich Herman.
14. All punctuation marks are disregarded. *Example:* O'Neal, Hank; Oneal, James; O'Neal, Leland.
15. All numeric characters, including dates, are filed in the beginning of the catalog before "A" in numerical order from lowest to highest. *For example: 3-D Stories, 99 Novels, 101 Tasty Treats, 1001 Health Tips, 1984 Revisited.* (See example in Figure 8.3)

Since filing practices vary from library to library, card catalog users should consult the library handbook or ask a reference librarian for explanations of the library's filing practices. For example, in many older card catalogs names beginning with M', Mc, or Mac are filed as if they are all spelled Mac. Some abbreviations are filed as they are spelled. *Mr.*, for example, would be filed under *Mister.* Dates and numbers are filed as they are pronounced; for example the date 1776 is filed as if written seventeen seventy-six, but the number 1,776 is filed as if it is written one thousand seven hundred seventy-six. In online catalogs entries are retrieved exactly as they are entered in the database. For example, *Mr.* would be retrieved as *Mr.* and not as *Mister.*

Online Catalogs

In many libraries the card catalog has been replaced either entirely or in part by an online catalog accessible by means of a computer terminal. Online catalogs were made possible by the advent of MARC (machine readable catalog) records in 1965. The Library of Congress developed the MARC format as a means of improving access to library information. Since that time it has been universally adopted by libraries throughout the world as a means for cataloging library materials. MARC records are stored on computer tapes (or in other electronic format) and retrieved by the use of a computer. Many libraries with online databases began creating MARC records around 1976, and have not completed the re-cataloging of pre-1976 materials in MARC format. As a result, it is not uncommon to find libraries with older materials in a card catalog and newer materials in an online catalog.

While the installation of an online catalog is expensive, it is easy to maintain and use. The records are updated on a continuing basis, and new materials are constantly being added. Unlike a card catalog which is limited to a single location, an online catalog can be accessed by terminals located in a number of different places, both within the library and in off-site locations. Online catalogs are easy to use; directions are either posted near the terminals or are part of the online database. The greatest advantage of an online catalog is that it provides access to library materials in ways not possible with a card catalog. In addition to the public catalog, online systems may have other capabilities. These include: (1) cataloging modules which allow the library to update the catalog on a daily basis; (2) acquisition modules which provide information concerning materials on order; (3) circulation modules which enable users to determine whether a book has been checked out; and (4) periodicals check-in capabilities which provide information on periodical ''holdings,'' and locations. For example, it tells which complete volumes of a periodical the library owns, what are the latest issues received, and whether there are missing issues or volumes. In addition it gives the location. In many cases online catalogs can be accessed from an off-site location such as a faculty office, dorm room, or another library. Online catalogs provide the library patrons with better library service and make doing research a much easier and faster process.

In many ways online catalogs are very similar to the other types of library catalogs that have already been mentioned. The description of materials is the same, and the subject headings are the same. The biggest difference is that the means of access is by searching a computer terminal rather than by looking for entries in a book, on microform, or on index cards. Most online catalogs can be accessed by author, title, and subject in essentially the same way as other types of catalogs. However, some online systems also have keyword and call number access. The information found on the computer screen for a catalog record is almost the same as that found on a catalog card or microfiche record, but it is often arranged in a different way. The arrangement depends on the kind of online system that is being used and the way the library has chosen to format the material on screens.

Some libraries have developed their own online catalog systems such as Melvyl at University of California-Berkeley and Socrates at Stanford, while others have purchased already developed software from vendors and adapted it for their particular needs. The examples on subsequent pages are from the NOTIS system which was developed at Northwestern University and from CLSI, Inc. Both of these systems are widely used by libraries throughout the United States.

Searching the Online Catalog

Not all online catalogs have the same features or the same commands. The *commands* are symbols and/or terms that are used to access the system. The examples following show how to search the NOTIS system:

Author search   a = author's name in inverted form.
Title search   t = exact title of the publication, except initial articles are
          ignored.
Subject search   s = appropriate subject heading from   *The Library of*
          Congress Subject Headings (LCSH)
Keyword search   k = individual words from any part of the record

All search terms must be followed by pressing the ENTER key which enables the command to be executed.

To access information in an online catalog, it is necessary to type in the exact string of characters in the database. For example, to retrieve the title *100 Great Fantasy Short Stories* one should type in:

> t = *100 Great Fantasy Short Stories*
>
>   not
>
> t = *One Hundred Great Fantasy Short Stories.*

To retrieve *One Last Look* one should type

> t = *One Last Look*
>
>   not
>
> t = *1 Last Look*

However, it is possible to shorten words or parts of words in the command. This is called *truncation.* Search terms are usually truncated from right to left. For example, *Journal of Nutrition Education* can be shortened to *Journal of Nutrition Ed,* but not to *Jl of Nutr Ed.* Truncation can be used if there is doubt about the spelling of an author's name or if only the last name of the author is known. One should guard against entering common names such as Smith or Jones without a first name or initial as this will result in a confusing number of entries in the name/title index. Truncation can be used also to find words in subjects or titles if the correct spelling or form is unknown.

When using an online catalog, it is not necessary to be concerned with the filing rules which are used in the card catalog since the system will search the database for the information requested without regard to the alphabetizing or the forms. Book titles which begin with the articles, ''a,'' ''an,'' or ''the,'' or the foreign language equivalents, are entered under the word following the article. Initials, acronyms, abbreviations, numbers, and dates appear in the catalog records as they are entered. All punctuation marks are disregarded by the computer. However, in some systems, divided subject headings must have two dashes (—) between the primary subject heading and all subdivisions.

The following screen reproductions are from the NOTIS[1] system currently being used in the Louisiana State University Libraries. The public catalog module has been named ''LOLA,'' an acronym for Library On-Line Access. This term is used on all of the online catalog screens.

---

1. Figures 5.18–5.34 are screen reproductions from the NOTIS System currently being used in the Louisiana State University Libraries. (Copyright 1990 by NOTIS Systems, Inc. Material reproduced by permission of the copyright holder and the Louisiana State University Libraries.)

Figure 5.18.   Introductory screen.

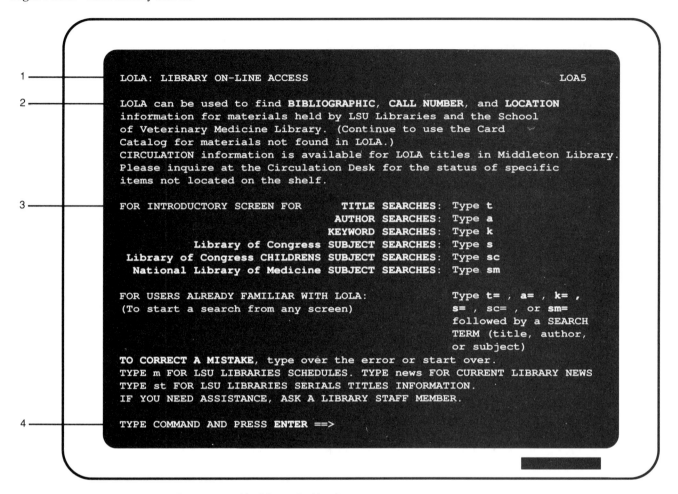

1. Acronym used for Library On-Line Access.
2. Introductory information provides general data about the system.
   Since this is necessarily brief, libraries often provide more comprehensive
   written instructions.
3. List of the kinds of searches available on the system and the commands
   needed to find materials by author, title, subject or keyword.
4. Information needed to access the database.

Figure 5.19. Author and title index screen.

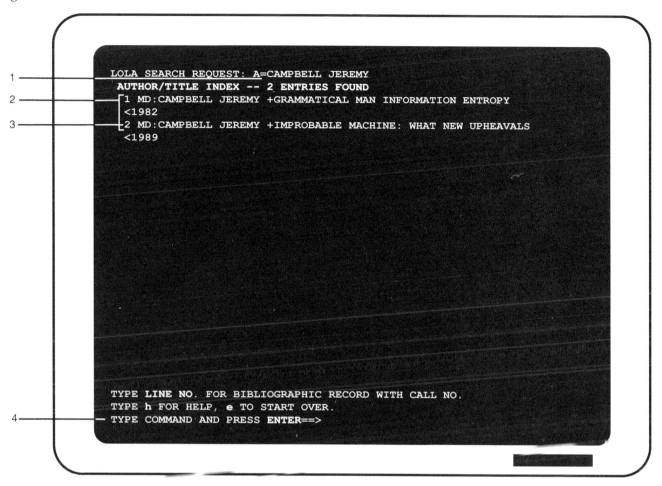

1. Command entered into the system to access this screen.
2. Numbers 1–2. List of book titles available in the database under the author's name.
3. Number entered to access the complete bibliographic record for the book, *The Improbable Machine* by Jeremy Campbell.
4. Instructions needed to enter the database.

Figure 5.20. Author or main entry bibliographic record screen.

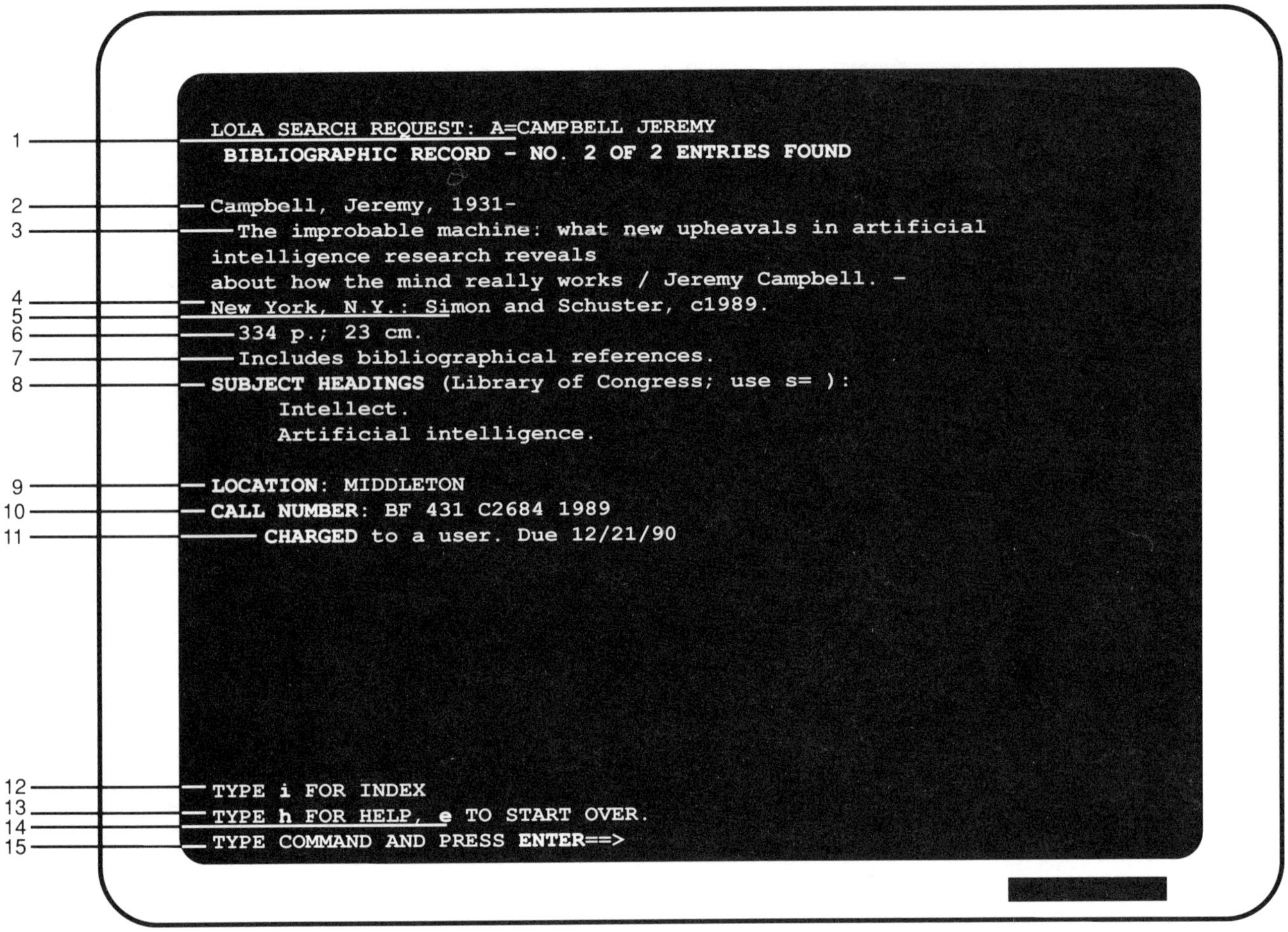

```
1 ──────── LOLA SEARCH REQUEST: A=CAMPBELL JEREMY
             BIBLIOGRAPHIC RECORD - NO. 2 OF 2 ENTRIES FOUND

2 ──────── Campbell, Jeremy, 1931-
3 ───────────── The improbable machine: what new upheavals in artificial
             intelligence research reveals
             about how the mind really works / Jeremy Campbell. -
4 ───────── New York, N.Y.: Simon and Schuster, c1989.
5 ─────────
6 ───────── 334 p.; 23 cm.
7 ───────── Includes bibliographical references.
8 ───────── SUBJECT HEADINGS (Library of Congress; use s= ):
                  Intellect.
                  Artificial intelligence.

9 ───────── LOCATION: MIDDLETON
10 ──────── CALL NUMBER: BF 431 C2684 1989
11 ───────────── CHARGED to a user. Due 12/21/90




12 ──────── TYPE i FOR INDEX
13 ──────── TYPE h FOR HELP, e TO START OVER.
14 ────────
15 ──────── TYPE COMMAND AND PRESS ENTER==>
```

1. Command entered into the system to produce the bibliographic record.
2. Author of the book.
3. Title of the book. This includes both the short title and subtitle.
4. Place of publication.
5. Publisher and copyright date.
6. Physical description. The book has 334 pages and is 23 cm. tall.
7. Book includes bibliographical references.
8. Subject headings under which this book and ones like it can be found.
9. Book is located in the Middleton Library.
10. Call number of the book.
11. Circulation information. Book checked out to user/due date.
12. Type "i" to go back to the author/title index screen (Figure 5.19).
13. Type "e" to go back to the introductory screen (Figure 5.18).
14. Type "h" to access the help screen. Help screens provide useful information for interpreting the system.
15. Type next command and press ENTER to access the system for another record.

Figure 5.21. Subject heading guide screen.

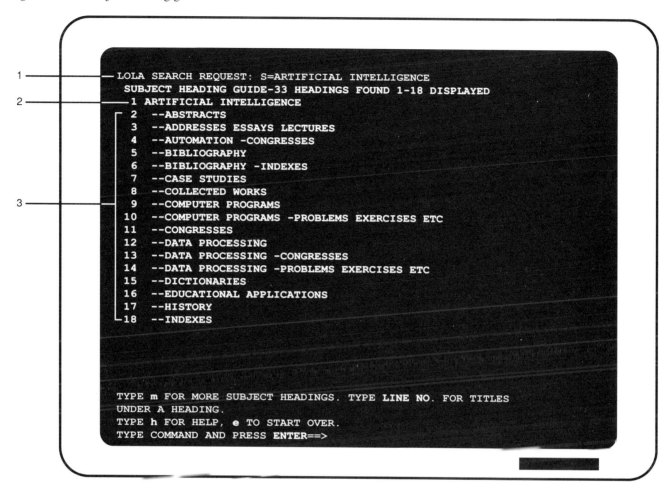

1. Command entered to access this screen.
2. Number entered to go to the subject/index screen.
3. Possible subheads available under this subject.

Figure 5.22.   Subject and title index screen.

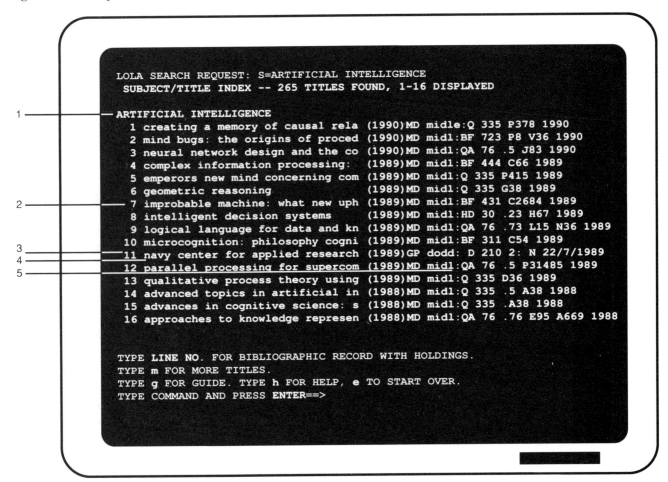

```
LOLA SEARCH REQUEST: S=ARTIFICIAL INTELLIGENCE
 SUBJECT/TITLE INDEX -- 265 TITLES FOUND, 1-16 DISPLAYED

ARTIFICIAL INTELLIGENCE
  1 creating a memory of causal rela (1990)MD midle:Q 335 P378 1990
  2 mind bugs: the origins of proced (1990)MD midl:BF 723 P8 V36 1990
  3 neural network design and the co (1990)MD midl:QA 76 .5 J83 1990
  4 complex information processing:  (1989)MD midl:BF 444 C66 1989
  5 emperors new mind concerning com (1989)MD midl:Q 335 P415 1989
  6 geometric reasoning              (1989)MD midl:Q 335 G38 1989
  7 improbable machine: what new uph (1989)MD midl:BF 431 C2684 1989
  8 intelligent decision systems     (1989)MD midl:HD 30 .23 H67 1989
  9 logical language for data and kn (1989)MD midl:QA 76 .73 L15 N36 1989
 10 microcognition: philosophy cogni (1989)MD midl:BF 311 C54 1989
 11 navy center for applied research (1989)GP dodd: D 210 2: N 22/7/1989
 12 parallel processing for supercom (1989)MD midl:QA 76 .5 P31485 1989
 13 qualitative process theory using (1989)MD midl:Q 335 D36 1989
 14 advanced topics in artificial in (1988)MD midl:Q 335 .5 A38 1988
 15 advances in cognitive science: s (1988)MD midl:Q 335 .A38 1988
 16 approaches to knowledge represen (1988)MD midl:QA 76 .76 E95 A669 1988



TYPE LINE NO. FOR BIBLIOGRAPHIC RECORD WITH HOLDINGS.
TYPE m FOR MORE TITLES.
TYPE g FOR GUIDE. TYPE h FOR HELP, e TO START OVER.
TYPE COMMAND AND PRESS ENTER==>
```

1. Number 1 entered to go from subject heading guide (Figure 5.21) to the subject/title index (Figure 5.22)
2. Number 7 selected to go to the bibliographic record screen (Figure 5.20)
3. Number 11 selected to go to the bibliographic record screen (Figure 5.23).
4. Example of a reference to a government publication. Call number is a SuDocs number. GP, dodd indicates that the book is in the documents collection.
5. Both MD and midl indicate that book is in the Middleton Library.

Figure 5.23. Bibliographic record for a government publication.

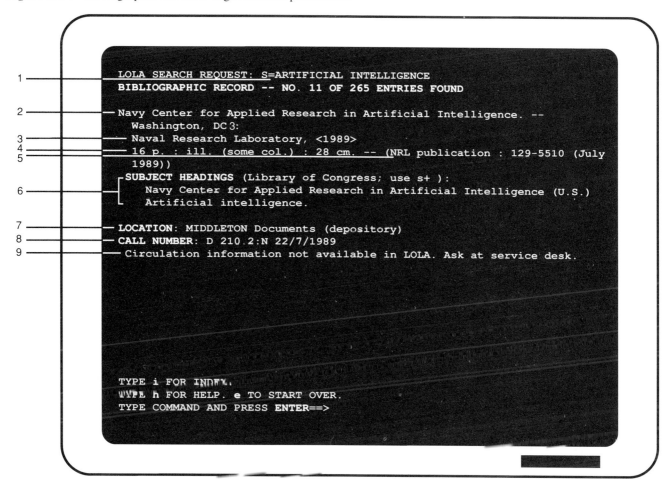

1. Subject heading.
2. Title of publication.
3. Place of publication publisher, and publication date.
4. Physical description. Publication has 16 pages;
   illustrated, some in color; 28 centimeters tall.
5. Part of the NRL publication series.
6. Subject headings under which book can be found. Note
   that Navy Center for Applied... is an added entry for a
   subject corporate name.
7. Located in Middleton Library Documents department. Library
   is a depository for U.S. Government publications.
8. SuDocs call number for book.
9. Circulation information not available.

Figure 5.24. Bibliographic record accessed by means of a title command.

1 —

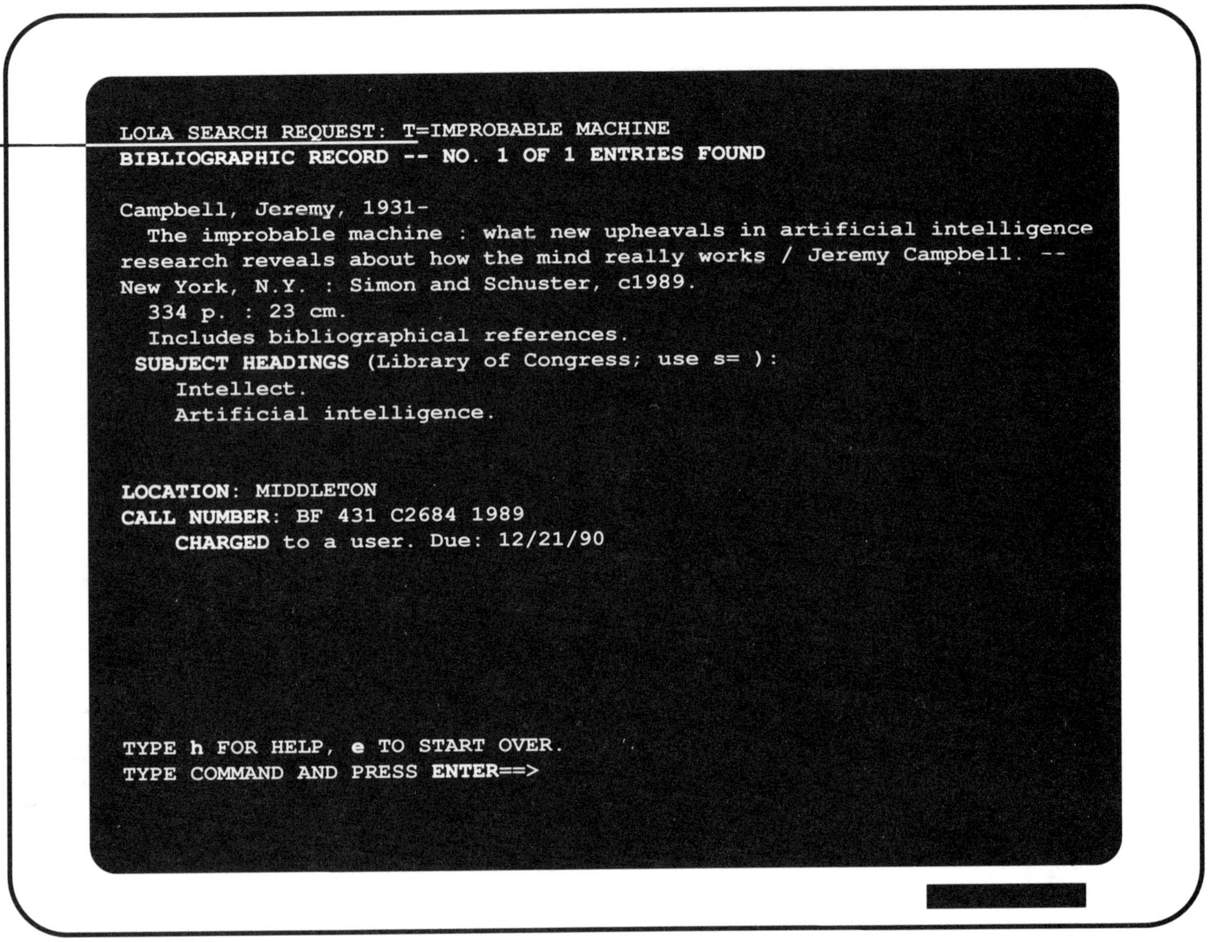

```
LOLA SEARCH REQUEST: T=IMPROBABLE MACHINE
BIBLIOGRAPHIC RECORD -- NO. 1 OF 1 ENTRIES FOUND

Campbell, Jeremy, 1931-
  The improbable machine : what new upheavals in artificial intelligence
research reveals about how the mind really works / Jeremy Campbell. --
New York, N.Y. : Simon and Schuster, c1989.
  334 p. : 23 cm.
  Includes bibliographical references.
 SUBJECT HEADINGS (Library of Congress; use s= ):
    Intellect.
    Artificial intelligence.


LOCATION: MIDDLETON
CALL NUMBER: BF 431 C2684 1989
    CHARGED to a user. Due: 12/21/90




TYPE h FOR HELP, e TO START OVER.
TYPE COMMAND AND PRESS ENTER==>
```

1. Command used to access the bibliographic record screen

Figure 5.25.   Introductory screen for keyword searches.

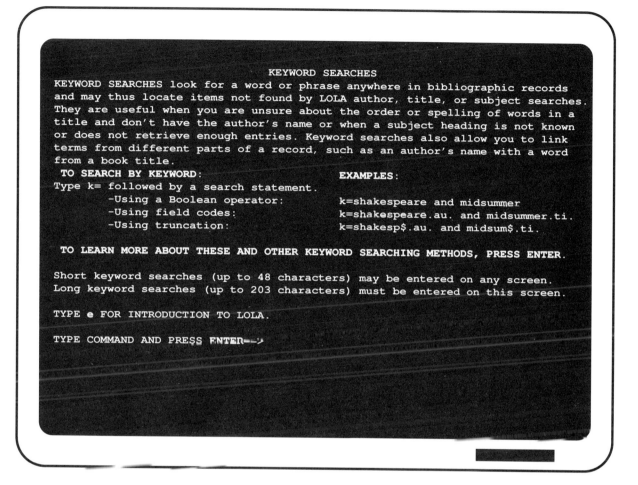

```
                        KEYWORD SEARCHES
KEYWORD SEARCHES look for a word or phrase anywhere in bibliographic records
and may thus locate items not found by LOLA author, title, or subject searches.
They are useful when you are unsure about the order or spelling of words in a
title and don't have the author's name or when a subject heading is not known
or does not retrieve enough entries. Keyword searches also allow you to link
terms from different parts of a record, such as an author's name with a word
from a book title.
  TO SEARCH BY KEYWORD:                       EXAMPLES:
Type k= followed by a search statement.
        -Using a Boolean operator:        k=shakespeare and midsummer
        -Using field codes:               k=shakespeare.au. and midsummer.ti.
        -Using truncation:                k=shakesp$.au. and midsum$.ti.

  TO LEARN MORE ABOUT THESE AND OTHER KEYWORD SEARCHING METHODS, PRESS ENTER.

Short keyword searches (up to 48 characters) may be entered on any screen.
Long keyword searches (up to 203 characters) must be entered on this screen.

TYPE e FOR INTRODUCTION TO LOLA.

TYPE COMMAND AND PRESS ENTER-->
```

Keyword Searching

Many systems have *keyword search* capabilities which enable the user to search by individual words or terms regardless of their order or where they appear in the database. Words in titles, authors' names, and subject fields can be searched individually or in combination with other words. The advantages of keyword searching are:

1. It is possible to find information even though the user has incomplete or partial information. For example, only part of a title is known, or the word order is incorrect, or the correct subject heading is not known.
2. One can narrow or refine a search in ways that are not possible with a catalog which permits searching only by controlled terms. Logical operators (Boolean logic) are used to link terms in order to specify the exact search desired.

Figure 5.26. Help screen for keyword searching using logical and positional operators.

```
   HELP FOR KEYWORD SEARCHES: USING LOGICAL AND POSITIONAL OPERATORS
You may formulate a search statement through use of logical (BOOLEAN) and
positional operators that specify the relationship of terms being searched.
They allow you to link terms from different parts, called fields, of a
bibliographic record. For example, you can search an author's name and a word
or words from the title in one search statement. If more than one term is
typed and no logical operator is used, the system assumes adjacency.
 LOGICAL BOOLEAN OPERTORS are; AND, OR and NOT      SEARCH STATEMENT EXAMPLES
 AND specifies that terms X AND Y must
     both be present in the same record:          shakespeare and midsummer
 OR specifies that either or both term X
and term Y be present in the same record:            dream or midsummer
 NOT specifies that term X but not term
     Y be present in the same record:               dream not shakespeare


 POSITIONAL OPERATORS are: ADJ and SAME
ADJ specifies that term X precede term
     Y, and in that order:                          midsummer adj nights
 SAME specifies that term X be in the
     same part of the record as term Y:             midsummer same dream

       PRESS ENTER FOR INFORMATION ON REFINING A SEARCH BY FIELD.

TYPE k TO BEGIN A KEYWORD SEARCH. TYPE e TO START OVER.
TYPE COMMAND AND PRESS ENTER==>
```

One thing one must guard against in keyword searching is the possibility of "false" hits or records. For example if the searcher wants to search "apple" as a keyword, the search will result in entries on the fruit, on Apple computers and on persons with the name Apple.

Keyword searching is performed by a series of commands which may vary from system to system. However, the basics of keyword searching and logical operators are standard for most systems. Figures 5.25–5.34 show the online instructions for keyword searching in a NOTIS online catalog.

Figure 5.27.   Help screen for refining a search by field in keyword searching.

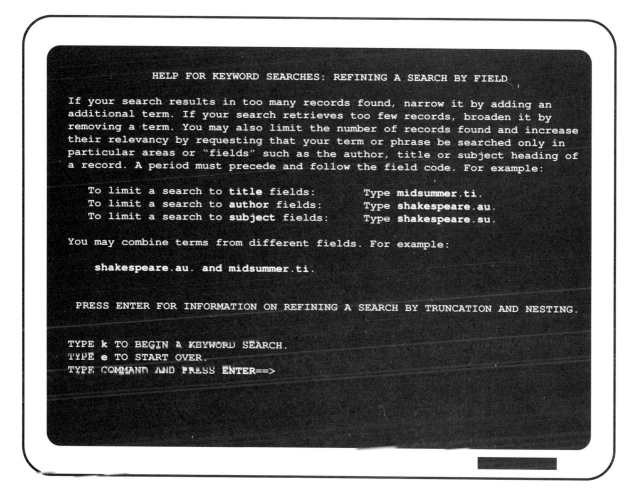

```
        HELP FOR KEYWORD SEARCHES: REFINING A SEARCH BY FIELD

If your search results in too many records found, narrow it by adding an
additional term. If your search retrieves too few records, broaden it by
removing a term. You may also limit the number of records found and increase
their relevancy by requesting that your term or phrase be searched only in
particular areas or "fields" such as the author, title or subject heading of
a record. A period must precede and follow the field code. For example:

    To limit a search to title fields:        Type midsummer.ti.
    To limit a search to author fields:       Type shakespeare.au.
    To limit a search to subject fields:      Type shakespeare.su.

You may combine terms from different fields. For example:

        shakespeare.au. and midsummer.ti.


  PRESS ENTER FOR INFORMATION ON REFINING A SEARCH BY TRUNCATION AND NESTING.


TYPE k TO BEGIN A KEYWORD SEARCH.
TYPE e TO START OVER.
TYPE COMMAND AND PRESS ENTER==>
```

Figure 5.28.   Help screen for refining a search by truncation and nesting.

```
   HELP FOR KEYWORD SEARCHES: REFINING A SEARCH BY TRUNCATION AND NESTING

TRUNCATION: A search term can be shortened by using "$" as a truncation
symbol. This allows one search to retrieve singular or plural forms or
different spellings of a word or name. For example:
          justif$ for justification or justify
          theat$ for theatre or theater
          system$ for system or systems or systematic



NESTING: Search statements can be efficiently structured by combining
several terms and operators into a single search statement. Parentheses must
be used to separate terms when more than one operator is used. This
technique is called nesting. For example:
          legal adj (costs or fees)
          (absenteeism or truancy) and (cost adj analysis)


          PRESS ENTER FOR KEYWORD SEARCH INPUT INSTRUCTIONS.


TYPE k TO BEGIN A KEYWORD SEARCH.
TYPE e TO START OVER.
TYPE COMMAND AND PRESS ENTER==>
```

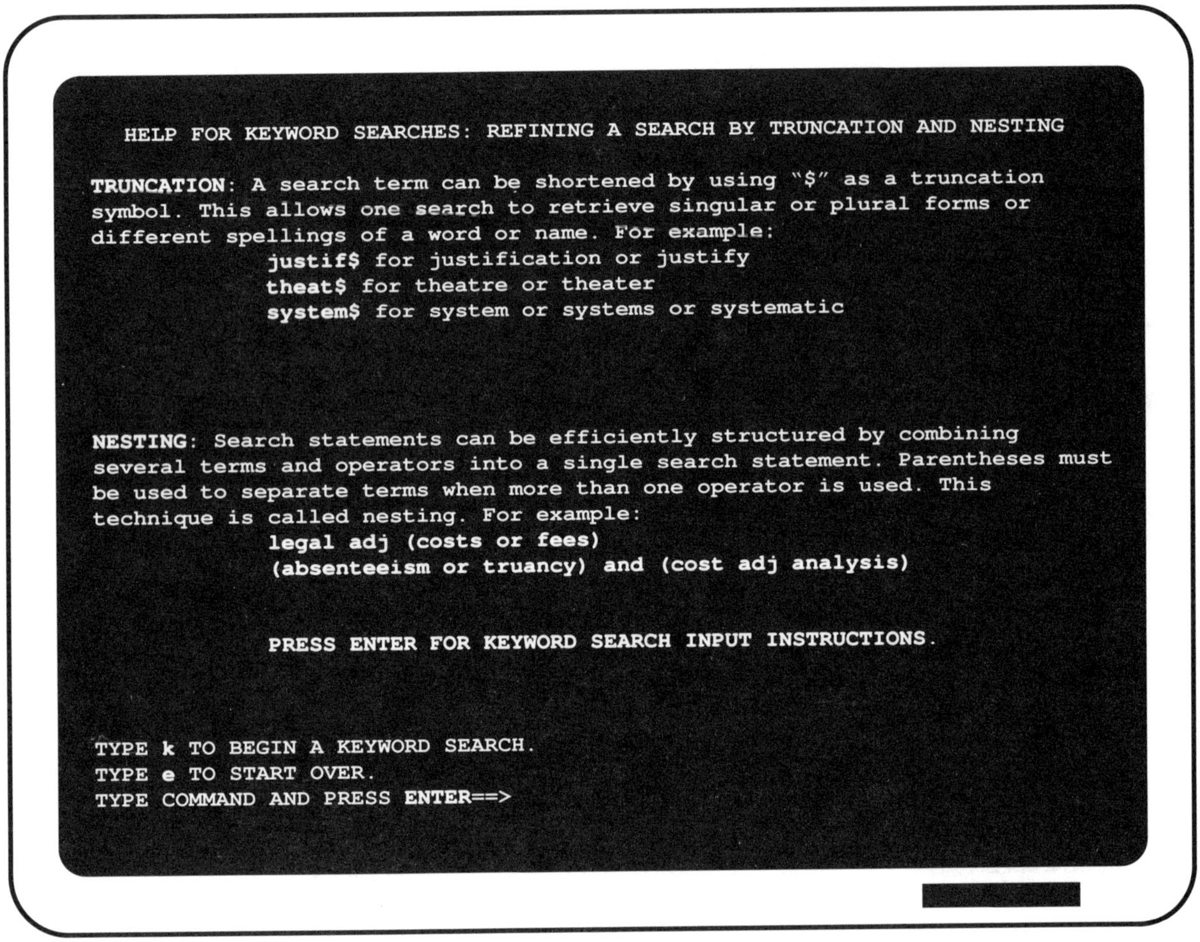

Figure 5.29. Help screen explaining input instructions for keyword searching.

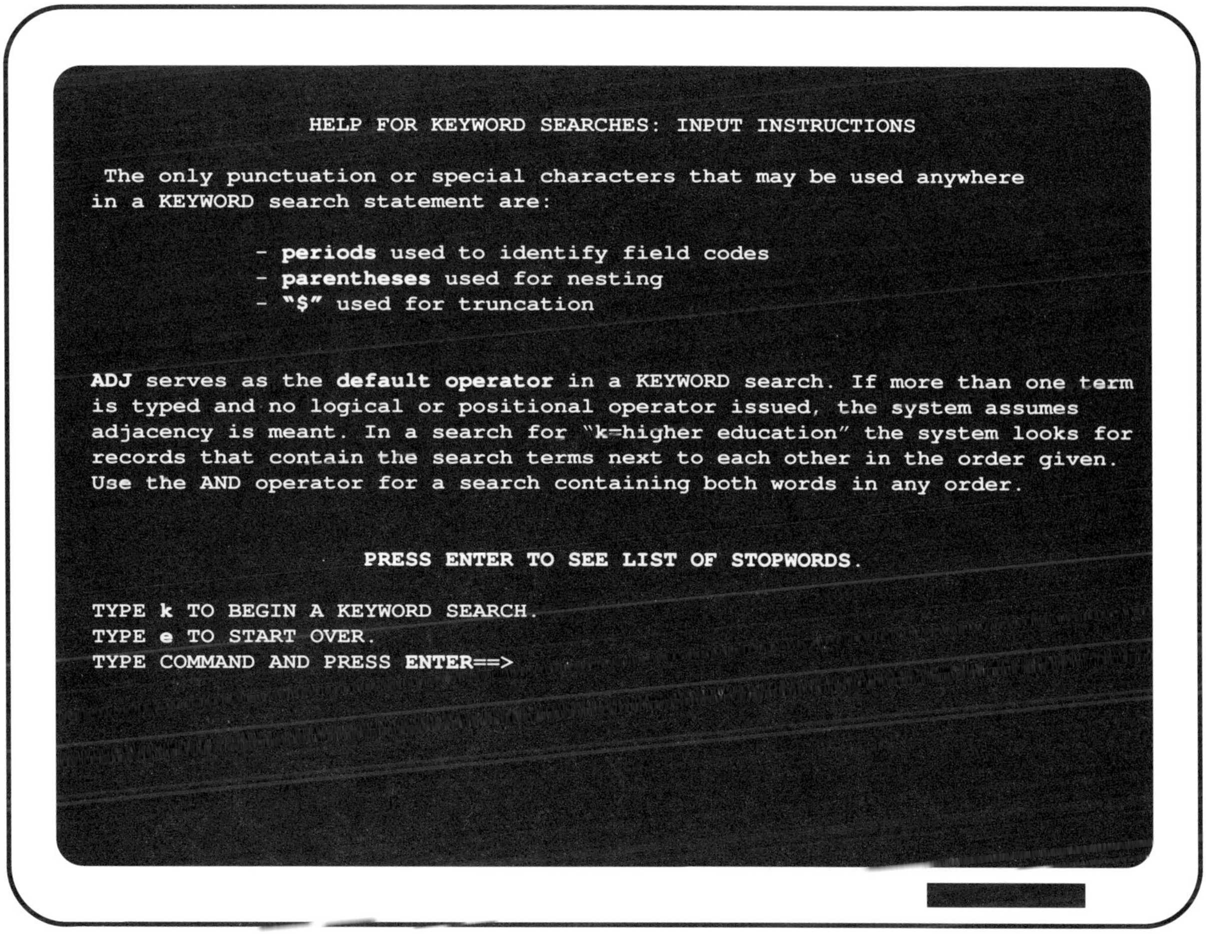

```
                HELP FOR KEYWORD SEARCHES: INPUT INSTRUCTIONS

  The only punctuation or special characters that may be used anywhere
in a KEYWORD search statement are:

              - periods used to identify field codes
              - parentheses used for nesting
              - "$" used for truncation


ADJ serves as the default operator in a KEYWORD search. If more than one term
is typed and no logical or positional operator issued, the system assumes
adjacency is meant. In a search for "k=higher education" the system looks for
records that contain the search terms next to each other in the order given.
Use the AND operator for a search containing both words in any order.


                  PRESS ENTER TO SEE LIST OF STOPWORDS.

TYPE k TO BEGIN A KEYWORD SEARCH.
TYPE e TO START OVER.
TYPE COMMAND AND PRESS ENTER==>
```

Figure 5.30.   Help screen explaining the use of stopwords and common terms in keyword searching.

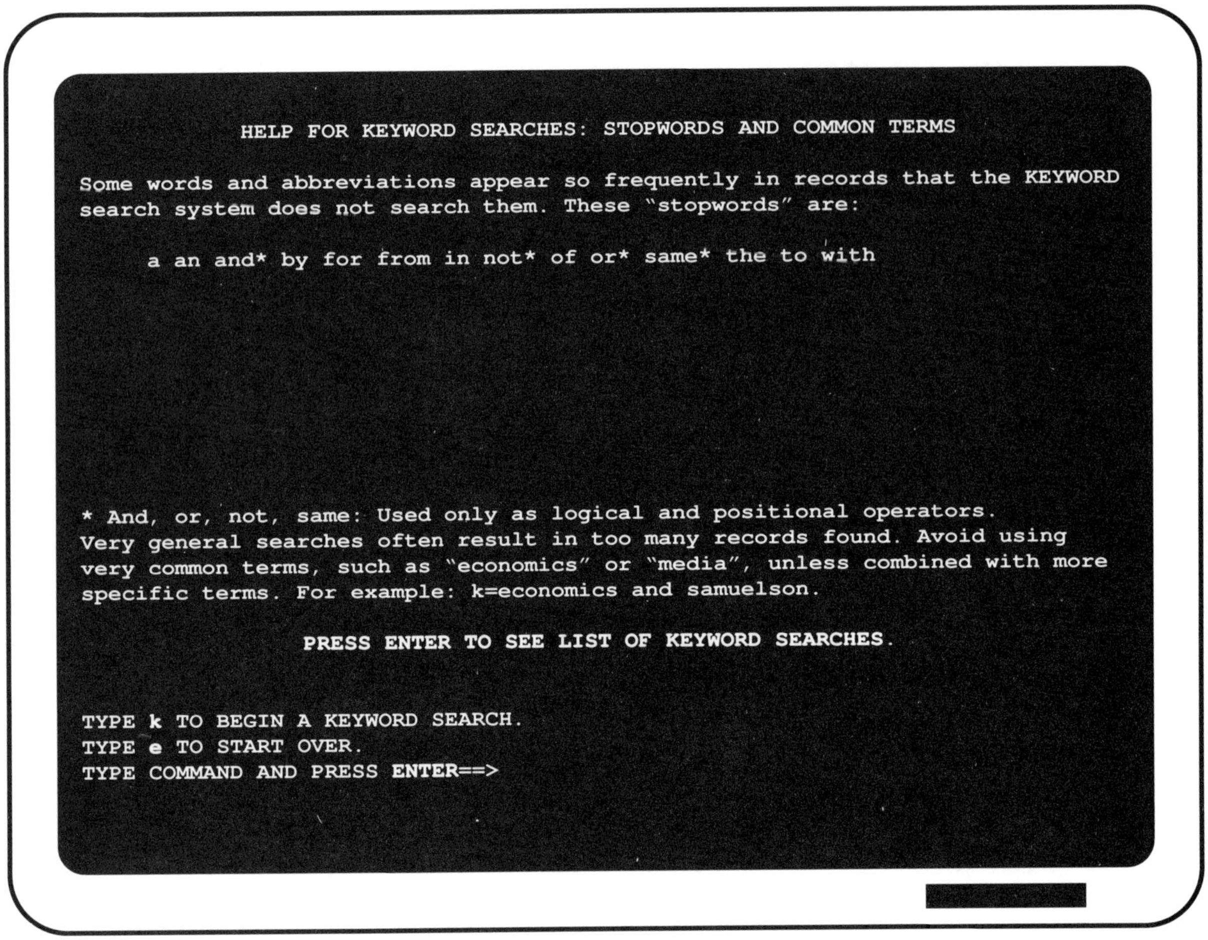

```
          HELP FOR KEYWORD SEARCHES: STOPWORDS AND COMMON TERMS

Some words and abbreviations appear so frequently in records that the KEYWORD
search system does not search them. These "stopwords" are:

    a an and* by for from in not* of or* same* the to with




* And, or, not, same: Used only as logical and positional operators.
Very general searches often result in too many records found. Avoid using
very common terms, such as "economics" or "media", unless combined with more
specific terms. For example: k=economics and samuelson.

           PRESS ENTER TO SEE LIST OF KEYWORD SEARCHES.


TYPE k TO BEGIN A KEYWORD SEARCH.
TYPE e TO START OVER.
TYPE COMMAND AND PRESS ENTER==>
```

Figure 5.31.   Examples of keyword searches.

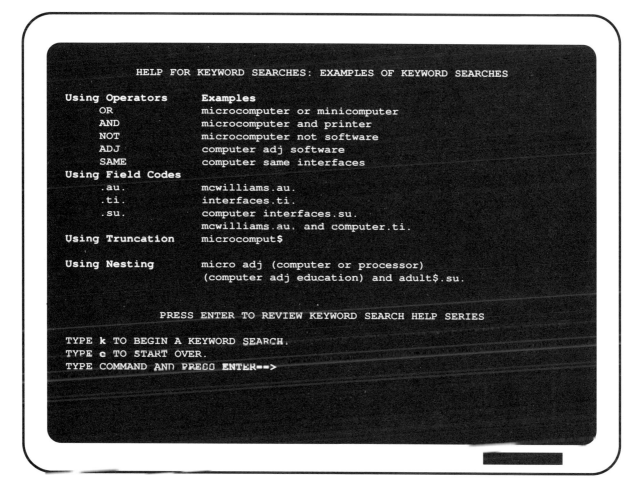

```
        HELP FOR KEYWORD SEARCHES: EXAMPLES OF KEYWORD SEARCHES

Using Operators       Examples
     OR               microcomputer or minicomputer
     AND              microcomputer and printer
     NOT              microcomputer not software
     ADJ              computer adj software
     SAME             computer same interfaces
Using Field Codes
     .au.             mcwilliams.au.
     .ti.             interfaces.ti.
     .su.             computer interfaces.su.
                      mcwilliams.au. and computer.ti.
Using Truncation      microcomput$

Using Nesting         micro adj (computer or processor)
                      (computer adj education) and adult$.su.


             PRESS ENTER TO REVIEW KEYWORD SEARCH HELP SERIES

TYPE k TO BEGIN A KEYWORD SEARCH.
TYPE c TO START OVER.
TYPE COMMAND AND PRESS ENTER==>
```

Figure 5.32.   Keyword search index screen.

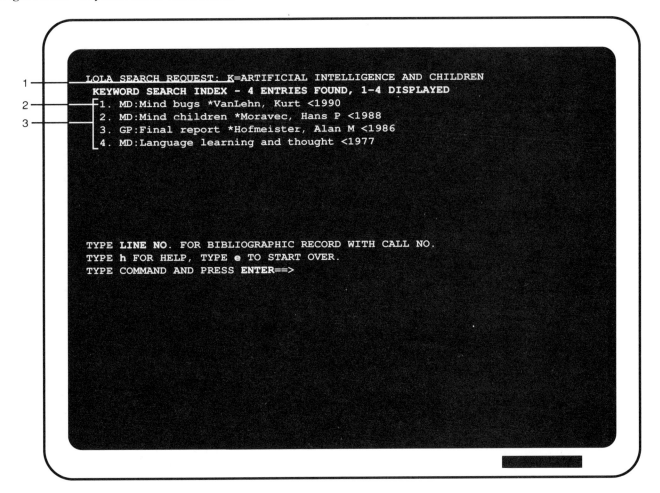

1. Keyword search term.
2. Number selected to access the bibliographic record
   screens. (Figure 5.33 anmd 5.34)
3. Titles, authors, and dates of books located
   by combining the words "artificial intelligence" and "children".

Figure 5.33.   Author or main entry bibliographic record screen.

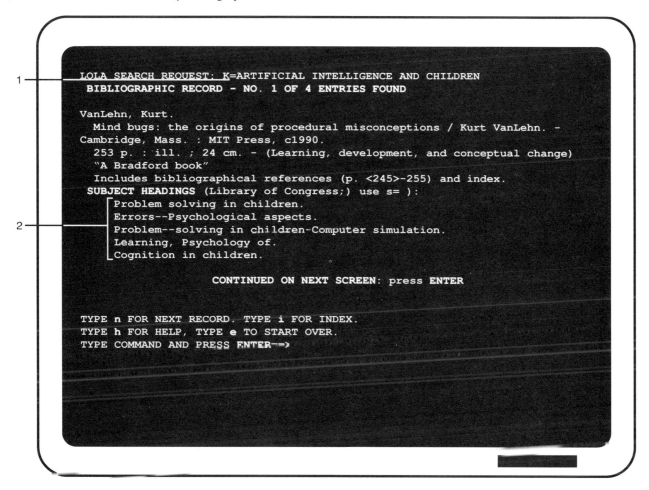

```
LOLA SEARCH REQUEST: K=ARTIFICIAL INTELLIGENCE AND CHILDREN
 BIBLIOGRAPHIC RECORD - NO. 1 OF 4 ENTRIES FOUND

VanLehn, Kurt.
  Mind bugs: the origins of procedural misconceptions / Kurt VanLehn. -
Cambridge, Mass. : MIT Press, c1990.
  253 p. : ill. ; 24 cm. - (Learning, development, and conceptual change)
 "A Bradford book"
  Includes bibliographical references (p. <245>-255) and index.
 SUBJECT HEADINGS (Library of Congress;) use s= ):
        Problem solving in children.
        Errors--Psychological aspects.
        Problem--solving in children-Computer simulation.
        Learning, Psychology of.
        Cognition in children.

             CONTINUED ON NEXT SCREEN: press ENTER


TYPE n FOR NEXT RECORD. TYPE i FOR INDEX.
TYPE h FOR HELP, TYPE e TO START OVER.
TYPE COMMAND AND PRESS ENTER--->
```

1. Keyword search term.
2. Subject headings which include the term "children".

Figure 5.34. Continuation of author or main entry bibliographic screen.

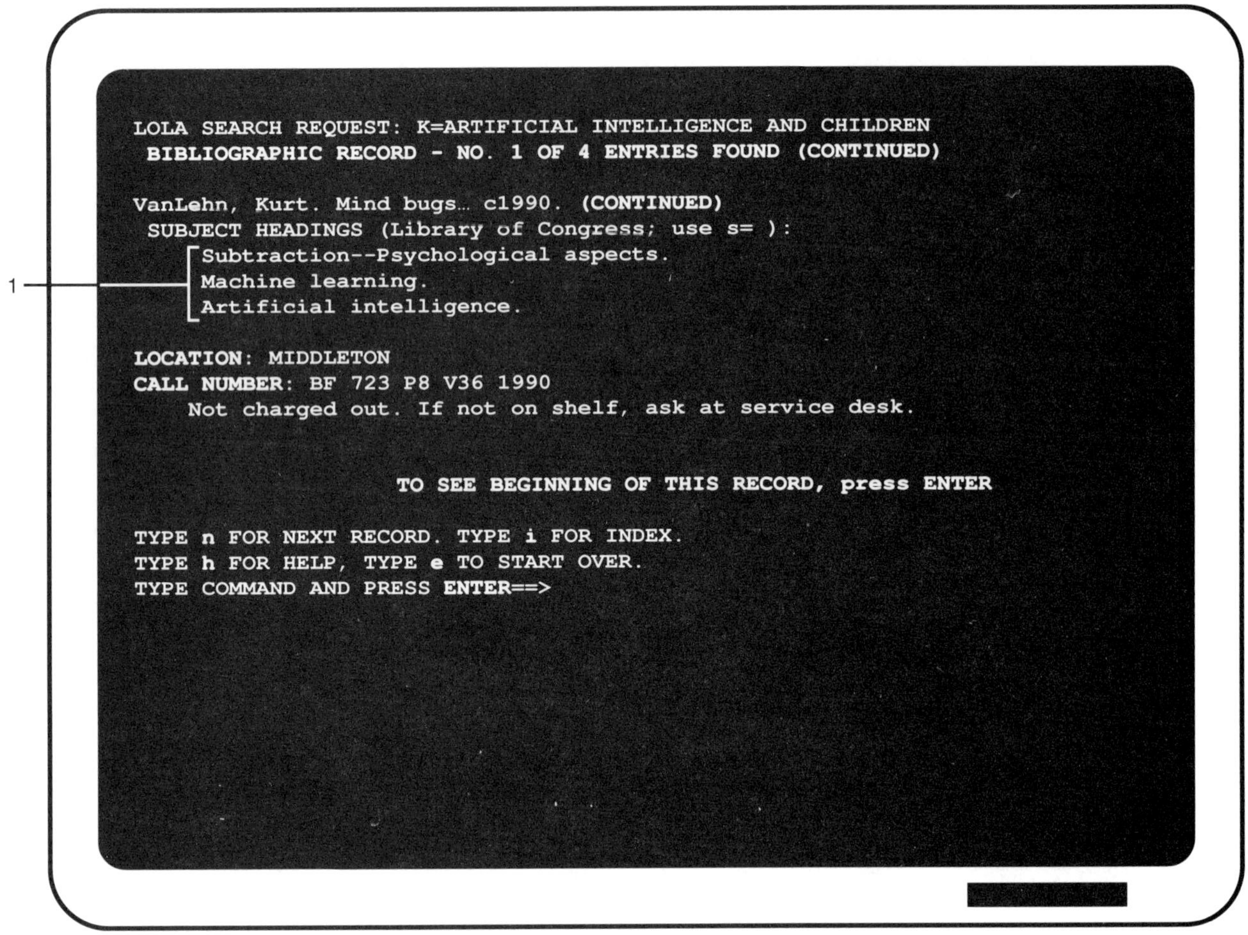
LOLA SEARCH REQUEST: K=ARTIFICIAL INTELLIGENCE AND CHILDREN
BIBLIOGRAPHIC RECORD - NO. 1 OF 4 ENTRIES FOUND (CONTINUED)
VanLehn, Kurt. Mind bugs... c1990. (CONTINUED)
SUBJECT HEADINGS (Library of Congress; use s=):
Subtraction--Psychological aspects.
Machine learning.
Artificial intelligence.
LOCATION: MIDDLETON
CALL NUMBER: BF 723 P8 V36 1990
Not charged out. If not on shelf, ask at service desk.
TO SEE BEGINNING OF THIS RECORD, press ENTER
TYPE n FOR NEXT RECORD. TYPE i FOR INDEX.
TYPE h FOR HELP, TYPE e TO START OVER.
TYPE COMMAND AND PRESS ENTER==>
1

1. Subject headings which include the term "artificial intelligence".

Menu Driven Systems and Labeled Screens

The screen reproductions in Figures 5.35–5.40 are from the CLSI[2] system which is a menu driven system. The menu allows the user to select from among several options on the screen. The example in Figure 5.35 shows the introductory menu with six categories from which to choose: (1) subject, (2) author, (3) title, (4) author and title, (5) all categories—author, title, subject, keyword, and call number, and (6) call number. The initial selection brings up another screen which has specific instructions. Each subsequent operation is performed by selecting items from a menu until the search is completed.

2. The screen reproductions are from the CLSI Inc. system currently being used by the East Baton Rouge Parish Library System. The material is reproduced with the permission of the copyright holder and the library.

Figure 5.35. Introductory screen.

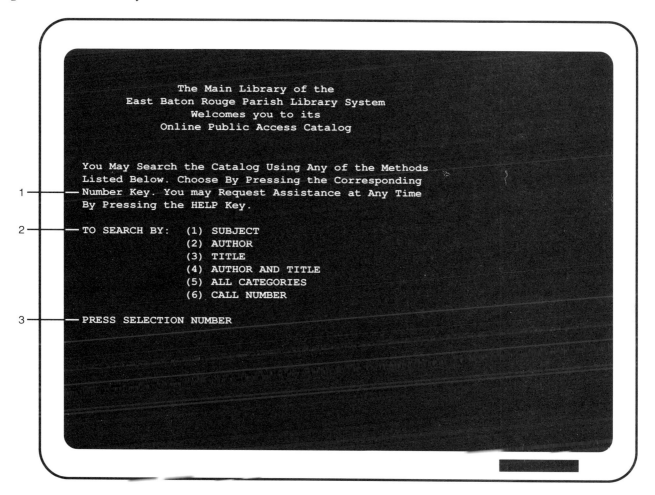

1. Introductory screen providing general information about the system. More information is available on the HELP screens.
2. List of kinds of searches available on the system.
3. Information needed to access the database.

Another feature of the CLSI system is that it provides labeled screens. That is, the items on the display are identified as to author, title, edition, imprint, subject, etc. (Figure 5.39). The examples of screens from the NOTIS System are not labeled and are similar to entries on a catalog card. (See Figure 5.20.) Labeled screens make it easier for the user to interpret information in catalog records.

Figure 5.36.   Subject screen.

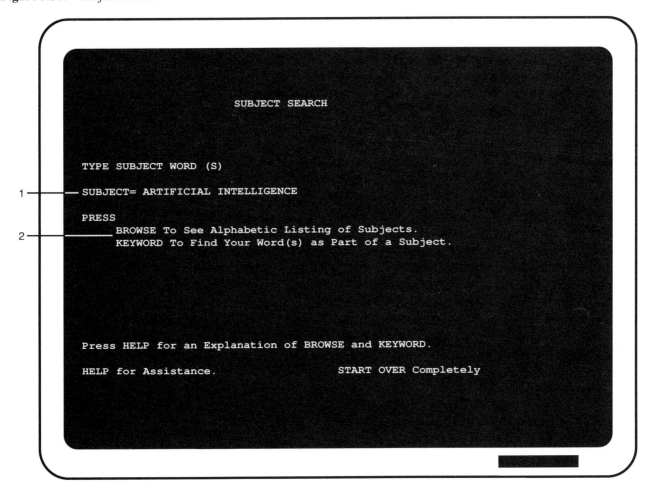

1. Subject to be searched.
2. Available options to find information on the subject.

Figure 5.37. Subject browse screen.

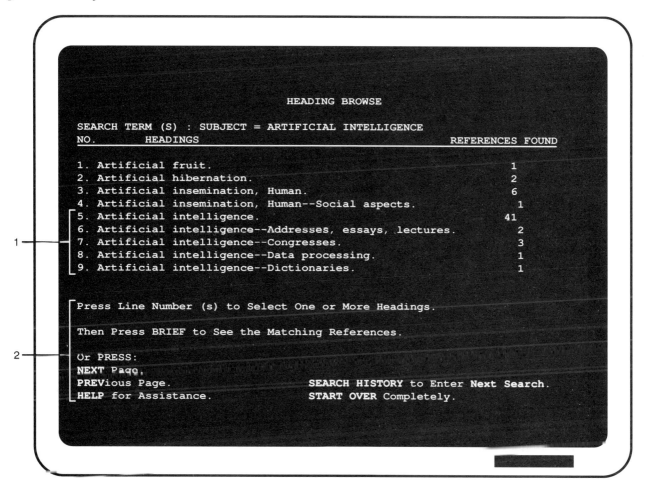

```
                          HEADING BROWSE

SEARCH TERM (S) : SUBJECT = ARTIFICIAL INTELLIGENCE
NO.        HEADINGS                                    REFERENCES FOUND

1. Artificial fruit.                                         1
2. Artificial hibernation.                                   2
3. Artificial insemination, Human.                           6
4. Artificial insemination, Human--Social aspects.           1
5. Artificial intelligence.                                 41
6. Artificial intelligence--Addresses, essays, lectures.     2
7. Artificial intelligence--Congresses.                      3
8. Artificial intelligence--Data processing.                 1
9. Artificial intelligence--Dictionaries.                    1


Press Line Number (s) to Select One or More Headings.

Then Press BRIEF to See the Matching References.

Or PRESS:
NEXT Page.
PREVious Page.                      SEARCH HISTORY to Enter Next Search.
HELP for Assistance.                START OVER Completely.
```

1. Different aspects of subject entered into the system.
2. Directions for accessing the system.

Figure 5.38. Short bibliographic screen.

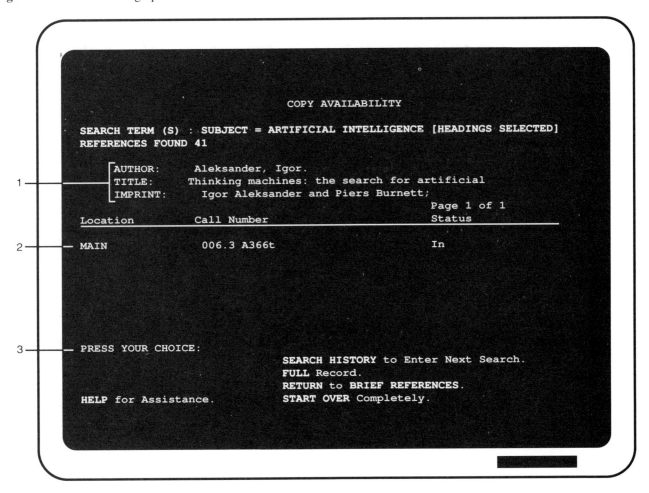

1. Abbreviated bibliographic record.
2. Location, call number, and availability of the book.
3. Information needed for further searching.

Figure 5.39.   Full bibliographic screen.

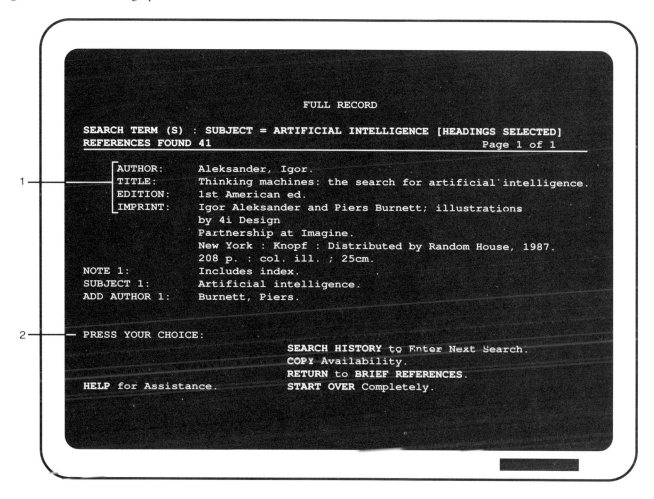

FULL RECORD

SEARCH TERM (S) : SUBJECT = ARTIFICIAL INTELLIGENCE [HEADINGS SELECTED]
REFERENCES FOUND 41   Page 1 of 1

1 —
    AUTHOR: Aleksander, Igor.
    TITLE: Thinking machines: the search for artificial intelligence.
    EDITION: 1st American ed.
    IMPRINT: Igor Aleksander and Piers Burnett; illustrations
                 by 4i Design
                 Partnership at Imagine.
                 New York : Knopf : Distributed by Random House, 1987.
                 208 p. : col. ill. ; 25cm.
    NOTE 1:   Includes index.
    SUBJECT 1:   Artificial intelligence.
    ADD AUTHOR 1: Burnett, Piers.

2 — PRESS YOUR CHOICE:

                              SEARCH HISTORY to Enter Next Search.
                              COPY Availability.
                              RETURN to BRIEF REFERENCES.
     HELP for Assistance.   START OVER Completely.

1. Labels denoting the parts of the record.
2. Directions for further searching.

Figure 5.40. Call number search.

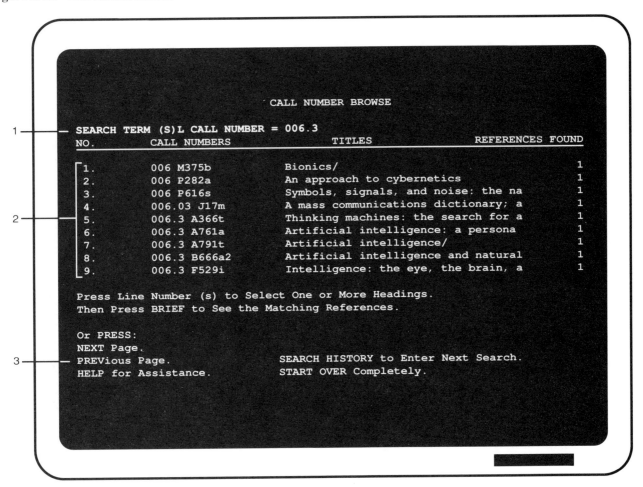

CALL NUMBER BROWSE

SEARCH TERM (S)L CALL NUMBER = 006.3

NO.	CALL NUMBERS	TITLES	REFERENCES FOUND
1.	006 M375b	Bionics/	1
2.	006 P282a	An approach to cybernetics	1
3.	006 P616s	Symbols, signals, and noise: the na	1
4.	006.03 J17m	A mass communications dictionary; a	1
5.	006.3 A366t	Thinking machines: the search for a	1
6.	006.3 A761a	Artificial intelligence: a persona	1
7.	006.3 A791t	Artificial intelligence/	1
8.	006.3 B666a2	Artificial intelligence and natural	1
9.	006.3 F529i	Intelligence: the eye, the brain, a	1

Press Line Number (s) to Select One or More Headings.
Then Press BRIEF to See the Matching References.

Or PRESS:
NEXT Page.
PREVious Page.   SEARCH HISTORY to Enter Next Search.
HELP for Assistance.   START OVER Completely.

1. Class number which was entered into the system.
2. First nine call numbers in the system beginning with 006.
3. Directions for further searching.

SUBJECT HEADINGS

Users of library catalogs who are not familiar with authors or titles of books must look for materials by subject. The greatest difficulty which the researcher will encounter is trying to determine under which subject heading the information is indexed. In catalogs with keyword searching this is not a problem; but in card catalogs, online catalogs, and some CD-ROM catalogs which do not have keyword searching, it is necessary to know something about the way subject headings are entered in the catalog. Organizations such as the American Library Association, H. W. Wilson Company, and the Library of Congress have published lists of standardized subject headings which are used extensively in library catalogs and indexes. Libraries and publishers of indexes and other reference materials use these standardized subject headings to promote uniformity among reference sources. Many times individual libraries and individual publishers add other subject headings to fit their particular needs, but the basic format remains the same. Copies of the subject heading lists that are being used by an individual library are usually placed near the library catalogs for the convenience of patrons. The *Library of Congress Subject Headings* (*LCSH*) is the list that is most commonly used in academic libraries.

The primary rule in looking for subject headings is to proceed from the specific to the general. The library catalog user should think of the topic in as precise terms as possible and try to determine the subject heading that would be the most appropriate. For example, to locate material on educating the blind, the student should look under the more precise subject heading *Blind Education* rather than the broad heading *Education*. It is helpful if one book on the subject can be located in the library catalog. The catalog record should be examined for a list of subjects covered in the book. These additional subject headings might lead to other useful materials on the subject.

If the library user is unable to find any material in the library's catalog on a topic, perhaps the wrong subject headings are being used. To check the accuracy of a subject heading or to get suggestions for other possible headings, the *Library of Congress Subject Headings* should be consulted. Commonly referred to as the "LC List of Subject Headings" or "LCSH," it lists subject headings used by the Library of Congress in their catalogs, as well as *see* references for terms not used, and *see also* references for related topics. Many libraries follow the practices used by the Library of Congress but add their own subject headings to fulfill special local needs. The subject headings used by the Library of Congress are based on some common practices which are helpful to know. These involve the kinds of subject headings and the order in which certain materials are usually entered. Some of these are discussed below.

Kinds of Subject Headings

There are three kinds of subject headings: *simple*, *inverted*, and *divided*.

1. The *simple* subject heading is one word or a phrase, for example: *Photography* or *Photography in oceanography*. The simple subject heading is used for books of a general nature or for subjects too specialized to be subdivided.
2. The *inverted* subject heading is a simple phrase subject heading which has been reversed for purposes of alphabetizing since it is desirable to have all aspects of a topic together in one area of the catalog. To accomplish this

the key word or the noun is listed first followed by the adjective, for example: *Photography, Commercial* or *Photography, Trick*. Thus, the subject headings for books on "commercial photography" and "trick photography" are filed with other subject headings on "photography."

3. The *divided* subject heading is used to indicate more precisely the content and sometimes the form of a book than is possible with either the simple or inverted subject headings. There are four types of subdivisions commonly used in divided subject headings: topical, geographical, form, and chronological.

    (1) The *topical* subdivision limits the primary subject heading to one aspect of the subject such as *Photography—Exposure* or *Photography—Films*.

    (2) A *geographic* subdivision narrows the subject to a particular area such as a country, state, or a smaller geographical designation, for example: *Photography—United States* or *Photography—New York*.

    (3) A *form* subdivision indicates the type or format of a publication such as *Photography—Periodicals* or *Photography—Dictionaries*.

    (4) The *chronological* subdivision is used when it is necessary to limit the subject to a certain date or time period. For example, a large subject such as American literature would be very unwieldy without chronological subdivisions.

Many times more than one type of subdivision is used in a single divided subject heading, for example: *Photography—United States—History—Bibliography* indicates to the catalog user that the publication represented by this subject heading is a bibliography on the history of photography in the United States. The student interested in finding a book which discusses the history of photography in the United States would not select a bibliography since it would list only sources of information. Instead, a subject heading having "handbook," "dictionaries," or no form subdivisions would be more appropriate. *Photography —Dictionaries* is a divided subject heading having only one subdivision. Since the term "dictionaries" is used to indicate encyclopedias as well as "true" dictionaries (i.e., books which simply define terms), terms such as "encyclopedia" or "encyclopedic dictionary" in the title often indicate that the work has more extensive information than simple definitions.

Order of Subject Headings

Some typical subject headings are:

American drama
American language
American literature—Revolutionary period 1775–1783
American literature—1783–1850
American literature—19th century—Bibliography
American literature—19th century—Dictionaries
American literature—20th century
American poetry

Notice that these subject headings are listed in chronological order and not in alphabetical order. The alphabetical arrangement is ignored when dates follow the subject heading. The above listings also illustrate the principle that literature, language, poetry, and drama are entered under the language of the work, not the country of origin.

Books or other publications which deal primarily with one particular country are entered under the name of that country. There are certain topical subdivisions which are commonly used with all countries. In addition, each of these subject headings can be narrowed further by adding chronological and/or form subdivisions.

For example:

United States—Antiquities
United States—Description and travel 1981–
United States—Economic conditions
United States—Foreign relations
United States—History
United States—Politics and government—Yearbooks
United States—Social conditions
United States—Social life and customs

Some subjects that are common to all cultures such as art, architecture, philosophy, and music are entered in the catalog as an inverted subject heading. The noun or name of the subject is followed by the name of the culture.

For example:

Art, American
Architecture, American
Music, American

Because of the complexities of forms used in subject headings, the library user should become familiar with the *Library of Congress Subject Headings.* Figure 5.41 is an example of an entry taken from the *Library of Congress Subject Headings* (Washington, D.C.: Library of Congress, 13th ed., 1990). The reference librarian should also be consulted for assistance with subject headings.

KEYWORD INDEXING

In addition to author, title, and subject access in the card catalog, COM, and computer generated catalogs, some library catalogs have a keyword index. *Keyword indexing* means that each significant word in the title, author, or subject fields of the publication can be retrieved. For example: the book by John Moyne, *Understanding Language: Man or Machine* (see Figure 5.1), can be retrieved from a title keyword index by looking under the keywords, "language," "man," and "machine" in addition to author, title, series, and the subject headings—"psycholinguistics," "linguistics—data processing," "comprehension," "artificial intelligence," and "grammar, comparative and general." This differs from subject indexing since subject headings are standardized and are part of a controlled vocabulary while keyword vocabulary depends upon whatever words are used in the title of the publication. Since keyword indexing adds tremendously to the size of the database it is not feasible to use this method of access in a card catalog. The catalog would increase dramatically in size and complexity and be extremely expensive to maintain.

Figure 5.41.   Library of Congress Subject Headings.

1. **Primary subject heading**. This heading is the correct terminology to use for this subject. These headings are always in dark type and hanging indention is used.

2. **UF**. This symbol indicates that "artificial intelligence" is used as a subject heading instead of the terms listed under this category.

3. **BT**. Broader terms are listed here. They relate to the primary subject heading but are broader in concept.

4. **RT**. Indicates that this term is related to the primary term.

5. **NT**. Narrower terms which relate to the primary term but are more limited in scope.

6. **Subdivisions of the subject**. These subjects are combined with the primary subject to form a more specific divided subject heading. For example "Artificial intelligence—Computer programs" is a more precise subject heading than "Artificial intellegence". These subdivisions are always preceded by a dash (—).

7. **May Subd Geog**. Indicates that a geographical subdivision may be added to this subject. Example: Artificial kidney—United States.

8. **Library of Congress Classification System** class numbers. These are letters or letter/number combinations that are appropriate for the subject and useful for browsing the shelves or using the shelf list.

9. **Scope note**. The range of material that is included under this term is discussed here. Often other terms are given that are useful for finding related material.

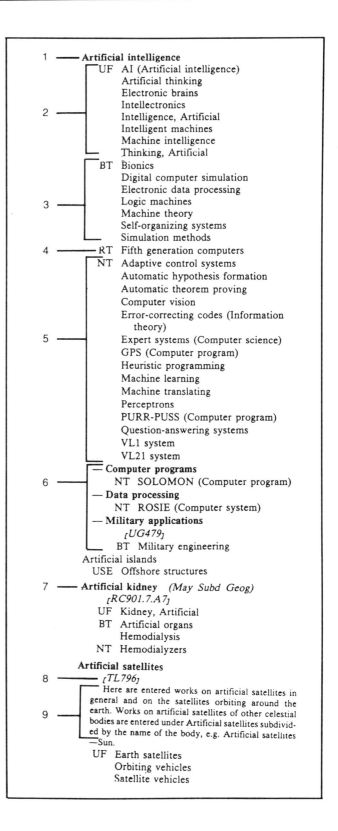

Keyword indexing is used in library catalogs that are computer based such as the COM and computer-generated book catalogs. Many online catalogs can be searched by keywords in a much more effective way. See pages 101-110 for the explanation on keyword searching.

MATERIALS THAT ARE NOT USUALLY FOUND IN LIBRARY CATALOGS

To use the library catalogs efficiently, library users must know what they cannot expect to find there, as well as what they can. It is also important for them to know the tools that will enable them to find materials not listed in the catalog. These will be discussed in subsequent chapters.

Most library catalogs do not have entries for the contents of anthologies. Anthologies are collections of literary works such as a group of plays, poems, speeches, short stories, or essays published in a single work. If the contents of these collections are included in the catalog, a set of entries is put in the catalog indicating the anthology in which the play, poem, short story, speech, or essay is found. For access to the contents of anthologies, one should consult indexes to literature in collections such as: *Play Index*, *Granger's Index to Poetry*, *Speech Index*, *Short Story Index*, and *Essay and General Literature Index*. A more complete list is found in Chapter 8.

Individual articles from periodicals and newspapers are not usually found in the library catalog, although some libraries may include databases for periodical indexes as part of their online catalog. In most cases articles in periodicals are listed in indexes such as *Reader's Guide to Periodical Literature*, *Humanities Index*, *Psychological Abstracts*, or the *New York Times Index*. Indexes to periodical literature are discussed in Chapter 8.

Some libraries which serve as depository libraries for government publications do not list the contents of the collection in the library catalog. To locate these materials it is necessary to consult special finding aids. Information on finding aids for government publications can be found in Chapter 9.

Figure 5.42. Steps in locating nonreference materials.

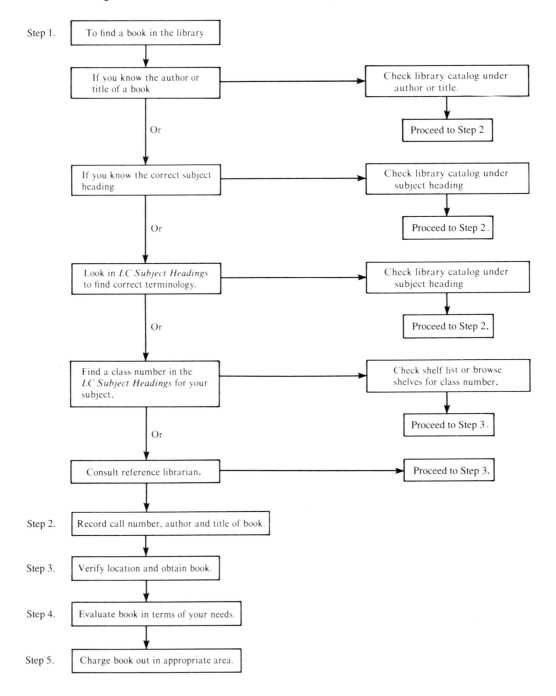

REVIEW QUESTIONS
CHAPTER 5

1. What is the purpose of the library catalog?

2. What are the advantages of the:

    a. card catalog

    b. online catalog

    c. COM catalog

    d. book catalog

    e. CD-ROM catalog

3. What are the disadvantages of the:

    a. card catalog

    b. online catalog

    c. COM catalog

    d. book catalog

4. Most books are represented by at least three different kinds of cards in the catalog. Name them.

5. What is a corporate entry or corporate author?

6. Which form of alphabetizing is used in a card catalog? In most dictionaries?

7. What kinds of entries are found in the online catalog?

8. Define ''commands'' as it applies to the online catalog.

9. How does keyword indexing differ from subject indexing?

10. What is the purpose of the *Library of Congress Subject Headings*?

INSTRUCTOR_____ NAME_____

HOUR & DAY _____

ALPHABETIZING EXERCISE

Arrange the following items in alphabetical order by using the word-by-word method in column 1 and by using the letter-by-letter method in column 2.

	Word by Word	*Letter by Letter*
1. natural law		
2. naturalism		
3. Newport Tower		
4. news services		
5. newspaper ethics		
6. Newfoundland		
7. Newark		
8. New Orleans		
9. native races		
10. Nabokov, Vladimir		
1. Greene, Graham		
2. Green Knight		
3. Greensboro		
4. Greenwich, England		
5. Great Britain		
6. Green Bans		
7. Great Lakes Reader		
8. Green, John Richard		
9. Greenland		
10. Greater Manchester		

FILING RULES EXERCISE

Rearrange the entries in each group in correct order by using the filing rules on pages 90–91. Cite the rule or rules used in the last column.

	Entries	*Rule used*

1. Armstrong-Jones, Anthony

2. Aalto, Alvar, 1898–

3. ABC Cook Book

4. Abbas, Ferhat

5. AT & T

6. ATAP

7. Armstrong, Neil

8. AMA Research Study

9. American Airlines

10. A V Guide

1. McDonald, Joseph

2. Les Misérables

3. McDonald's, Inc.

4. Macartnew, Fred

5. M'Kendrick, Andrew

6. Minute Man

7. Mrs. Mike

8. Mr. Lincoln's Army

9. Mr. Audubon's Lucy

10. The Minute Minder

	Entries	*Rule used*

1. 1001 Lost Treasures

2. One Whaling Family

3. The Nineteen Twenties

4. On 5 & 10 a Day

5. The 1984-style Library

6. 1933: Characters in Crisis

7. One-hoss Shay

8. Northwest Passage

9. North Dakota

10. One Kind of Freedom

1. St. John's Wood

2. Sandberg, Peter Lars 1934–

3. The 6800 Microprocessor

4. Silverwork

5. The SIECUS Circle

6. 66 Weekend Wood Furniture Projects

7. Silver Queen Saloon

8. Shakespeare, William, 1564–1616

9. 17 Ben Gurion

10. Shakespeare to Hardy

LIBRARY OF CONGRESS SUBJECT HEADINGS EXERCISE

Using the latest edition of the *Library of Congress Subject Headings* available in your library, list the subject headings and possible subheadings which are appropriate for the topic you have chosen. Write NA (not applicable) for any term which does not apply.

1. Subject heading or headings:

2. Was there a class letter or a class letter/number following any of the subject headings? If yes, record them here.

3. List subdivisions under the topic given, if any (preceded by a dash):

4. Copy one "used for the term following" (UF):

5. Copy one related broad term (RT):

6. Copy broader term (BT):

7. Copy one narrower term (NT):

8. Does the subject heading have a scope note? If so, what does it say?

9. Consult the library catalog and determine which of the subject headings you have selected for items 1, 3, 4, 5, 6, and 7 are being used in the catalog. List them.

TYPES OF SUBJECT HEADINGS EXERCISE

Listed below are different types of subject headings used in the library catalog. After each subject heading write whether it is a/an *simple* heading, *inverted* heading, *divided* heading, or *combination* of inverted and divided headings. *Circle* all of the form subdivisions.

PSYCHOLOGY

PSYCHOLOGY—ABSTRACTS

PSYCHOLOGY AND LITERATURE

PSYCHOLOGY, APPLIED

PSYCHOLOGY, APPLIED—PERIODICALS

PSYCHOLOGY, APPLIED—RESEARCH

PSYCHOLOGY AS A PROFESSION

PSYCHOLOGY—BIBLIOGRAPHY

PSYCHOLOGY—CASES, CLINICAL REPORTS, STATISTICS

PSYCHOLOGY, COMPARATIVE

PSYCHOLOGY—DICTIONARIES

PSYCHOLOGY—DIRECTORIES

PSYCHOLOGY—HANDBOOKS, MANUALS, ETC.

PSYCHOLOGY—HISTORY

PSYCHOLOGY IN LITERATURE

PSYCHOLOGY—INDEXES

PSYCHOLOGY, INDUSTRIAL

PSYCHOLOGY, PATHOLOGICAL

PSYCHOLOGY—PERIODICALS

PSYCHOLOGY—PERIODICALS—INDEXES

PSYCHOLOGY, RELIGIOUS

PSYCHOLOGY—STUDY AND TEACHING

PSYCHOLOGY—YEARBOOKS

CARD CATALOG EXERCISE

```
TJ
163      Hall, Charles A. S.
.2          Energy and resource quality : the
H344     ecology of the economic process /
1986     Charles A.S. Hall, Cutler J. Cleveland,
         Robert Kaufmann. -- New York : Wiley,
         c1986.
             xxi, 577 p. : ill. ; 29 cm. --
         (Environmental science and technology)
             "A Wiley-Interscience publication."
             Bibliography: p. 535-568.
             Includes index.
             ISBN 0-471-08790-4
             1. Power resources.  2. Industry--
         Power supply.  3. Human ecology.
         I. Cleveland, Cutler J.  II. Kaufmann,
         Robert (Robert K.)  III. Title
         IV. Series
```

Using the information on the catalog card reproduced above, answer the following questions about the book it represents:

1. Call number: _____

2. Analyze the call number. What does TJ stand for? _____

   163.2

   H344? 1986? _____

   _____

3. Classification system used: _____

4. Author/authors: _____

5. Complete title of book: _____

6. Imprint: _____

7. Physical description: _____

8. Is this book illustrated? Justify your answer. _____

_____

9. Is the book part of a series? Justify your answer. _____

_____

10. Does it have a list of sources? Justify your answer. _____

_____

11. Under how many different subject headings can this book be found? _____

Name them. _____

_____

12. Give two reasons why the subject headings on the card are important to the catalog user:

(a) _____

_____

(b) _____

_____

13. Write a bibliographic citation for this book. (See examples in Chapter 11.)

ONLINE OR CD-ROM CATALOG EXERCISE

Select five of the following subjects and using the online or CD-ROM catalog, determine whether or not the library has any books on these subjects. Record the titles and the dates of the most recent books found and the commands or search terms used to find them.

Subject	Title/date	Command or search term used
Drug abuse		
Computer science		
Chemical detectors		
American fiction		
Aviation accidents		
Industrial hygiene		
Economic conditions in Great Britain		
Politics and government in Canada		
Microcomputer programming		
Child development		

Look up the authors listed below in the online or CD-ROM catalog. If the library has any of their books, record the titles and dates of the most recent ones found and commands used.

Author	Title/date	Command or search term used
John Kenneth Galbraith		
Ernest Hemingway		
Henry Louis Mencken		
Virginia Woolf		
Truman Capote		
Erle Stanley Gardner		
Margaret Mead		

Author	Title/date	Command or search term used
William F. Buckley		
Arthur Schlessinger, Jr.		
Thomas Mann		

Look in the online or CD-ROM catalog for the book titles listed below. If the library owns them, record the date of the latest edition and the command used.

Title	Date	Command or search term used
1. *JAMA, Journal of the American Medical Association*		
2. *The New Encyclopaedia Britannica*		
3. *CRC Handbook of Chemistry and Physics*		
4. *Gardner's Art Through the Ages*		
5. *McGraw-Hill Encyclopedia of Energy*		
6. *Twentieth Century Authors*		
7. *The 1990s and Beyond*		
8. *MLA Handbook for Writers of Research Papers*		
9. *2001: A Space Odyssey*		
10. *A Midsummer Night's Dream*		

LIBRARY CATALOG EXERCISE

Locate two nonreference books on a topic you have chosen in the library catalog. If you are not sure of the correct terminology, consult the *Library of Congress Subject Headings*. Fill in the blanks using the information from the books you have located. If the books you have selected do not have one or more of the items listed below, write NA (not applicable) in the blank.

First book:

1. Subject heading used: _____

2. Call number: _____

3. Author(s) or editor: _____

4. Complete title of book: _____

5. Imprint: _____

6. Series (if any): _____

7. Subject headings listed in tracings: _____

　　　_____

8. Write bibliographic citation. See Chapter 11 for examples.

Second book:

1. Subject heading used: _____

2. Call number: _____

3. Author(s) or editor: _____

4. Complete title of book: _____

5. Imprint: _____

6. Series (if any): _____

7. Subject headings listed in tracings: _____

   _____

8. Write bibliographic citation. See Chapter 11 for examples.

Finding and Using
Reference Sources

6

A PREVIEW

Some of the library's most frequently used resources are standard reference works. This chapter seeks to identify the major relevant reference works in a variety of areas and to instruct the library user in effective methods of retrieving information from reference sources. A second objective of this chapter is to develop the researcher's ability to make critical judgments in the selection and use of reference materials.

Reference sources can be broadly defined as those materials which are used to find quick answers to questions and to locate facts. If one wants the derivation of a word, it can be found in a reference book. To find out when the sun rises in the Mohave desert, one consults a reference book. The latest information on the treatment of the common cold can be located in a reference source. While reference collections in libraries vary greatly, depending on the type of library and the information needs of the library's clientele, there are certain characteristics which set reference sources apart. These are:

1. Books which are designed to be consulted rather than being read straight through and which provide facts and figures in an easy-to-find format. These usually include encyclopedias, dictionaries, directories, guides, atlases, etc.
2. Books which can be read straight through, but which have reference value; that is, they provide concise information to frequently asked questions, or they contain valuable information for particular subject areas. These include handbooks and manuals.
3. Sources which serve as guides to information. These include indexes and bibliographies.

Certain non-book materials are also used for reference. These include information in electronic format such as CD-ROMs, online catalogs, online databases, and information in other formats such as microforms and video tapes.

It is helpful to think of reference sources as falling into two broad categories: (1) general reference sources and (2) subject reference sources. Those materials that are general in scope provide information in one source on a wide variety of topics. *The New Encyclopaedia Britannica* and *World Almanac* are examples of general reference books. One can find information on almost any topic in these sources. Subject reference sources cover a single subject field. The *New Grove Dictionary of Musical Instruments* and *Black's Law Dictionary* are examples of reference works which are devoted to single subject areas.

Both general and subject reference sources can be further categorized as being direct or indirect sources of information. A direct source provides the information in such a way that it is not necessary to consult another source. An indirect source serves as a guide to information which is located in other sources. Examples of direct access sources are:

almanacs
atlases
biographical dictionaries
dictionaries
directories
encyclopedias
gazetteers
guidebooks
handbooks
manuals
yearbooks

Examples of indirect access sources are:

abstracts
bibliographies
concordances
indexes

USING REFERENCE SOURCES

One can see from the preceding discussion that the collection of materials found in a typical reference department varies widely, both in content and in format. Although the collection varies, there are some features of the individual works which are common to all of them. Knowing these features will make the collection less forbidding. It is often the case that users do not make effective use of reference sources simply because they do not understand some basic characteristics of reference sources. Some of the more important qualities to look for in a reference book are noted below:

1. *Scope of coverage.* There are a number of points to consider in determining the scope, or level and range of coverage. The scope of the reference work must match that of the research question. Does the work include sufficient material to answer the question? Is there sufficient detail to cover all the points needed for an answer? There are several ways to determine the scope of a work: (a) The introduction, the preface, and the table of contents all tell something about the scope or coverage of the work and about the author's intent. Manuals or instruction books which accompany non-book materials serve the same purpose as the introductory pages of books. (b) The title of a work will help to determine its scope. One should keep in mind that subject reference works tend to give greater coverage to the topics which they cover than more general works. For example, the

article on artificial intelligence in the *McGraw-Hill Encyclopedia of Science and Technology* is more detailed than that in *Encyclopedia Americana*. One can check the title for words or phrases which provide clues to the contents. (c) The text itself might be perused to determine the extent of details and the type of coverage. Periodical articles from a subject index such as *ABI/Inform* tend to be more scholarly than those in a general index such as *InfoTrac*. Therefore, for a more scholarly approach to current information on bank loans the user would select *ABI/Inform*. Sometimes it might be necessary to make comparisons to determine which sources match the reference need.

2. *Timeliness.* If currency is important to the researcher's needs, the *copyright date* should be used to determine whether or not the information contained in a book is current. As a rule, the contents of a reference book are about a year older than the copyright date since it takes approximately a year before a book is published after a copyright is secured. The publication date which is found on the verso, or reverse side, of the title page of a work is not an accurate indicator of the up-to-dateness of a book's contents. One should be wary of the copyright date of a so-called "revised edition." Although the extent of the revision may vary, a revised edition with a new copyright may indicate only minor changes. It is common practice for publishers of reference books to update only parts of a reference work with each new edition. The terms "completely revised edition" or "enlarged edition" are indicative of more extensive revisions.

3. *Arrangement*—Reference books may be arranged or organized in three ways: *alphabetically*, *topically*, or *chronologically*. If arranged alphabetically, subjects or words appear in simple alphabetical order; dictionaries are typically arranged in this fashion. Some reference books arranged in alphabetical order often include a separate index to help locate sub-topics within the work. For example, *Webster's New World Dictionary* has a single alphabetical arrangement without a separate index while the *World Book Encyclopedia* includes a separate index volume. If organized *topically*, subjects are listed in order by broad categories. Reference works arranged by topics almost always have a separate index which is used to find specific subjects within the broad categories. *The Encyclopedia of Crime and Justice* and *Sociological Abstracts* are examples of this type of arrangement. Some works are arranged *chronologically* by date or time periods; historical works are often arranged in this way. Langer's *Encyclopedia of World History*, for example, is arranged by time periods.

4. *Author.* Knowing something about the author can be useful for determining the reliability of information. Occasionally reference books are written by one author, but more often, they are the work of several authors under the direction of an editor. Individual articles are usually signed by the author or authors responsible. Often the author's full name is given along with a brief biographical note indicating education, professional position, and a list of the author's other works. Sometimes that information appears elsewhere in the book or even in a separate volume if the work is a multi-volume one. In *The New Encyclopaedia Britannica*, for example, only the author's initials appear at the end of the article; the full name and biographical information are found in a separate volume.

5. *Bibliographies.* Bibliographies are helpful in providing the researcher with a list of materials for further consideration, they also tell the reader that the

author has researched the topic, which is an indication of the reliability of the information. Bibliographies may be found at the end of each article, at the end of a section in some topically arranged works, at the end of the entire work, or perhaps as an appendix to the work.

6. *Cross references.* Cross references include the *see* and *see also* references which direct the reader to similar or related topics. The *see* reference guides the reader from a term that is not used to one that is used. A *see also* reference suggests other terms to consult for additional information. Both of these are useful in gathering information.

FINDING REFERENCE SOURCES

There are several strategies to use in locating information in the reference collection: (1) using the library catalog; (2) browsing the reference shelves; (3) checking the shelf list or other call number file of materials; (4) consulting a guide to reference books; and (5) asking a reference librarian.

The library catalog should be consulted when one knows the title of a reference source but not its location. The catalog is also used to find titles of works when one knows only the subject. If the topic is not found in the catalog, it may be because it is too specific or it may be that the topic is not used as a subject in the catalog. For example, to find information on growing tomatoes for commercial uses, it may be necessary to look under a broad category. In the example in Figure 6.1 the researcher might begin with the most specific term, "tomatoes" and, if nothing is found, expand the term until its broadest concept, "science," is reached.

The *Library of Congress Subject Headings* (*LCSH*) suggests *related terms* (*RT*), *narrow terms* (*NT*), and *broader terms* (*BT*) to be used in locating topics in the library catalog. The terms "use" and "used for" indicate the proper terminology to be used in locating a subject heading. Reference books are listed in the library catalog by subject and then by the type of reference book. The examples below illustrate the subject headings with their corresponding subdivisions:

TOMATOES—YEARBOOKS
AGRICULTURE—HANDBOOKS, MANUALS, ETC.
SCIENCE—DICTIONARIES

Figure 6.1. Broadening subject headings.

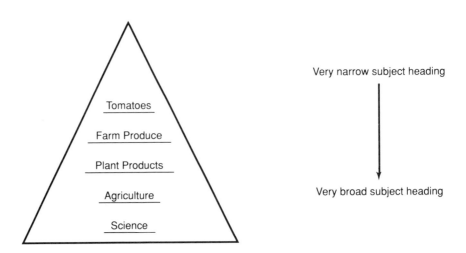

A second strategy is to browse the shelves in the reference collection using the Dewey Decimal or the Library of Congress class number appropriate to the desired subject. Class numbers may be found in the library catalog or the *LCSH*. Some reference departments keep frequently used materials on "ready reference" shelves or on special index tables, making it necessary to browse in several different areas.

Another useful strategy is to consult the public shelf list if one is available. The shelf list is a record of the books owned by the library; it is arranged by call number, that is, by the way works are arranged on the shelf. If the library uses a card catalog, book catalog, or COM catalog, the shelf list will be in a separate file. On the other hand, if the library has an online catalog or a CD-ROM catalog, the shelf list will be a part of the database, and may usually be found in the call number index. For example, if the library's materials are classified in the Dewey Decimal system, the researcher looking for reference books on architecture would look in the 720 section for those works with a reference location symbol. In a library which uses the LC classification system, it would be necessary for the same researcher to look through the NA section for books on architecture that are located in the reference collection. By using the shelf list the researcher finds out which books the library owns in a particular classification. Checking the shelves does not alert one to those works which the library owns but are not in the appropriate place on the shelf.

A fourth strategy is to consult a guide to reference books. The guides list reference sources by subject and often include subdivisions by type such as encyclopedias, handbooks, manuals, etc. Listed below are some of the more useful guides:

American Reference Books Annual. Englewood, CO: Libraries Unlimited, 1970-.

> Annual publication listing general reference books as well as those in the humanities, social sciences, and sciences. Each entry contains a comprehensive review of the work. Contains an author/title index and a subject index.

First Stop: The Master Index to Subject Encyclopedias. Phoenix: Oryx, 1989.
> Useful for background material. Analyzes over 400 different titles including not only encyclopedias but dictionaries, handbooks, and yearbooks as well. Contains keyword index.

Sheehy, Eugene P. *Guide to Reference Books.* 10th ed. Chicago: American Library Association, 1986.

> Guide to reference books arranged by broad subject headings with further subdivisions according to type of work, specific subject headings, and/or geographical location. Each entry is annotated. Includes author, title, and subject index.

Walford, Albert J., ed. *Guide to Reference Material.* 5th ed. 3 vols. London: Library Association, 1989-.

> Each of the three volumes is devoted to a different discipline—vol. 1, science and technology; vol. 2, social and historical science; vol. 3, generalia, language and literature, and the arts. Entries are annotated and each volume has an author/title index and a subject index.

Figure 6.2. Steps in locating reference books.

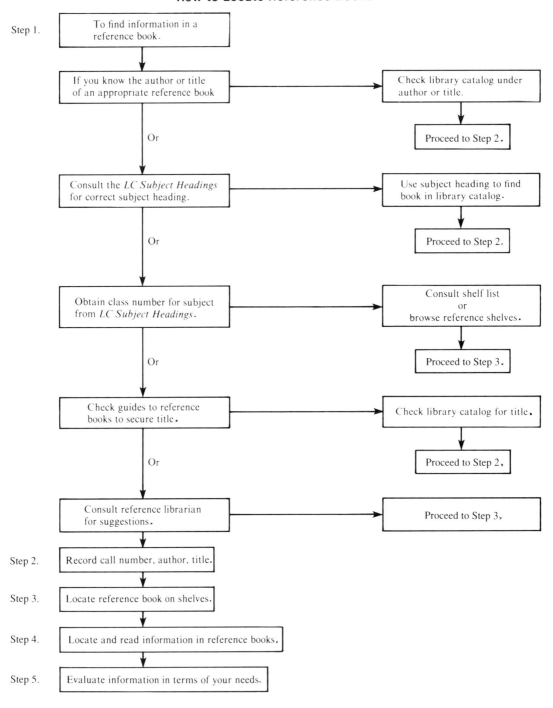

The final strategy mentioned above, but not the least important, is to ask the reference librarian for assistance. Reference librarians are information specialists who are trained to analyze patrons' research needs and assist them in locating different sources of information. When seeking information from the reference librarian, the researcher should be as specific as possible in stating what is wanted. Much valuable time is lost if the questions are vague or poorly formulated.

HOW TO SELECT A REFERENCE SOURCE

The strategies outlined above will lead us to a variety of reference sources. The researcher still must determine those sources which will be most useful. It is helpful to start the search by first analyzing the question to determine what sort of information is needed. For example, a student doing research on the first U.S. flight to the moon should use several types of reference sources in order to find suitable materials. Figure 6.3 illustrates some of the sources that might be used to find suitable materials:

Figure 6.3. Choosing reference sources.

Topic: Information on the first U.S. flight to the moon.

Needed information		*Appropriate reference sources*
Overview article on the flight	—— consult ——→	Subject or general encyclopedia
Statistics on the size of the payload and the amount of fuel required	—— consult ——→	Statistical handbook, yearbook, or almanac
Biographical information on the astronauts	—— consult ——→	Biographical index or dictionary, library catalog
Contemporary account of flight in periodicals and newspapers	—— consult ——→	Periodical and newspaper indexes
Pre- and post-flight analysis of mission	—— consult ——→	Library catalog, periodical and newspaper indexes, abstracts, atlas
Definition of technical terms used in references	—— consult ——→	Dictionary

EVALUATING REFERENCE SOURCES

The user will ordinarily select the particular reference work which meets his/her information needs. What is being asked? What reference source contains the answers to that question? Once the researcher finds a source that supplies the information, it is essential that he/she exercise some critical judgment regarding the work. Is the information accurate? Is it up-to-date? Have primary sources been used or is the work based only on secondary sources? Is the information clearly presented? It is difficult for users to determine the worth of a particular reference source because they are dealing primarily with unknowns. However, the following guidelines are useful in evaluating references sources:

1. *Authority.* Was the article written by someone who is an expert in the field? A signed article is usually an indication of reliable information. Information about authors can usually be found in the reference book itself; but if this is not the case, biographical information can be found elsewhere, such as in biographical dictionaries and biographical indexes. The library catalog will indicate other works by the same author.
2. *Completeness of information.* Are all aspects of the subject covered or have obvious facts been omitted? These questions may be difficult for the novice researcher to answer, but comparing information in one source with that in another may reveal additional details.
3. *Accuracy.* Is the information correct, or are there obvious errors in the information? Again, it may be necessary to sample several sources to determine if there are inconsistencies in reporting such things as times, dates,

places, etc. Statistical information is vulnerable to such inaccuracies, and one might do well to verify statistical information in more than one source whenever this is possible.

4. *Currency.* Is the information up-to-date or have discoveries been made or events taken place since the copyright date of the book? To determine currency of information found in a reference book, one might check journal articles on the same topic to see if there have been new events or developments.

5. *Objective or biased treatment.* Do facts support the author's viewpoint or is a biased viewpoint being presented? Knowing something about the author's background, training, and other works is useful in determining possible bias. Often this information can be obtained from biographical dictionaries and indexes. The periodical indexes and abstracts might be checked to see if the author has written biased literature or if there has been controversy surrounding his/her publications.

6. *Publisher.* Is the publisher well known in the field? When many of the reference sources on a subject are published by the same commercial publisher, learned or technical society, or university press, it can usually be assumed that the materials are authoritative.

7. *Documentation.* Are the sources used in the research listed? This is important if the student wishes to verify the author's sources. For some reference books, *primary,* or original, sources are preferred. In others, *secondary* sources, or sources removed two or more stages from the original, are acceptable. For example, books of statistics are usually compiled from primary sources; encyclopedia articles, on the other hand, are usually based on secondary sources. In either case, it is important that the author give the source of the information, either in notes or in a bibliography listing the sources. Sometimes bibliographies also include other sources in addition to those which the author used in the research.

8. *Illustrations.* Does the reference source contain pictures, drawings, maps, statistical tables, etc. which would enhance its usefulness? The use of illustrations not only makes a book more interesting but often makes a significant contribution to the understanding of the materials being presented.

9. *Language.* Are the articles written in a clear, concise, and easily understood style? Good reference books explain technical and specialized terms fully within the text or in a separate glossary.

10. *Ease of Use.* Does the reference source have an easy-to-use format? Whether the arrangement is alphabetical, topical, chronological, or a combination of one or more of these, a table of contents, index, and good cross references make it possible to locate information much more efficiently.

TYPES OF REFERENCE BOOKS

In any library one finds that considerable emphasis is placed on the reference collection. Each year thousands of reference materials are published, and the librarian attempts to select those sources which will be of greatest use to the library users. Because information needs vary, the reference collection is necessarily diverse. It consists of various types of reference sources designed to yield different kinds of information. On the following pages, these different types of reference sources are discussed in more detail. Whether looking for quick facts or conducting extensive research, it is helpful to know the types of reference sources which are available and which will be most useful for the particular reference need.

DICTIONARIES

Probably the most frequently and widely used type of reference book is a *dictionary*. This is no doubt true because all communication depends on language, which in turn, is made up of words. Reference books which tell us about words are called *dictionaries*. Dictionaries are used to verify words and to confirm spelling, definition, and pronunciation. They are also used to find out how words are used, to locate synonyms and antonyms, and to trace the origin of words. In a dictionary one can find whether a word is no longer in use or has specialized uses. Some dictionaries contain short biographical facts about well-known people, identification of fictional characters, and geographical information. A useful feature in most dictionaries is the guide to pronunciation and a list of abbreviations which usually appear in the front of the dictionary. Many dictionaries are updated by addenda which indicates new words added since the last printing.

There are five broad categories of dictionaries: general dictionaries, historical dictionaries, specialized dictionaries, subject dictionaries and foreign language dictionaries. These are discussed below with representative titles provided for each category. To locate other dictionaries one can look in the library catalog under the heading "dictionaries" or under a subject heading followed by "dictionaries" as a form subdivision.

For example:

DICTIONARIES
COMPUTERS—DICTIONARIES
FRENCH LANGUAGE—DICTIONARIES

General Dictionaries

Most of us are familiar with the general dictionary. It is the dictionary that lists the words of a language with the proper spelling, pronunciation, definition, and grammatical usage. Some general dictionaries also include etymology and related terminology. Dictionaries may be *abridged* or *unabridged*, depending on the extent of coverage. An unabridged dictionary attempts to list all, or nearly all, the words in a language. Additionally, it provides extensive information about each word. An abridged dictionary is a condensation of an unabridged dictionary or a limited version of a dictionary. For example, *Webster's Ninth New Collegiate Dictionary* is a condensation of the unabridged *Webster's Third New International*. Its coverage is limited to words suitable for college level. *The American Heritage Dictionary* limits its coverage to words that are considered more "American" and more reflective of the changing nature of language than some other more traditional dictionaries. While unabridged dictionaries are more comprehensive and thorough in their coverage, they lack the portability of the shorter abridged dictionaries. They are not up-dated as frequently as abridged dictionaries and might not be as useful for finding newer words, particularly those useful in business or in science.

Unabridged

The Random House Dictionary of the English Language. 2nd ed. New York: Random House, 1987.

Up-to-date, easy to read dictionary with good illustrations. Supplement includes French, Spanish, Italian, and German dictionaries, a style manual, and a world atlas. Names of people are included in the main body of the work.

Webster's Third New International Dictionary of the English Language. Springfield, MA: Merriam, 1986.

A comprehensive dictionary containing all the principal words used in the English language. Provides pronunciations as well as definitions. A separate pronunciation guide is found in the front. Features numerous tables within the text such as gestation periods, chemical elements, geologic periods, signs of the zodiac, time charts, etc. Some illustrations included in the text.

The World Book Dictionary. 2 vols. Chicago: Free Enterprise Educational Corp., 1984.

225,000 terms with easy to use format with thumb tabs. Gives current pronunciations with few special symbols. Supplementary pages include instructions for punctuation, capitalization, grammar, and effective writing.

Abridged

The American Heritage Dictionary. 2nd college ed. Boston: Houghton Mifflin, 1985.

Dictionary designed for "American English." Definitions often accompanied by illustrations. Contains several essays on the use of language. Features a separate style manual, list of abbreviations, geographic entries, and biographical entries.

Webster's Ninth New Collegiate Dictionary. Springfield, MA: Merriam, 1988.

A newer but abbreviated version of *Webster's Third New International Dictionary.* An important new feature is that it gives dates indicating when a word came into use. In some cases quotations are used to clarify the meanings of words. Contains a guide to pronunciation and explanatory notes in the preliminary pages. Lists of abbreviations, personal names, geographical names, colleges and universities, and a style manual are found in the back of the book.

Historical Dictionaries

Historical dictionaries place emphasis on the historical perspectives of words and phrases. These often contain useful information about words not found in the traditional dictionary.

Craigie, Sir William A., and James R. Hulbert. *Dictionary of American English on Historical Principles.* 4 vols. Chicago: University of Chicago Press, 1936–1944.

Historical dictionary containing words or phrases that are purely American in origin or ones which are used more frequently in this country than elsewhere. Many of the words were coined to denote certain events or movements in the country's history. Gives date that the word came into the language, quotations illustrating the meaning of the word, and alternate definitions.

Oxford English Dictionary. 2nd ed. 20 vols. New York: Clarendon, 1989.

Comprehensive record of the words used in the English language from the twelfth century to the present time. Quotations demonstrate how words were used during different time periods. Excellent source for quotations using words in a particular context.

Specialized Dictionaries

In addition to the traditional dictionaries, there are a great number of specialized dictionaries which approach the study of words from a different perspective. That is, they present a different point of view depending on the purpose of the dictionary. For example, a thesaurus would come under this category since it groups synonyms together. A few of these specialized dictionaries are listed below.

New Dictionary of American Slang. New York: Harper and Row, 1986.

Extensive list of American slang terms with definitions, parts of speech, examples, and, in some cases, the date of origin. Good introductory essay on slang.

Partridge, Eric. *Dictionary of Slang and Unconventional English.* 8th ed. London: Kegan Paul, 1984.

Emphasis is on British slang although some American terms are included. Where possible, date and place of origin are given. Multiple meanings are included when applicable.

Roget, Peter Mark. *Roget's Thesaurus of English Words and Phrases.* London: Longman, 1987.

Classified list of terms in the English language with synonyms indicating different possible meanings and usage of the word. Includes index of words in the main body of the work. Does not define words but indicates their meanings through their usage.

Subject Dictionaries

Subject dictionaries are devoted primarily to a subject field and give the terminology most useful in that field. Many of these dictionaries are updated frequently to keep current with changing terminology and new developments.

Black, Henry Campbell. *Black's Law Dictionary.* 6th ed. St. Paul: West, 1990.

Comprehensive dictionary defining terms used in law and related subjects. Some definitions are quite extensive while others are brief. Good cross references. Pronunciation guide in the front arranged alphabetically.

Dorland's Illustrated Medical Dictionary. 27th ed. Philadelphia: Saunders, 1987.

> Defines medical terms giving pronunciations, alternate definitions, if any, and origin of the word. Numerous plates showing detailed drawings of parts of the human body such as bones, blood vessels, nerves, and vital organs.

Shafritz, Jay M., Richard P. Koeppe, and Elizabeth W. Soper. *The Facts on File Dictionary of Education.* New York: Facts on File, 1988.

> Concise definitions of terms currently used in education. Some charts and cross references. Includes some acronyms and biographical material.

Foreign Language Dictionaries

Foreign language dictionaries can be found for virtually every written language. Foreign language dictionaries may be written entirely in the language covered, or they may be English-foreign language. Just as with English language dictionaries, there are a wide variety of foreign language dictionaries. A few representative works are listed below.

Cambridge Dizionario Italiano-Inglese, Inglese-Italiano. Milano: Signorelli, 1985.

> Comprehensive up-to-date dictionary which includes both classical and idiomatic terms. English-Italian section includes pronunciations.

Collins-Robert French-English, English-French Dictionary. 2nd ed. Glasgow: Collins, 1987.

> Emphasizes contemporary rather than classical terms in both languages. "Style labels" indicate when a term may have stylistic complexities, e.g., local idioms that cannot be literally translated. Includes phrases as well as single words.

Falla, P. S., ed. *The Oxford English-Russian Dictionary.* New York: Oxford, 1984.

Wheeler, Marcus. *The Oxford Russian-English Dictionary.* 2nd ed. New York: Oxford, 1984.

> These two volumes can be used together to alternate between the two languages—English and Russian. Designed primarily for English speaking students. Includes both geographical and personal names.

The New Velázquez Spanish and English Dictionary. Piscataway, NJ: New Century, 1985.

> Includes not only classical Spanish words but terms that are in common use in both Spanish America and the United States. Lists both Spanish and English words with their alternate language equivalent.

The Oxford-Duden Pictorial English-Japanese Dictionary. New York: Oxford, 1984.

> Series of labelled drawings accompanied by both the English and Japanese words for each of the numbered parts. Very broad in coverage and ranges from clothing and common household items to concepts in science and technology.

ENCYCLOPEDIAS

The word "encyclopedia" is almost a synonym for "reference book." It is usually the first book that comes to mind when one thinks of "reference." The term "encyclopedia" is of Greek origin and means "instruction in the circle of arts and sciences." Encyclopedias attempt to cover knowledge, or branches of knowledge, in a comprehensive, but summary, fashion. Encyclopedias are useful for providing facts and for giving a broad overview of a topic. For these reasons, most researchers will find them indispensable when beginning a research project. While there is no one encyclopedia which is the "perfect" reference book, some encyclopedias have features which enhance their quality and make them superior to others. Many encyclopedias have articles which are written and signed by specialists in their fields, a sign of authoritativeness. The articles are frequently accompanied by bibliographies, maps, and illustrations. Most encyclopedias are kept up-to-date by continuous revisions. That is, new material is inserted with each new printing, which in many cases means annually. Completely revised editions are issued less frequently.

Because they cover such a broad range of knowledge, many encyclopedias are multivolume works. The topics within the scope of the work are covered in separate articles which are arranged either alphabetically or by broad topics. A separate index, which lists more specific topics, is standard for most encyclopedias.

There are two basic types of encyclopedias, general or subject. General encyclopedias cover a wide spectrum of knowledge, while subject encyclopedias are restricted to one subject or one aspect of a subject. To locate encyclopedias in the library catalog one should look under the heading "dictionaries." Some of the works listed under that heading will be true dictionaries, but others will be encyclopedias. For example, the *Encyclopedia of Artificial Intelligence* is listed under the heading: ARTIFICIAL INTELLIGENCE—DICTIONARIES. Examples of different types of encyclopedias are listed below.

General

Academic American Encyclopedia. 21 vols. Danbury, CT.: Grolier, 1990.

Comprehensive general encyclopedia featuring broad coverage of both contemporary and historical events, biographical sketches, and current technology. Emphasis is on science and technology and the arts and humanities. Many colored photographs. Available on CD-ROM.

Encyclopedia Americana. 30 vols. Danbury, CT: Grolier. 1990.

The first encyclopedia published in the United States. It covers the arts and humanities as well as scientific development. Signed articles by experts in the field. Unique feature is the "century" articles which discuss the outstanding events and trends of various time periods. For example, all of the accomplishments and events of the nineteenth century are discussed in an article under that heading. Long articles contain a table of contents for easy reference. Supplemented by *Americana Annual.*

The New Encyclopaedia Britannica. 15th ed. 32 vols. Chicago: Encyclopaedia Britannica, 1990.

The fifteenth edition consists of three parts with a two-volume index. Volume 30, the *Propaedia* is an "Outline of Knowledge," which serves as a topical approach to the articles in volumes 1–12, the *Micropaedia*, and in volumes 13–29, the *Macropaedia*. The twelve-volume *Micropaedia* contains brief entries with cross references to the longer articles in the *Macropaedia*. The *Macropaedia* volumes contain long comprehensive articles complete with bibliographies. Articles are signed with initials which can be identified by referring to volume 30. Supplemented by *Britannica Book of the Year*.

World Book Encyclopedia. 22 vols. Chicago: World Book, 1990.

Designed for elementary through high school students, but because of its extremely wide coverage, it is excellent for general reference. Major articles provide subject headings for related articles, an outline of the subject, and review questions. Numerous diagrams and pictures, good cross references, and signed articles. Updated by *World Book Yearbook*.

Subject Encyclopedias

Encyclopedia of Bioethics. 4 vols. in 2. New York: Free Press, 1978.

Lengthy signed articles with good cross references and bibliographies. Covers the ethical concerns with human problems such as abortion, aging, human experimentation, population policies, reproductive technologies, etc.

Encyclopedia of Psychology. 4 vols. New York: Wiley, 1984.

Volumes 1–3 alphabetically arranged by specific topics. Some articles signed and have short bibliographies. Volume 4 contains an extensive bibliography, an author index, and a subject index.

Encyclopedia of World Art. 17 vols. New York: McGraw-Hill, 1959–1987.

A collection of critical essays on all aspects of art from ancient times to the present. Discusses trends and schools of artistic thought as well as methods of conservation and restoration. Some biographical information. Each article is signed and has a bibliography. Approximately half of each volume is devoted to reproductions of art works. Some illustrations in color.

International Encyclopedia of the Social Sciences. 18 vols. in 9 and a *Biographical Supplement*. New York: Macmillan, 1979.

Long scholarly articles with bibliographies covering all aspects of the social sciences from anthropology to statistics. Treats narrow subjects within the broad subjects. Good cross references. The *Biographical Supplement* contains a classified subject list to the alphabetically arranged biographies.

McGraw-Hill Encyclopedia of Science and Technology. 6th ed. 20 vols. New York: McGraw-Hill, 1987.

Covers all aspects of science and technology. Scholarly yet non-technical articles most of which are signed. Contains illustrations, bibliographies, and cross references. Volume 20 contains topical and analytical indexes and a section on scientific notation. Kept up-to-date by *McGraw-Hill Yearbook of Science and Technology*.

ALMANACS AND YEARBOOKS

Almanacs and yearbooks are important because they provide a wide variety of miscellaneous type information in a succinct and timely manner. They are usually published regularly and provide information on events and developments during the span of their publication coverage. Many of them provide statistical type information. Almanacs are listed in the library catalog under the heading ''almanacs.''

For Example:

ALMANACS, AMERICAN

Yearbooks are listed as a form heading following the subject.

For example:

PETROLEUM—YEARBOOKS

Almanacs

Almanacs are usually one volume works containing statistical data and a compilation of specific facts. Some almanacs update previous editions but continue to include the data from previous years, while others include only data from the current year. Almanacs such as *The World Almanac* and *Information Please* cover a wide range of topics such as facts and figures on governmental affairs, entertainment, and notable persons as well as unusual or noteworthy facts. Other almanacs, such as *Farmer's Almanac*, are limited to a specific field. A few typical almanacs are listed below:

Information Please Almanac, Atlas and Yearbook. 1947 to date. Boston: Houghton Mifflin, 1947-.

> Volume is arranged by broad subjects such as astronomy, economics and business, nutrition and health, religion, science, etc. Articles include both discussion and statistical material. Each issue contains signed articles dealing with important issues of the period such as biotechnology, space exploration, consumer affairs, environmental problems, and energy concerns. Some maps and a few pictures. Includes a subject index.

Whitaker, Joseph, ed. *An Almanack.* 1868 to date. London: Whitaker, 1868-.

> British counterpart of *The World Almanac.* This annual publication is a compilation of excerpts from news stories, statistical information, and events of the preceding year. Emphasis is on Great Britain and Europe but contains information on the United States. Includes some pictures.

The World Almanac and Book of Facts. 1868 to date. New York: World-Almanac, 1868-.

> Covers a wide variety of subjects. An excellent source for statistics which are updated annually. Features a chronology of events that took place during the preceding year. Contains biographical information on U.S. presidents. Includes a few maps and some pictures. Index located at the front of the book.

Yearbooks

Yearbooks tend to cover trends and events of the previous year. Some yearbooks supplement encyclopedias in that they provide the latest trends and developments. Yearbooks, like almanacs and other books of facts and statistics, may be general in coverage, or they may be limited to one subject or restricted to one geographical area. The list below is a sampler of various types of year-books.

Americana Annual. 1923 to date. New York: Encyclopedia Americana, 1923-.

> Published annually as a supplement to the encyclopedia. Has long signed articles discussing the year's political, economic, scientific and cultural developments. Includes a list of significant monthly events. Extensive biographical material on people in the news and of major figures who have died during the year.

Britannica Book of the Year. 1938 to date. Chicago: Encyclopaedia Britannica, 1938-.

> Annual supplement to the encyclopedia. Includes several feature articles on newsworthy events. The "Year in Review" section covers the major events of the year as well as biographical information on people in the news. A separate section entitled "Britannica World Data" provides up-to-date statistical information on all countries of the world. Articles are signed and a list of contributors is provided.

Europa Year Book: A World Survey. 2 vols. 1926 to date. London: Europa Publications, 1926-.

> Provides information on the organization and activities of the United Nations and other international organizations. The chapters on the major countries of the world discuss such things as government, economic affairs, social welfare, education, and recent history. Includes statistics.

Statesmen's Year Book: Statistical and Historical Annual of the States of the World. 1864 to date. New York: St. Martin's, 1864-.

> Handy reference source for information on various countries of the world. Gives brief history, statistical information, area and population, climate, constitution and government, and natural resources. For the United States, the information is not only for the whole country, but also for each state.

Statistical Abstract of the United States. 1878 to date. Washington: GPO, 1879-.

> Issued annually by the U.S. Bureau of the Census. Consists of a compilation of social, political, and economic statistics gathered from both private and government sources. Most tables give comparative information from prior years. Many of the statistics are from primary sources; all information is documented.

HANDBOOKS AND MANUALS

Handbooks and manuals are difficult to categorize because they are so varied. They usually deal specifically with one subject or with one subject area. There are many reference books which fall into this category, and they cover a wide range of topics. The library catalog lists handbooks and manuals under the form subdivision "handbooks manuals etc."

For example:

COMPUTERS—HANDBOOKS MANUALS ETC.

Handbooks

A *handbook* usually treats one specific subject in a brief fashion or presents a broad survey of a subject. The original *handbook* was a book that was designed to be held in the hand, so the coverage of the subject must necessarily be limited by the size of the book. Some reference books have the word "encyclopedia" in their title but are actually handbooks. For example, *Benét's Reader's Encyclopedia* is considered to be a handbook because it provides a brief treatment of the field of literature in one volume. Handbooks with both broad and narrow coverage are listed below.

Benét's Reader's Encyclopedia. 3rd ed. New York: Harper & Row, 1987.

> Primarily concerned with literature but useful for identifying movements and important people in art and music. Contains references to literary characters and plot summaries. International in scope, but emphasis is on American and British works.

Cambridge Guide to World Theatre. New York: Cambridge University Press, 1988.

> Alphabetically arranged listing of names of people prominent in the theater, famous theaters, titles of plays, festivals, etc. Short articles signed with initials which are identified in the front of the volume. Some pictures.

Columbia Literary History of the United States. New York: Columbia University Press, 1988.

> Discusses the nation's literary history from pre- colonial time of the American Indian through the 1980s. Essays are signed and the authors are further identified in the "Notes on Contributors" section. Comprehensive index.

Gray, Henry. *Anatomy of the Human Body.* Philadelphia: Lee and Febiger, 1985.

> Standard medical handbook used to identify and study parts of the human body. Divided into 18 main sections with numerous subsections. Articles are unsigned but bibliographies are furnished. Many illustrations.

Manuals

A *manual* is a specific reference book which tells how-to-do something. It may also describe how something operates, or provide descriptions of the inner workings of an organization. Another way to think of a manual is as an instruction book. Manuals and handbooks frequently resemble one another in their form and content and these terms are frequently interchangeable. For example, the *MLA Handbook for Writers of Research Papers* is a book which gives rules and examples to be followed when preparing and documenting reports, term papers, theses, etc. It may be thought of as a manual or a handbook.

Gibaldi, Joseph and Walter S. Achtert. *MLA Handbook for Writers of Research Papers.* 3rd ed. New York: Modern Language Association of America, 1988.

An authoritative manual which explains the mechanics of preparing, organizing, and writing research papers using the methods and forms prescribed by the Modern Language Association. Contains examples for documenting both print and non-print materials such as films, computer software, recordings, etc.

Robert, Henry M. *Robert's Rules of Order*. Newly revised. Glenview, IL: Scott, Foresman, 1990.

The definitive guide since 1876 to standard parliamentary procedure used by organizations to conduct business meetings. The introduction explains the history and development of parliamentary rules while the center section codifies procedures for conducting meetings. Other chapters explain the duties of organization officers, committee members, and board members.

Turabian, Kate L. *A Manual for Writers of Term Papers, Theses, and Dissertations*. 5th ed. Chicago: University of Chicago Press, 1987.

Guide to writing and assembling a research paper. Includes directions and examples of bibliographic forms, footnotes, and other citations for both published and unpublished materials.

United States Government Manual. 1935 to date. Washington: GPO, 1935-.

Official guide to the organization of the United States government. Lists all of the government agencies, both official and semi-official, along with the names, addresses, and phone numbers of their top personnel. Contains a copy of the U.S. Constitution, a list of abbreviations useful for identifying government agencies, an index of names, and an agency/subject index.

ATLASES, GAZETTEERS, AND GUIDEBOOKS

Geographic reference sources are useful in providing information about places in the world. These sources include atlases, gazetteers, and guidebooks which tell us about the physical geography of a place; the vegetation and natural resources; the economic, social and cultural conditions; the government; travel and leisure; and historical development. Much of the information found in geographical reference books can also be found in other reference books such as encyclopedias and almanacs, but the specific geographical reference sources often include additional information not found in these more general sources. For example, atlases include maps of various kinds—political, topographic, and demographic. Ordinarily one will not find these detailed maps in an encyclopedia. One can look under the heading "atlases" in the library catalog. The subheading "maps" is also useful for finding atlases. Gazetteers appear under the heading "gazetteer," and guidebooks appear as a main heading or as a form subheading following the term "description and travel."

For example:

ATLASES, FRENCH
EUROPE—DESCRIPTION AND TRAVEL—GUIDEBOOKS
GAZETTEERS

The types of geographical reference sources are discussed below with representative titles of each.

Atlases

An *atlas* is a book of maps, although some atlases contain supplementary materials such as population, indexes to place locations, and distance charts. There are two basic types of atlases—historical and current. The list below contains examples of both kinds.

Goode's World Atlas. 18th ed. Chicago: Rand McNally, 1990.

An easy-to-use volume arranged in four major divisions: (1) world thematic maps dealing with the world's climate, raw material distribution, landform, languages, and religions; (2) regional maps which cover the political and topographical features of the continents and the countries within those continents; (3) plate tectonics and ocean floor maps; and (4) maps covering the major cities of the world. Includes a comprehensive index.

Rand McNally Cosmopolitan World Atlas. Chicago: Rand McNally, 1987.

Good discussions with aerial photographs of geologic phenomena such as earthquake zones, volcanoes, glaciers, and floods. Has a section of thematic maps on such subjects as population, religion, languages, agriculture, energy production and consumption, and climate.

Rand McNally Commercial Atlas and Marketing Guide. 1876 to date. Chicago: Rand McNally, 1876-.

An annual publication containing business and commercial data. Useful for information on transportation, communication, economic conditions, and population. Contains state and national maps as well as maps of some American and Canadian cities. International in scope, but emphasis is on the United States.

Shepherd, William R. *Historical Atlas*. 9th ed. rev. New York: Barnes & Noble, 1980.

Collection of chronologically arranged maps of the world dating from approximately 3000 BC to the 20th century. Includes plans of Rome (350 AD) and Athens (420 BC). Contains both political and physical maps.

The Times Atlas of the World. New York: Times Books, 1985.

Contains physical and political maps of the world. Includes star charts, discussions of the solar system, and descriptions of the space flights. Comprehensive index of place names and their locations.

The Times Atlas of World History. Rev. ed. Maplewood, NJ: Hammond, 1984.

Consists of political and cultural maps beginning with the origin of humankind through the 1980s. Includes chronological charts of geographic regions depicting the major political and cultural events from 9000 BC to 1984 AD.

Gazetteers

A gazetteer is a listing of geographical places with explanatory material. In addition to location, a gazetteer usually describes the physical features of a place and gives statistical information. Some gazetteers such as the *Encyclopedia of Historic Places* provide historical information about places. Gazetteers frequently supplement atlases or are a part of a volume which contains maps. Several of the various types of gazetteers are listed below.

Canby, Courtlandt. *Encyclopedia of Historic Places.* 2 vols. New York: Facts on File, 1984.

> Lists in alphabetical order names of places of historical significance such as battle sites, archaeological sites, shrines, cities, towns, and countries. Gives geographic location and historical significance. Cross references from former names to present ones. Some illustrations.

Chambers World Gazetteer: An A-Z of Geographical Information. 5th ed. Edinburgh: Chambers, 1988.

> Alphabetical list of countries, towns, cities, and areas with descriptions of each. Helpful preface notes with specimen entry. Contains some maps and measurement conversion charts.

Webster's New Geographical Dictionary. Springfield, MA: Merriam, 1988.

> Alphabetically arranged list of place names with locations and pronunciations. Information for each state of the U.S. includes list of counties, products manufactured, natural resources, etc.; other countries of the world have similar listings under the country's name. Some maps.

Guidebooks

Guidebooks provide detailed descriptions of places and are intended primarily for the traveller. However, their value as a source of geographical information should not be overlooked. While they list interesting places to see and provide travel information such as hotel and restaurant accommodations and travel routes, they also provide historical information and details about places which might not be found elsewhere. In addition to being more detailed than other sources, they are usually more up-to-date. Most guidebooks are updated annually to include only the most recent information. Guidebooks series are considered reliable because the continued sale of these works depends on their accuracy. Some of the better known series are listed below.

Baedeker Guidebooks. 1828 to date. Englewood Cliffs, NJ: Prentice-Hall, 1828-.

> One of the oldest series of guidebooks still being published. Provides information about individual countries, groups of countries, and cities. Gives the history of the area, places to see, places to stay, and restaurants. Many pictures and maps. Columnar arrangement for easy consultation.

Fodor's Travel Guides. 1936 to date. New York: McKay, 1936-.

> Volumes cover various regions and cities of the United States, Europe, Asia, South America, and the Caribbean. Offers suggestions for transportation to and from an area and places of interest to visit. Discusses local customs and history. Contains maps of cities and lists of lodging places and restaurants. Well illustrated. Frequently revised.

McLanathan, Richard B. K. *World Art in American Museums.* Garden City, NJ: Doubleday, 1983.

Guide to art collections in museums in the U.S. and Canada. Arranged in three parts: Section I contains the names of museums alphabetically arranged by state and province; Section II is in ten parts arranged by artistic period; Section III is an alphabetical list of artists with biographical notes and a list of the locations of their works. Some pictures and maps.

Mobil Travel Guide. 8 vols. New York: Prentice-Hall, 1990.

Each volume covers a different area of the United States and Canada. Contains regional road maps, information on local accommodations, restaurants, places to see, and local events. Some city maps. Each volume is arranged by state and then alphabetically by city and town names.

DIRECTORIES

There are thousands of directories published and distributed each year, ranging from the telephone directory of even the smallest town to directories international in coverage. Libraries cannot possibly acquire all the directories which are published, so they must select those which will be of informational value to their users. Directories are used to supply information about persons, organizations or institutions, and companies. Entries in directories range from simple listing of names to more extensive information such as addresses, history, or ganization charts, product description, and publications. People use directories for a variety of reasons: to locate names and addresses, to find marketing information, to find out about organizations and government agencies, etc. Catalogs sometimes serve the same functions as directories in that they list products, organizations, etc. Directories may also provide valuable historical information. For example, it is possible to track the development of a product by looking in back issues of manufacturers' directories. Genealogists track names of ancestors by looking in old city directories or telephone directories. Directories for specialized uses can be located in the library catalog under the subject heading followed by the form subdivision "directories."

For example:

LAWYERS—DIRECTORIES
COMPUTERS—CATALOGS
COMPUTERS—DIRECTORIES

There are also guides to directories such as the *Directory of Directories* which are useful for finding directories. The list below contains representative titles from among the many specialized or subject directories.

The College Blue Book. 3 vols. 22nd ed. New York: Macmillan, 1989.

Directory of colleges and universities in the United States and Canada. Lists schools by state and province, professional accreditation, degrees offered. A separate volume describes each of the institutions listed in the other two volumes.

Congressional Directory. 1809 to date. Washington: GPO, 1809-.

Published for each session of Congress. Contains names, addresses, committee assignments, and biographical sketches of members of Congress.

Also includes names and addresses of top officials in all government agencies, international organizations, diplomatic missions, and the press corps. Contains maps of each Congressional district.

Encyclopedia of Associations. 1956 to date. Detroit: Gale, 1956-.

Multivolume directory of active organizations in the United States and Canada. Has a separate volume for international organizations. Arranged by broad subject areas with separate organization name, executive name, keyword, and geographic indexes.

Patterson's American Education. 1990 ed. Mount Prospect, IL: Education Directories, Inc., 1989.

Directory of secondary schools in the United States. Includes middle schools, high schools, technical schools, colleges and universities both public and private. Arranged alphabetically by state and then by school district.

Thomas' Register of American Manufacturers. 1905 to date. New York: Thomas Publishing, 1905-.

Multivolume lists of products and services available from American companies. Includes product and brand name indexes, company profiles, and a file of company catalogs. Issued annually.

The World of Learning, 1990. 40th ed. London: Europa, 1989.

Directory of research organizations, libraries and archives, colleges and universities, learned societies, museums, and art galleries found throughout the world. Arranged alphabetically by country. Includes names, addresses and some annotations.

BIBLIOGRAPHIES

Bibliographies are compilations of sources of information. They call attention to the literature on a specific subject or by a specific author. The sources listed in bibliographies consist of a variety of formats—books, periodicals, newspaper articles, films, recordings, CD-ROMs, personal interviews, etc. The bibliographies themselves appear in a number of forms—listings at the end of periodical or reference book articles; periodical articles devoted exclusively to listing of information sources; listings at the end of book chapters or at the end of the book, and entire books that are lists of sources of information. Some bibliographies are annotated—a short descriptive or critical statement is included; others are simple alphabetical listings of references. Bibliographies of bibliographies serve as a reference guide to locating bibliographies. The value of bibliographies to the researcher should be readily apparent. They list the sources an author used to find information on a specific topic and/or they direct the reader to other sources of information. It is not uncommon to find full length bibliographies in the regular collection along with the books on a particular subject. Some libraries, however, maintain a separate bibliography collection within the reference collection. To find bibliographies devoted exclusively to a specific topic, one should look in the library catalog for the specific heading, followed by the form sub-division ''bibliographies.''

For example:

ARTIFICIAL INTELLIGENCE—BIBLIOGRAPHIES

To locate the general bibliographies one should look for ''bibliographies'' in the library catalog.

The examples following list typical reference books that are devoted exclusively to listing sources of information.

Books in Print. 1940 to date. New York: Bowker, 1948-.

> Published annually, lists books currently available from publishers. Contains separate author, title, and subject lists. Useful for determining what is available in different subject areas. Good for verifying author's names and titles of books.

Cumulative Book Index. 1928/32 to date. New York: Wilson, 1933-.

> Author, title, subject listing of books published in the English language throughout the world. Gives full bibliographic information along with standard numbers useful for ordering books. Book titles beginning with numbers or dates are listed before the alphabetical listing. Published eleven times a year and cumulated into an annual volume.

Paperbound Books in Print. 1955 to date. New York: Bowker, 1955-.

> List of paperbound books by author, title, and subject. Each entry gives full bibliographic information such as author, title, date, etc. Entries include the standard numbers used for ordering and the American Bookseller's Association subject classification number.

CONCORDANCES

A *concordance* is an alphabetical list of keywords and phrases found in the works of one author or in a collection of writings. A concordance differs from an index in that it is usually more exhaustive and it includes the context in which the word or phrase appears in the body of the work. A concordance might be used to compare the ways in which an author has used certain words or phrases. For example, the Shakespearean scholar who wishes to analyze the playwright's philosophy of political power could use a concordance to locate those works and the context in which the word ''power'' appears. There are a number of concordances to the *Bible* which help readers find references to words and phrases. It is possible that electronic publishing will make concordances obsolete. Scholars will be able to search electronically for keywords in works that are in electronic format. For example, if the *Bible* were available in electronic format the researcher could search for keywords on the computer which would bring up all occurrences of the words being searched.

Concordances are located in the library catalog under the heading ''concordance'' and as a form subdivision.

For example:

CONCORDANCES
BIBLE—CONCORDANCES

New American Standard Exhaustive Concordance of the Bible. Nashville: Holman, 1981.

>Lists words and phrases found in the *New American Standard Bible*, giving the book, chapter, verse, and a reference number to the words listed in the Hebrew/Aramaic and Greek dictionaries found in the back of the book. The dictionaries show how the word was used in the original language.

Spevack, Marvin. *The Harvard Concordance to Shakespeare.* Cambridge, MA: Belknap, 1973.

>Alphabetical list of the words used in Shakespeare's plays and poems. Indicates the work or works in which the word appears and the act, scene, verse, and line of the play, or, in the case of poetry, the verse and line numbers. Also indicates the frequency with which the word was used.

BIOGRAPHICAL DICTIONARIES

Biographical dictionaries are sources of information about the lives of people. Chapter 7 provides information on biographical dictionaries and other biographical sources.

INDEXES AND ABSTRACTS

Indexes and abstracts are special types of reference sources which are used for finding information; that is, they point to information in other sources. These are discussed in Chapter 8.

SELECTED SUBJECT REFERENCE BOOKS

Agriculture

Agricultural Statistics. 1963-.
The Agrochemicals Handbook. 2nd. ed. 1987.
Farm Chemicals Handbook. 1990.
Handbook of Engineering in Agriculture. 3 vols. 1988.
Handbook of Soils and Climate in Agriculture. 1982.
Yearbook of Agriculture. 1894-.

Anthropology

Dictionary of Human Geography. 2nd ed. 1986.
Encyclopedia of Human Evolution and Prehistory. 1988.
A Hundred Years of Anthropology. 1974.

Archaeology

Atlas of Archaeology. 1982.
Cambridge Encyclopedia of Archaeology. 1980.
Dictionary of Terms and Techniques in Archaeology. 1980.
Keyguide to Information Sources in Archaeology. 1985.
Larousse Encyclopedia of Archaeology. 1983.

Architecture

The Architecture of the United States. 3 vols. 1981.
Encyclopedia of Architecture: Design, Engineering, and Construction. 2 vols. 1989.
Encyclopedia of American Architecture. 1980.
Handbook of Sports and Recreational Building Design. 1981.
A History of Western Architecture. 1986.
Macmillan Encyclopedia of Architects. 4 vols. 1982.
Means Illustrated Construction Dictionary. 1985.

Art and Interior Design

American Art Analog. 3 vols. 1986.
Art Across America. 1990.
The Book of Art. 10 vols. 1985.
Conran Directory of Design. 1985.
Contemporary Arts. 1989.
Gardner's Art Through the Ages. 8th ed. 1986.
Guide to Textiles for Interior Designers. 1983.
Human Factors Design Handbook. 1981.
Interior Design in the 20th Century. 1986.
The Oxford Dictionary of Art. 1988.
Penguin Companion to the Arts in the Twentieth Century. 1985.
Random House Dictionary of Art and Artists. 1990.

Astronomy

Cambridge Atlas of Astronomy. 1988.
Encyclopedia of Astronomy and Astrophysics. 1989.
Illustrated Encyclopedia of the Universe. 1983.
International Encyclopedia of Astronomy. 1987.

Aviation and Aerospace

Aerospace Facts and Figures. 1989.
Aerospace Medicine and Biology. 1986.
Aerospace Yearbook. 1919-.
Illustrated Encyclopedia of Space Technology. 1981.
Jane's All the World Aircraft, 1899–1989. 1988.
World's Aviation Directory. 2 vols. 1989.

Biology

Cambridge Encyclopedia of Life Sciences. 1985.
Dr. Burgess's Atlas of Marine Aquarium Fishes. 1988.
Fishes of the World. 1984.

Botany

A Dictionary of Botany. 1984.
A Dictionary of Plant Pathology. 1989.
Marshall Cavendish's Illustrated Encyclopedia of Plants and Earth Sciences. 10 vols. 1988.

Business and Economics

Accountant's Cost Handbook. 1983.
Accountant's Handbook. 7th ed. 1990.
Advertising Age Yearbook. Vol. 1-, 1981-.
American Advertising: A Reference Guide. 1988.
Beacham's Marketing Reference. 1986.
Business Rankings Annual. 1989-.
The Dartnell Personnel Administration Handbook. 3rd ed. 1985.
Data Sources for Business and Market Analysis. 3rd ed. 1983.
Dictionary of Accounting Terms. 1987.
Dictionary of Business and Economics. Rev. ed. 1986.
Dictionary of Business and Management. 2nd ed. 1983.
Dictionary of Finance. 1988.
Dow Jones-Irwin Business and Investment Almanac. 1982-.
Encyclopedia of Banking and Finance. 8th ed. 1983.
Encyclopedia of Business Information Sources. 7th ed. 1988.
Encyclopedia of Economics. 1982.
Exporters' Encyclopedia. 1989/90.
Handbook of Business Information: A Guide for Librarians, Students and Researchers. 1988.
How to Use the Business Library, with Sources of Business Information. 5th ed. 1984.
Insurance Almanac. 1913-.
International Directory of Company Histories. 5 vols. 1988.
Macmillan Dictionary of Modern Economics. 3rd ed. 1986.
Moody's Manuals of Investments. 1909-.
Standard and Poor's Corporation Descriptions. 1941-.

Chemistry and Physics

Beilstein's Handbook of Organic Chemistry. 4th ed. 1989.
CRC Handbook of Chemistry and Physics. 1988.
Concise Dictionary of Physics. 1985.
Encyclopedia of Chemistry. 4th ed. 1984.
The Encyclopedia of Electrochemistry of the Elements. 15 vols. 1973-.
Encyclopedia of Physics. 2nd ed. 1990.
Hawley's Condensed Chemical Dictionary. 11th ed. 1987.
Lange's Handbook of Chemistry. 13th ed. 1985.

Computer Science

Computer Dictionary. 4th ed. 1985.
Encyclopedia of Artificial Intelligence. 2 vols. 1987.
Encyclopedia of Computer Science and Engineering. 1983.
Encyclopedia of Computer Science and Technology. vol. 1- 1975-.
Encyclopedia of Computers and Data Processing. 1978-.
Handbook of Artificial Intelligence. 3 vols. 1981–1982.
Handbook of Industrial Robotics. 1985.
Software Reviews on File. 1985-.
Standard Handbook of Industrial Automation. 1986.

Criminal Justice

Dictionary of Criminology. 1983.
The Encyclopedia of Child Abuse. 1989.
The Encyclopedia of Crime and Justice. 4 vols. 1983.
The Encyclopedia of Psychoactive Drugs. 25 vols. 1985–1988.
Forensic Science Handbook. 1988.
Handbook on Crime and Delinquency Prevention. 1987.
International Handbook of Contemporary Developments in Criminology. 2 vols.
    1983.
The Police Dictionary and Encyclopedia. 1988.

Education

American Educators Encyclopedia. 1982.
Critical Dictionary of Educational Concepts. 1986.
Dictionary of Developmental and Educational Psychology. 1986.
Education Yearbook. 1972/73-.
Encyclopedia of Careers and Vocational Guidance. 3 vols. 7th ed. 1987.
Encyclopedia of Education. 10 vols. 1971.
Encyclopedia of Educational Research. 4 vols. 1982.
Encyclopedia of Physical Education, Fitness and Sports. 4 vols. 1977–1985.
Encyclopedia of Special Education. 3 vols. 1987.
International Encyclopedia of Education. 10 vols. 1985.
International Encyclopedia of Higher Education. 10 vols. 1977.
International Handbook of Education Systems. 3 vols. 1983/1984.
Mental Measurements Yearbook. 1958-.
Professional Careers Sourcebook. 1990.
TESS: The Educational Software Selector. 1984 Supplement. 1988.
World Education Encyclopedia. 1988.
Yearbook of Special Education. 6th ed. 1980.

Energy

Dictionary of Energy. 1988.
Energy Handbook. 1984.
McGraw-Hill Encyclopedia of Energy. 2nd ed. 1981.
Solar Energy Handbook. 1984.
United States Energy Atlas. 1986.

Engineering and Technology

Civil Engineers Reference Book. 1989.
Electrical Engineering Handbook. 1985.
Electronics Engineers' Handbook. 3rd ed. 1989.
Encyclopedia of Materials Science and Engineering. 8 vols. 1986.
Handbook of Concrete Engineering. 2nd ed. 1985.
Handbook of Industrial Engineering. 2nd ed. 1985.
Handbook of Metal Forming. 1985.
Hazardous Chemicals on File. 3 vols. 1988.
Juran's Quality Control Handbook. 4th ed. 1988.
Marks' Standard Handbook for Mechanical Engineers. 9th ed. 1987.
Metals Handbook. 10th ed. 1990.

SAE Handbook. 4 vols. 1990.
Standard Handbook for Civil Engineers. 3rd ed. 1983.

Environment and Ecology

The Earth Report: The Essential Guide to Global Ecological Issues. 1988.
Encyclopedia of Climatology. 1987.
Encyclopedia of Environmental Science and Engineering. 3 vols. 1983.
Encyclopedia of the Environment. 1988.
Guide to State Environment Programs. 1988.
McGraw-Hill Encyclopedia of Environmental Science. 1980.
Water Encyclopedia. 2nd ed. 1990.
The Weather Almanac. 5th ed. 1987.

Ethnology

Atlas of World Cultures. 1989.
Dictionary of Asian American History. 1986.
Dictionary of Mexican American History. 1981.
Encyclopedia of Black America. 1981.
Handbook of North American Indians. 1978-.
Harvard Encyclopedia of American Ethnic Groups. 1980.
Negro Almanac: A Reference Work of the African-American. 5th ed. 1989.

Food and Nutrition

Bowes and Church's Food Values of Portions Commonly Used. 15th ed. 1989.
CRC Handbook of Food Additives. 2nd ed. 1986.
Craig Claiborne's The New York Times Food Encyclopedia. 1985.
Directory of Food and Nutrition Information Services and Resources. 1984.
Encyclopedia of Food Engineering. 2nd ed. 1986.
Foods and Food Production Encyclopedia. 1982.
Foods and Nutrition Encyclopedia. 2 vols. 1983.
Handbook of Vitamins: Nutritional, Biochemical and Clinical Aspects. 1984.
The Nutrition and Health Encyclopedia. 1989.

Forestry

Encyclopedia of American Forest and Conservation History. 2 vols. 1983.
Forestry Handbook. 2nd ed. 1984.
Oxford Encyclopedia of Trees of the World. 1981.

Genealogy

Ancestry's Red Book: American State, County, and Town Resources. 1989.
A Dictionary of Heraldry. 1987.
A Dictionary of Surnames. 1988.
The Library: A Guide to the LDS Family History Library. 1988.
Passenger and Immigration Lists Index. 1901. Cumulated supplements 1986–
    1990.
Source: A Guidebook of American Genealogy. 1984.

Geography

Cities of the World. 4 vols. 1982-.
Cambridge Encyclopedia of Africa. 1981.
Cambridge Encyclopedia of Latin America and the Caribbean. 1987.
Dictionary of Concepts in Physical Geography. 1988.
Dictionary of Human Geography. 1986.
Encyclopaedic Dictionary of Physical Geography. 1985.
Harper Atlas of World History. 1987.
Manual of Remote Sensing. 2 vols. 1983.
Worldmark Encyclopedia of the Nations. 5 vols. 7th ed. 1988.
Worldmark Encyclopedia of the States. 1986.

Geology

Dictionary of Geology. 6th ed. 1986.
Encyclopedia of Applied Geology. 1984.
Encyclopedia of Earth Sciences series. vol. 1- 1966-.
Encyclopedia of Minerals. 2nd ed. 1990.
International Petroleum Encyclopedia. 1989.
McGraw-Hill Encyclopedia of the Geological Sciences. 2nd ed. 1988.
Oilfields of the World. 3rd ed. 1986.

History: the Americas

Annals of America. 21 vols. 1976–1987.
Cambridge History of Latin America. 5 vols. 1983–1986.
The Canadian Encyclopedia. 4 vols. 1988.
Dictionary of Indian Tribes of the Americas. 4 vols. 1980.
Dictionary of Mexican American History. 1981.
Documents of American History. 10th ed. 1988.
Encyclopedia of American Economic History. 3 vols. 1980.
Encyclopedia of American History. 6th ed. 1982.
Encyclopedia of American Political History. 3 vols. 1984.
Encyclopedia of Southern Culture. 1989.
Great Events from History: American Series. 3 vols. 1975.
International Library of Afro-American Life and History. 10 vols. 1978.
The New Iberian World. 5 vols. 1984.

History: the World

Africa South of the Sahara. 18th ed. 1988.
The Annual Register: A Record of World Events. 1788-.
Collins Australian Encyclopedia. 1984.
Dictionary of the Middle Ages. 13 vols. 1989.
Encyclopedia of Asian History. 4 vols. 1988.
Encyclopedia of Historic Places. 2 vols. 1984.
Encyclopedia of the Holocaust. 4 vols. 1990.
Encyclopedia of the Third World. 3 vols. 1987.
Great Events from History: Ancient and Medieval Series—4000 BC to 1500 AD.
    3 vols. 1972.
Great Events from History: Modern European Series—1469–1969. 3 vols. 1973.

Great Events from History: Worldwide Twentieth Century Series—1900–1979.
   3 vols. 1980.
Great Soviet Encyclopedia. 31 vols. 3rd ed. 1982.
Historical Dictionary of France from the 1815 Restoration to the Second Empire. 2 vols. 1987.
Historical Dictionary of the French Second Empire 1852–1870. 1985.
Historical Dictionary of the Third French Republic 1870–1940. 2 vols. 1986.
The Middle East and North Africa. 1990.
Victorian Britain: An Encyclopedia. 1988.
World Opinion Update. 1977-.

Horticulture

A Colour Atlas of Fruit Pests, Their Recognition, Biology and Control. 1984.
Complete Handbook of Garden Plants. 1984.
Herbs, Spices and Medicinal Plants. 2 vols. 1986.
Horticultural Research International. 1986.
The New York Botanical Garden Illustrated Encyclopedia of Horticulture.
   10 vols. 1984.

Journalism

Broadcast Communications Dictionary. 3rd ed. 1989.
Communication Yearbook. vol. 1- 1977-.
Editorials on File. vol. 1- 1970-.
Encyclopedia of American Journalism. 1983.
Facts on File: A Weekly World News Digest with Cumulative Index. 1940-.
The Gallup Poll: Public Opinion. 1935-.
Historical Dictionary of Censorship in the United States. 1985.
International Encyclopedia of Communications. 4 vols. 1989.
Keesing's Record of World Events. 1931-.
Professional's Guide to Public Relations Sources. 1988.
What They Said: A Yearbook of Spoken Opinion. 1969-.

Language and Literature

Annals of American Literature. 1986.
Barnhart Dictionary of Etymology. 1987.
Black American Writers, Past and Present. 2 vols. 1975.
Bloomsbury Guide to English Literature. 1989.
Cambridge Encyclopedia of Language. 1987.
Cambridge Guide to English Literature. 1986.
Cambridge History of American Literature. 3 vols. 1978.
Cambridge History of Classical Literature. 2 vols. 1982–1985.
Cambridge History of English Literature. 15 vols. 1963–1965.
Columbia Dictionary of Modern European Literature. 2nd ed. 1980.
Concise Oxford Dictionary of English Etymology. 1986.
Contemporary Literary Criticism. 8 vols. 1973-.
Critical Survey of Mystery and Detective Fiction. 4 vols. 1989.
Critical Survey of Poetry: English Language Series. 4 vols. 1989.
Critical Survey of Poetry: Foreign Language Series. 5 vols. 1984.
The Critical Temper: A Survey of Modern Criticism of English and American Literature from the Beginnings to the Twentieth Century. 5 vols. 1969–1989.

Encyclopedia of Mystery and Detection. 1984.
Encyclopedia of World Literature in the 20th Century. 4 vols. in 5. 1981–1984.
Familiar Quotations (Bartlett's). 15th ed. Rev. 1980.
Far Eastern Literature in the 20th Century. 1986.
Handbook of Russian Literature. 1985.
Harbrace College Handbook. 11th ed. 1990.
Harper Handbook to Literature. 1985.
Languages of the World. Rev. ed. 1986.
Library of Literary Criticism: English and American Authors. 4 vols. 1966.
Library of Literary Criticism: Modern Black Writers. 1978.
Library of Literary Criticism: Modern British Literature. 4 vols. 1966–75.
Library of Literary Criticism: Modern Latin American Literature. 1975.
Literary Terms: A Dictionary. 3rd ed. 1989.
Oxford Companion to American Literature. 5th ed. 1983.
Oxford Companion to Canadian Literature. 1983.
Oxford Companion to English Literature. 5th ed. 1985.
Oxford Dictionary of English Etymology. 1966.
Poetry Criticism. 1990.
Poetry Handbook: A Dictionary of Terms. 4th ed. 1981.
Princeton Handbook of Poetic Terms. 1986.
Twentieth Century Science Fiction Writers. 2nd ed. 1986.
Webster's Dictionary of English Usage. 1989.

Law

Constitutional Law Dictionary. 2 vols. 1985.
Guide to American Law: Everyone's Legal Encyclopedia. 1983-1985.
Legal Traditions and Systems: An International Handbook. 1986.
Mass Communication Law: Cases and Comment. 5th ed. 1990.
Research in Law, Deviance and Control. 7 vols. 1978–1987.

Library and Information Science

ALA World Encyclopedia of Library and Information Services. 1986.
Books in Print: Authors and Titles. 8 vols. 1989–1990.
Books in Print: Subject Guide. 4 vols. 1989–1990.
Directory of Library and Information Professionals. 2 vols. 1988.
Encyclopedia of Legal Information Sources. 1988.
Encyclopedia of Library and Information Science. 44 vols. 1968-1987.
Forthcoming Books. 1966-.
Paperbound Books in Print. 2 vols. 1955-.
The Reader's Adviser: A Layman's Guide to Literature. 6 vols. 1986–1988.

Mathematics

CRC Handbook of Mathematical Science. 1962-.
Concise Dictionary of Mathematics. 1990.
Encyclopedic Dictionary of Mathematics. 2 vols. 1987.
Prentice-Hall Encyclopedia of Mathematics. 1982.
VNR Concise Encyclopedia of Mathematics. 2nd ed. 1989.

Medicine

AIDS Information Sourcebook. 1988.
American Medical Assn. Encyclopedia of Medicine. 1989.
Consumer Health Information Source Book. 3rd ed. 1990.
Cyclopedia of Medicine, Surgery, Specialties. 15 vols. 1964-.
Dictionary of Behavior Therapy Techniques. 1985.
Dictionary of Medical Syndromes. 3rd ed. 1990.
Encyclopedia and Dictionary of Medicine, Nursing, and Allied Health. 4th ed.
    1987.
Medical and Health Annual. 1977-.
Melloni's Illustrated Medical Dictionary. 2nd ed. 1985.
Merck Manual of Diagnosis and Therapy. 1899-.
Modells' Drugs in Current Use and New Drugs. 1990.
Physician's Desk Reference Book. 1947-.
Stedman's Medical Dictionary. 25th ed. 1990.
A Year in Nutritional Medicine. 1986-.

Military Science

The Almanac of World Military Power. 4th ed. 1980.
Dictionary of Battles. 1985.
Encyclopedia of Military History. 2nd ed. 1986.
Facts on File Dictionary of Military Science. 1989.

Motion Pictures, Radio, and Television

Blacks in American Films and Television: An Encyclopedia. 1988.
Broadcasting Yearbook. 1990.
The Complete Film Dictionary. 1987.
Contemporary Theatre, Film and Television. 1984.
Dictionary of Audio, Radio and Video. 1981.
Encyclopedia of Television. 3 vols. 1985–1986.
Film Facts. 1980.
Halliwell's Filmgoers Companion. 9th ed. 1989.
International Television and Video Almanac. 1956-.
Magill's Cinema Annual. 1981-.
Magill's Survey of Cinema: English Language Films. 2nd series, 6 vols. 1981.
Magill's Survey of Cinema: Foreign Language Films. 8 vols. 1986.
Magill's Survey of Cinema: Silent Films. 2 vols. 1982.
Radio's Golden Years: The Encyclopedia of Radio Programs, 1930-1960. 1981.
The Video Sourcebook. 10th ed. 1989.

Music

The Definitive Kobbé's Opera Book. 1987.
The Encyclopedia of Folk, Country, and Western Music. 1983.
Gänzl's Book of Musical Theatre. 1989.
Illustrated Encyclopedia of Rock 'n' Roll. 2 vols. 1982.
New Grove Dictionary of American Music. 4 vols. 1986.
New Grove Dictionary of Jazz. 2 vols. 1988.
New Grove Dictionary of Music and Musicians. 20 vols. 1980.
New Grove Dictionary of Musical Instruments. 3 vols. 1984.

New Harvard Dictionary of Music. 1986.
The New Oxford Companion to Music. 2 vols. 1983.
Norton/Grove Concise Encyclopedia of Music. 1988.

Mythology, Folklore, Parapsychology

The Arthurian Encyclopedia. 1986.
Brewer's Dictionary of Phrase and Fable. 1981.
Dictionary of Classical Mythology. 1986.
Dictionary of Mysticism and the Occult. 1985.
The Donning International Encyclopedic Psychic Dictionary. 1986.
Encyclopedia of the Occult. 1986.
Folklore of American Holidays. 1987.
Handbook of American Folklore. 1983.
Man, Myth, and Magic. 12 vols. 1985.

Oceanography

CRC Practical Handbook of Marine Science. 1989.
Facts on File Dictionary of Marine Science. 1988.
McGraw-Hill Encyclopedia of Ocean and Atmospheric Sciences. 1980.
Ocean World Encyclopedia. 1980.

Philosophy

Dictionary of Philosophy. 2nd ed. 1986.
Dictionary of Philosophy and Religion: Eastern and Western Thought. 1980.
Dictionary of the History of Ideas. 5 vols. 1980.
Encyclopedia of Philosophy. 8 vols. in 4. 1972.
Handbook of World Philosophy. 1980.
World Philosophy: Essay-reviews of 225 Major Works. 5 vols. 1982.

Political Science

Almanac of American Politics. 1972-.
Black Elected Officials: A National Roster. 1970-.
Blackwell Encyclopedia of Political Thought. 1987.
Congress A to Z: CQ's Ready Reference Encyclopedia. 1988.
The Constitutional Law Dictionary. 2 vols. 1985.
Countries of the World and Their Leaders Yearbook. 1980-.
County Year Book. 1975-.
Demographic Yearbook. 1949-.
Dorsey Dictionary of American Government and Politics. 1988.
Encyclopedic Dictionary of American Government. 3rd ed. 1986.
Historical Atlas of Political Parties in the United States Congress, 1789–1989. 1989.
Municipal Yearbook. 1934-.
Politics in America. 1982-.
Presidential Elections Since 1789. 1983.
World Encyclopedia of Peace. 4 vols. 1986.
World Encyclopedia of Political Systems and Parties. 2 vols. 1987.

Psychology

American Handbook of Psychiatry. 8 vols. 2nd ed. 1974–1986.
Encyclopedia of Phobias, Fears, and Anxieties. 1989.
Encyclopedia of Psychology (Corsini). 4 vols. 1984.
Handbook of Developmental Psychology. 1982.
Handbook of Mental Health and Aging. 1980.
International Encyclopedia of Psychiatry, Psychology, Psychoanalysis & Neurology. 12 vols. and supplement. 1977-1984.
International Handbook of Psychology. 1987.
Oxford Companion to the Mind. 1987.

Religion

Encyclopedia of Judaism. 1989.
Encyclopedia of Religion. 15 vols. 1987.
Encyclopedia of Religion and Ethics. 13 vols. 1962.
New Catholic Encyclopedia. 18 vols. 1967–1989.
New Dictionary of Theology. 1987.
Westminster Dictionary of Christian Ethics. 1986.

Science—General

Asimov's Chronology of Science and Discovery. 1989.
Britannica Yearbook of Science and the Future. 1968-.
Dictionary of the History of Science. 1981.
Encyclopedia of Physical Science and Technology. 15 vols. 1987.
Hammond Barnhart Dictionary of Science. 1986.
Scientific and Technical Information Sources (Chen). 1987.
Van Nostrand's Scientific Encyclopedia. 7th ed. 1989.

Sociology and Social Work

American Social Attitudes: Data Sourcebook 1947–1978. 1980.
Encyclopedia of Aging. 1987.
Encyclopedia of Social Work. 2 vols. 1986.
Genocide: A Critical Bibliographic Review. 1988.
Handbook on the Aged in the United States. 1984.
International Encyclopedia of Sociology. 1985.
Social Science Encyclopedia. 1985.
Sourcebook on Pornography. 1989.
Sources of Information in the Social Sciences. 1986.

Speech

Dictionary of Speech and Hearing: Anatomy and Physiology. 1975.
Gallaudet Encyclopedia of Deaf People and Deafness. 3 vols. 1987.
Handbook of Speech Pathology and Audiology. 1971.

Statistics

Demographic Yearbook. 1949-.
Encyclopedia of Statistical Sciences. 9 vols. 1982–1988.
The New Book of American Rankings. 1984.

State Demographics. 1984.
Statistical Record of Black America. 1990.
Statistics Sources: A Subject Guide to Data on Industrial, Business and Other Topics. 10th ed. 1986.
The World in Figures. 1987.

Textiles

American Cotton Handbook. 3rd ed. 1965–66.
Encyclopedia of Textiles. 3rd ed. 1980.
Handbook of Textile Fibres. 2 vols. 5th ed. 1988.

Theater

Best Plays and the Yearbook of Drama in America. 1894/99-.
Black Plays. 1987.
Black Playwrights 1821–1977: An Annotated Bibliography of Plays. 1977.
Cambridge Guide to World Theatre. 1988.
Contemporary Dramatists. 2nd ed. 1977.
The Drama Dictionary. 1988.
Encyclopedia of the American Theater 1900–1975. 1980.
Historical Encyclopedia of Costume. 1988.
McGraw-Hill Encyclopedia of World Drama. 5 vols. 5th ed. 1984.
The Reader's Encyclopedia of World Drama. 1975.
Stage Management and Theatrecraft: A Stage Manager's Handbook. 4th ed. 1988.
Theatre World, 1987–1988 Season. 1989.

Urban Affairs

Book of World City Rankings. 1986.
Encyclopedia of American Cities. 1980.
Urban America: A Historical Bibliography. 1983.

Women's Studies

Almanac of American Women in the 20th Century. 1987.
American Political Women. 1980.
Directory of Financial Aids for Women. 1989–1990.
A Feminist Dictionary. 1985.
Handbook of International Data on Women. 1976.
The Nature of Women: An Encyclopedia and Guide to the Literature. 1980.
Women: A Bibliography (Ballou). 1986.
Women of Achievement. 1981.
The Women's Annual, the Year in Review. 1980-.
Women's Studies Encyclopedia. 1989.

Zoology

Dictionary of Ethology. 1989.
Encyclopedia of Mammals. 1984.
Encyclopedia of the Animal World. 11 vols. 1980.
Grzimek's Animal Life Encyclopedia. 13 vols. 1972–1975.
Grzimek's Encyclopedia of Mammals. 5 vols. 1990.

Mammals of North America. 2nd ed. 2 vols. 1981.
Mammals of the World. 4th ed. 2 vols. 1983.
The New Larousse Encyclopedia of Animal Life. Rev. ed. 1980.
Oxford Companion to Animal Behavior. 1987.

REVIEW QUESTIONS
CHAPTER 6

1. How do reference books differ in usage from the books normally found in the stacks?

2. How does one determine the scope of a reference book?

3. Why is it important to determine the date of the reference source being used in research?

4. Name three ways that reference books might be arranged.

5. Why is it important to look for signed articles in a reference book?

6. Why are bibliographies useful additions to articles found in reference sources?

7. Why is it important to have cross references in a reference source?

8. When looking for reference books in the library catalog, what form subdivisions in the subject heading would be useful?

9. What are some of the items you would look for when evaluating a reference source?

10. Name three strategies that can be used to locate materials in the reference collection.

11. List four different types of reference books and describe the main characteristics of each.

TYPES OF REFERENCE SOURCES EXERCISE

Various kinds of information may be obtained from many different reference sources. Name the type of reference source or sources in which you would probably find the following information. A source may be used more than once and may include nonbook sources discussed in earlier chapters.

EXAMPLE: Meaning and pronunciation of words   Dictionary

1. Brief, miscellaneous facts.   _____

2. List of references on a specific topic.   _____

3. Current nonperiodical articles in political science.   _____

4. Broad survey of a topic.   _____

5. Recent map of a foreign country.   _____

6. Brief description of the Ganges River in India.   _____

7. Books covering a particular subject.   _____

8. Pamphlets or leaflets on a subject.   _____

9. Illustrations of famous works of art.   _____

10. Materials published by the American Medical Association.   _____

11. Events or trends of the preceding year.   _____

12. List of manufacturers of air conditioners.   _____

13. Population figures from the 1990 census.   _____

14. Capital of a foreign country and its population.   _____

15. How to conduct an experiment in physics.   _____

16. Short discussion of the function of the U.S. Department of the Interior.   _____

17. Addresses of U.S. government officials.   _____

18. Location of words used in Shakespeare's plays. _____

19. Short discussion of the purpose of a catalytic converter in a car. _____

20. A book that contains definitions of technical terms used in a special field. _____

LOCATING REFERENCE BOOKS EXERCISE

Assignment

Locate two different reference books which contain information on your topic. *DO NOT* use an abstract, index, bibliography, biographical dictionary, concordance, general dictionary or a general encyclopedia. Consult the flow chart on page 146 for ideas on how to locate materials. Give the information listed below for each book:

Since reference books often are not listed under specific subject headings, what broad subject heading would be appropriate to your topic? _____

_____

First reference book

1. Method used to locate book _____

_____

2. Library catalog entry used _____

3. Call number (and out-of-place location, if any) _____

_____

4. Author (or) editor of the book _____

5. Title of the book _____

6. Imprint _____

7. Single or multivolume _____

8. What is the arrangement of the book (alphabetical, topical, chronological)? _____

9. What subjects are covered in the book? _____

_____

10. Give the title of an article on your topic _____

_____

11. Author of article (if any) _____

12. Volume number (if applicable) and inclusive pages of article _____

_____

Second reference book

1. Method used to locate book _____

   _____

2. Library catalog entry used _____

3. Call number (and out-of-place location, if any) _____

   _____

4. Author (or) editor of the book _____

5. Title of the book _____

6. Imprint _____

7. Single or multivolume _____

8. What is the arrangement of the book (alphabetical, topical, chronological)? _____

9. What subjects are covered in the book? _____

   _____

10. Give the title of an article on your topic _____

   _____

11. Author of article (if any) _____

12. Volume number (if applicable) and inclusive pages of article _____

   _____

EVALUATING REFERENCE BOOKS EXERCISE

1. Select a topic from the list of subjects beginning on page 164. Locate information on the topic in each of the types of reference sources and give the requested information about each.

Topic _____

a. *Abridged dictionary*

Title and date:

Unabridged dictionary

Title and date:

Compare the two sources. How was the information similar? How did it differ?

Write a bibliographic citation for each of the sources used.

b. *General encyclopedia*

Title and date:

Subject encyclopedia

Title and date:

Compare the two sources. How was the information similar? How did it differ?

Write a bibliographic citation for each of the sources used.

c. *Subject or general bibliography*

Title and date:

Arrangement (alphabetically, topically, chronologically):

Number of references in bibliography:

Bibliographic citation:

d. *Handbook or manual*

Title and date:

Write a brief summary of the information located.

Bibliographic citation:

2. Using a state or a city as a topic, look up information in each of the types of reference sources listed below and give the requested information about each.

Topic: _____

a. *Almanac*

Title and date of almanac:

Population:

b. *Yearbook*

Title and date:

Population:

Compare the two sources. How was the information similar? How did it differ?

Write a bibliographic citation for each of the sources used.

3. Using a country as a topic, look up information in each of the types of reference sources listed below and give the requested information about each.

Topic: _____

a. *Atlas*

Title and date:

Population:

b. *Gazetteer*

Title and date:

Population:

Compare the two sources. How was the information similar? How did it differ?

Write a bibliographic citation for each of the sources used.

Guide to Biographical Sources

A PREVIEW

In one way or another, virtually all the library's information has a human dimension. This human aspect requires that the library make available a great deal of biographical information about the lives of individuals, both living and dead. This chapter's objective is to survey the library's tools for accessing and using biographical data and to guide the researcher in selecting appropriate biographical information.

KEY TERMS

Biographical Information
Search Strategy for
 Biographical Information
Biographical Dictionaries
Biographical Indexes

Probably the most frequently asked reference question in a library deals with biographical information. People want to know about the lives of other people, both the famous and the not-so-famous. The popular literature is rich with sources which satisfy that need. Biography makes for wonderful reading, but more than that, it is an important source in the research process. Research on most subjects can be approached through the lives of individuals who have shaped developments in the field. For example, to learn about the development of the polio vaccine, one must read about Jonas Salk. Biographical information is so important to the contribution of knowledge that it can be found in almost all reference sources, such as dictionaries, almanacs, and encyclopedias; there are full length books written about people's lives; information about individuals appear in the daily newspapers and in magazines and journals; additionally, there are *biographical dictionaries* which are devoted exclusively to presenting facts about the lives of individuals.

The search strategy for finding biographical information depends on the question being asked and the extent of information needed. Below are some steps (not necessarily in order) to assist in finding biographical information:

1. look in the appropriate biographical dictionary;
2. try a reference book such as a general or subject encyclopedia;
3. consult the library catalog to see if the library owns a book by or about the individual;
4. use a specialized biographical index such as *Biography Index*;
5. check the general and/or appropriate subject indexes and abstracts to locate articles by or about the individual;
6. look for information in a newspaper index;
7. ask a reference librarian for help.

It is not difficult to find biographical information on noteworthy persons. Articles about famous persons appear in a number of sources, including encyclopedias and dictionaries. It is the not-so-famous which cause problems. It is helpful if certain basic information about the person is known such as nationality, profession, and whether the person is living or not. Knowing this information will allow the researcher to select the appropriate source without having to go through all the steps outlined above. The library catalog is helpful as a guide to biographical works. Usually, biographies about individuals are listed by the name of the individual with no form subdivision.

For example:

SALK, JONAS

Biographical dictionaries are listed under the heading:

BIOGRAPHY—DICTIONARIES

Subject biographical dictionaries are entered as a form subdivision:

PSYCHOLOGISTS—BIOGRAPHY

Some biographical dictionaries may be found under the form heading for directories. For example the entry for *American Men and Women of Science* is:

SCIENTISTS, AMERICAN—DIRECTORIES

BIOGRAPHICAL DICTIONARIES

Biographical dictionaries are works which contain information about people. They may be published as single volumes or as multiple volumes. Some are monographs which are published only once while others are serial publications which are issued on a monthly, quarterly, annual, or biennial basis. The *Biographical Directory of the American Congress*, 1774–1989, is an example of a single volume monographic work; the *Dictionary of American Biography* is a monograph which is published in multiple volumes. *Who's Who in America* and *Current Biography* are serial publications which are issued biennially and monthly respectively.

Most biographical dictionaries are arranged alphabetically, and many have additional specialized indexes which list the names of the biographees by occupation or profession, geographical area, or place of employment. For example, if the person is employed by a university, the name would be listed under the name of the institution as well as in the alphabetical arrangement. Some biographical dictionaries such as *Twentieth Century Authors* contain pictures of the biographee. The length of the entries in biographical dictionaries varies; for example, the entries in the *International Who's Who* consist of a few brief facts about the person, while those in the *Dictionary of National Biography* are long, descriptive, signed articles with bibliographies. Retrospective biographical dictionaries such as *Webster's New Biographical Dictionary* include only persons who are no longer living, others such as *Contemporary Authors* contain information on persons of the present day. Some biographical dictionaries list both

JEFFERSON, Thomas, a Delegate from Virginia and a Vice President and 3d President of the United States; born in "Shadwell," Va., in April 1743; attended a preparatory school; graduated from William and Mary College, Williamsburg, Va., in 1762; studied law; was admitted to the bar and commenced practice in 1767; member, colonial House of Burgesses 1769–1775; prominent in pre-Revolutionary movements; Member of the Continental Congress in 1775 and 1776; chairman of the committee that drew up the Declaration of Independence in the summer of 1776 and made the first draft; signer of the Declaration of Independence; resigned soon after and returned to his estate, "Monticello"; Governor of Virginia 1779–1781; member, State house of delegates 1782; again a Member of the Continental Congress 1783–1784; appointed a Minister Plenipotentiary to France in 1784, and then sole Minister to the King of France in 1785, for three years; Secretary of State of the United States in the Cabinet of President George Washington 1789–1793; elected Vice President of the United States and served under President John Adams 1797–1801; elected President of the United States in 1801 by the House of Representatives on the thirty-sixth ballot; reelected in 1805 and served from March 4, 1801, to March 3, 1809; retired to his estate, "Monticello," in Virginia; active in founding the University of Virginia at Charlottesville; died at "Monticello," Albemarle County, Va., July 4, 1826; interment in the grounds of "Monticello."

Bibliography: *DAB*; Malone, Dumas. *Jefferson and the Ordeal of Liberty.* Boston: Little Brown, 1962; Jefferson, Thomas. *The Papers of Thomas Jefferson.* Edited by Julian Boyd, Charles Cullen, and Dickinson Adams. 22 vols. to date. Princeton: Princeton University Press, 1950–

Figure 7.1. Excerpt from *Biographical Directory of the American Congress, 1774–1989.* P. 1257.

living and non-living persons; The *Biographical Directory of the United States Congress, 1774–1989* is an example of such a work. (See Figure 7.1.)

The following list contains representative titles of various types of biographical dictionaries. These are only a few of the many biographical sources found in a typical library.

General Biographical Dictionaries

Current Biography. 1940 to date. New York: H.W. Wilson, 1940-.

Published eleven times a year with an annual cumulative volume. Features people in the news: politicians, sports figures, entertainers, scientists, etc. The articles about the individuals are non-critical but comprehensive. Each article is accompanied by a photograph and a short bibliography. The annual cumulative volume contains the contents of the eleven preceding issues plus a section of obituaries and a multi-year cumulative index.

International Who's Who. 1935 to date. London: Europa, 1935-

This annual publication contains biographical information on people from all over the world. Articles are short and unsigned. Includes an obituary section listing those persons who have died since the preceding volume was published. Includes a list of the world's reigning royal families.

Who's Who: An Annual Biographical Dictionary. 1897 to date. New York: St. Martin's, 1897-.

Alphabetical listing of outstanding British subjects as well as some prominent international figures. Gives pertinent personal and professional data. Contains list of obituaries and a list of the present royal family.

Who's Who in America. 1899 to date. Chicago: Marquis, 1899-.

Published biennially with a supplement issued on the "off year." Lists notable Americans and some international figures. Arrangement is alphabetical with geographic, professional area, retiree, and necrology indexes. Entries are brief and non-critical.

Retrospective Biographical Dictionaries

Dictionary of American Biography. 20 vols. New York: Scribner, 1928-1936. *Supplements 1-8, 1944-1988.*

Published under the auspices of the American Council of Learned Societies, this scholarly and comprehensive work provides biographical information about notable Americans no longer living. Contains long scholarly signed articles with extensive bibliographies. Includes noteworthy persons from the colonial period to 1970. Supplement eight was published in two volumes and includes specialized indexes to all of the preceding volumes.

Dictionary of National Biography. 22 vols. London: Oxford, 1950. *Supplements 2-8, 1912-1990.*

Originally published in 1895 but has been reprinted at irregular intervals along with the eight supplements which have been issued to date. Premier source for historical biographical information on outstanding British subjects. Includes some non-British persons who are important in British history. Long, critical, scholarly signed articles with bibliographies.

Webster's New Biographical Dictionary. Springfield, MA: Merriam, 1988.

This new edition contains biographical information on approximately 30,000 notable personages beginning with the year 3100 B.C. to the twentieth century. World-wide in scope but most useful for American, British, and Canadian subjects. Articles are short and include birth and death dates, notable accomplishments, and pronunciations of names.

Who Was Who. 1907-1980. 7 vols. New York: St. Martin's, 1929-1981.

Companion volumes to *Who's Who*; contains reprints of articles about people listed in *Who's Who* who have died since the last compilation. Usually only the death date has been added but occasionally supplemental new material is included. Cumulative index to all seven volumes was published in 1981.

Who Was Who in America. Historical Volume 1607-1896. Chicago: Marquis, 1963.

Short biographical sketches of both Americans and non-Americans who were influential in the history of the United States. Contains lists of the names of the early governors, the U.S. presidents and vice-presidents, Supreme Court Justices, and cabinet officers.

Who Was Who in America with World Notables. 1897–1989. Wilmette, IL: Marquis, 1942–1989.

Compilation of the biographies of people no longer living which originally appeared in *Who's Who in America*. Death dates and, in some cases, other new information have been added. An index to all volumes of *Who Was Who in America 1607–1989* was published in 1989.

Subject Biographical Dictionaries

American Men and Women of Science. 1971 to date. New York: Bowker, 1971-.

Multivolume biographical dictionary listing people who are prominent in the physical and biological sciences. Articles are short and list personal data, accomplishments, and publications. Unsigned and non-critical.

Biographical Directory of the United States Congress, 1774–1989. Washington: GPO, 1989.

Short biographical sketches of the members of Congress beginning with the Continental Congress and continuing through the 100th Congress. Some entries have bibliographies. Contains listings of the executive officers and cabinet members beginning with the administration of George Washington and going through that of Ronald Reagan.

Contemporary Authors. Detroit: Gale, 1962-.

Comprehensive source for biographical as well as bibliographical information on current writers of both fiction and non-fiction. Also includes authors who are currently writing for newspapers, magazines, motion pictures, theater, and television. Separate annual cumulative index contains references to all previous volumes as well as some other biographical sources published by Gale.

Directory of American Scholars. 8th ed. 4 vols. New York: Bowker, 1982.

Contains profiles of American and Canadian scholars who are actively working in the humanities and the social sciences. Each volume is devoted to a different subject area—Volume I: history; Volume II: English, speech and drama; Volume III: foreign languages, linguistics, and philology; Volume IV: philosophy, religion, and law. Each volume contains a geographic index. In addition, Volume IV has a cumulative index to the scholars listed in all volumes.

Twentieth Century Authors. New York: H.W. Wilson, 1941. *First Supplement*, 1955.

Universal in scope, but limited to authors working in this century. Provides photograph, list of works completed, and a bibliography of sources used to compile the article. Articles are unsigned. Alphabetically arranged by author's name.

World Authors, 1975–1980. New York. H.W. Wilson, 1985.

Continues *Twentieth Century Authors* with a similar arrangement and scope. Set includes three separately issued volumes covering the years 1950–1970, 1970-1975, and 1975–1980.

BIOGRAPHICAL INDEXES

One effective way to access biographical information is through the use of an index which is devoted exclusively to biographical information. *Biographical indexes* are indirect sources of information; that is, they do not contain information about people, rather they provide references to sources which do. They index the biographical literature which appears in books, periodicals, newspapers and reference sources. Biographical indexes may cover a particular subject or they may be general in coverage. For example, *Performing Arts Biography Master Index* provides references to articles about people who are outstanding in the theater arts, while *Biography and Genealogy Master Index* covers persons of all professions, occupations, nationalities, and time periods.

The coverage of some biographical indexes is limited to certain types of literature. For example, *People in History* indexes only history journals and dissertations, while *Biography Index* is very broad in scope and indexes both periodicals and books. Figure 7.2, taken from *Biography Index*, is typical of the format of a biographical index.

The following is a list of useful biographical indexes. One should keep in mind that other indexes also contain references to biographical sources. Many of these are listed in Chapter 8.

Artist Biographies Master Index. Gale Biographical Index Series # 9. Detroit: Gale, 1986.

> Provides references to biographical material on artists working in all aspects of art—fine arts, illustration, ceramics, craft, folk art, and architecture. Sources include biographical dictionaries, encyclopedias, directories, and indexes. Both historical and contemporary artists are included.

Author Biographies Master Index. 2 vols. Gale Biographical Index Series # 3. Detroit: Gale, 1984.

> Useful source for references to biographical information on authors of all nationalities and all periods. Indexes biographical information in biographical dictionaries, encyclopedias, and directories. Includes information found in bibliographies and criticisms.

Biography and Genealogy Master Index. 2nd ed. 8 vols. Gale Biographical Index Series # 1. Detroit: Gale, 1980. *Annual Supplement*, 1981-.

> Name index to biographical dictionaries, subject encyclopedias, literary criticism, and other biographical indexes such as *Biography Index*. Provides names and dates of biography sources. Universal in scope.

Biography Index. 1946 to date. New York: H.W. Wilson, 1947-.

> Quarterly index to biographical information appearing in books and periodicals. Covers wide range of occupations. Arranged alphabetically, entries include birth and death dates (if available), occupation, and contributions to society. A separate index by occupations is located in the back of the book. Quarterly indexes are cumulated into biennial volumes.

Business Biography Master Index. Gale Biographical Index Series # 10. Detroit: Gale, 1987.

Lists prominent persons in the field of business. Coverage is primarily contemporary, but includes a few historical figures. Sources include biographical dictionaries, encyclopedias, and directories. Predominately American in scope with a few international figures.

Historical Biographical Dictionaries Master Index. Gale Biographical Index Series # 7. Detroit: Gale, 1980.

Alphabetically arranged index to information on prominent persons now deceased. Indexed sources include biographical dictionaries, encyclopedias, and other reference sources. Coverage is primarily American, but a few non-Americans are also included.

Journalist Biographical Master Index. Gale Biographical Index Series # 4. Detroit: Gale, 1979.

Indexes biographical information for people working in either the print or the broadcast media. Includes historical as well as contemporary journalists. Sources include biographical dictionaries and directories.

Marquis Who's Who Index to Who's Who Books. 1985 to date. Wilmette, IL: Marquis, 1985-.

Annual index to the various Marquis *Who's Who* biographical dictionaries. Each volume lists names of individuals covered in the series during the prior year. If the person is listed in more than one dictionary, the references are given in chronological order. This index eliminates the need to go through all of the Marquis publications to find a particular reference.

People in History: An Index to U.S. and Canadian Biographies in History Journals and Dissertations. 2 vols. Santa Barbara, CA: ABC-CLIO, 1988.

Arranged alphabetically by name of the biographee, each entry includes the author and title of the article, title of the source, and a brief abstract of the article. Volume 2 contains separate author and subject indexes.

People in World History: An Index to Biographies in History Journals and Dissertations Covering All Countries of the World Except Canada and the U.S. 2 vols. Santa Barbara, CA: ABC-CLIO, 1989.

Each entry gives the author and title of the article, the title of the source, subject, and a brief abstract. Entries are arranged alphabetically by the subject of the article. Separate subject and author indexes in the second volume.

Performing Arts Biography Master Index. 2nd ed. Gale Biographical Index Series # 5. Detroit: Gale, 1981.

References to biographical information on persons working in the theatre, films and television, or the concert stage. Sources indexed include biographical dictionaries, subject encyclopedias, and directories.

Twentieth-Century Authors Biographies Master Index. Gale Biographical Index Series # 8. Detroit: Gale, 1984.

Similar to the *Author Biographies Master Index*, but includes only contemporary authors. International in scope. Indexes biographical dictionaries, encyclopedias, criticisms, etc.

Figure 7.2. Selected reference from *Biography Index*. (Copyright 1990 by the H. W. Wilson Co. Material reproduced by permission of the publisher.)

Biography Index

FEBRUARY 1990

A

Abbey, Edward, 1927-1989, author
Obituary
Natl Parks por 63:42 My/Je '89
Sierra 74:100-1 My/Je '89
Abbot, Willis John, 1863-1934, author and journalist
Biographical dictionary of American journalism; edited by Joseph P. McKerns. Greenwood Press 1989 p1-3 bibl
Abbott, Jim, baseball player
Brofman, R. One for the Angels. il pors *Life* 12:118+ Je '89
Abbott, Lyman, 1835-1922, clergyman
Biographical dictionary of American journalism; edited by Joseph P. McKerns. Greenwood Press 1989 p3-4 bibl
Abbott, Robert S., 1868-1940, journalist
Biographical dictionary of American journalism; edited by Joseph P. McKerns. Greenwood Press 1989 p4-6 bibl
Abdul-Jabbar, Kareem, 1947-, basketball player
Kareem Abdul-Jabbar: what will he do after basketball? il pors *Jet* 76:46-8+ Je 26 '89
Lyons, D. C. Kareem's last hurrah. il pors *Ebony* 44:102+ My '89
Renaud, L. A fitting farewell. por *Macleans* 102:51 My 22 '89
Abel, Elie, Canadian journalist and educator
Biographical dictionary of American journalism; edited by Joseph P. McKerns. Greenwood Press 1989 p6-7 bibl
Abernathy, Ralph D., clergyman and civil rights leader
Abernathy, Ralph D. And the walls came tumbling down; an autobiography. Harper & Row 1989 638p il
A fight among Dr. King's faithful. por *Newsweek* 114:31 O 23 '89
Hampton, H. Dr. King's best friend. por *N Y Times Book Rev* p3 O 29 '89
Tattletale memoir. por *Time* 134:42 O 23 '89
Able, David, handicapped child
Grant, M. When the spirit takes wing. il pors *People Wkly* 31:50-5 My 15 '89
Abraham, F. Murray, actor
Copelin, D. "F" is for Farid: an interview with F. Murray Abraham. pors *Cineaste* 17 no1:[supp] 14-16 '89
Abraham, Gerald, 1904-1988, English musicologist
Obituary
19th Century Music 12:188-9 Fall '88
Abu Nidal, Palestinian revolutionary
Brand, D. Finis for the master terrorist? por *Time* 134:69 D 11 '89
Abu Suud, Khaled, Kuwaiti government official
Master of the money game. por *Fortune* 120:184+ Jl 31 '89
Acevedo Díaz, Eduardo, 1851-1921, Uruguayan author
Ruffinelli, Jorge. Eduardo Acevedo Díaz. (In Latin American writers. Scribner 1989 p299-303) bibl
Achitoff, Louis, d. 1989, aviation expert and government employee
Obituary
N Y Times p44 N 26 '89
Achucarro, Joaquin, 1932-, Spanish pianist
Elder, D. Joaquin Achucarro: the spirit and passion of Spain. il por *Clavier* 28:10-13 My/Je '89
Ackerley, J. R. (Joe Randolph), 1896-1967, English author
Jenkyns, R. Dog days. *New Repub* 201:31-4 D 18 '89
Lurie, A. Love with the perfect dog. por *N Y Times Book Rev* p12 N 12 '89
Parker, Peter. Ackerley; the life of J.R. Ackerley. Farrar, Straus & Giroux 1989 465p il
Ackerley, Joe Randolph *See* Ackerley, J. R. (Joe Randolph), 1896-1967
Ackerman, Arthur F., 1903-1989, pediatrician
Obituary
N Y Times pD-17 Ag 25 '89

Acosta, Joseph de, 1540-1600, Spanish missionary and historian
Arocena, Luis A. Father Joseph de Acosta. (In Latin American writers. Scribner 1989 p47-51) bibl
Adams, Abigail, 1744-1818, wife of John Adams and mother of John Quincy Adams
Gelles, E. B. Gossip: an eighteenth-century case. *J Soc Hist* 22:667-83 Summ '89
Juvenile literature
Lindsay, Rae. The presidents' first ladies. Watts 1989 p29-37 bibl il pors
Adams, Abigail, d. 1813, daughter of John and Abigail Adams
Gelles, E. B. Gossip: an eighteenth-century case. *J Soc Hist* 22:667-83 Summ '89
Adams, Ansel, 1902-1984, photographer
Biographical dictionary of American journalism; edited by Joseph P. McKerns. Greenwood Press 1989 p7-8 bibl
Adams, Brooks, 1848-1927, historian
Auchincloss, Louis. The Vanderbilt era; profiles of a gilded age. Scribner 1989 p163-74 il pors
Adams, Charles Francis, 1835-1915, lawyer, railroad executive and historian
Auchincloss, Louis. The Vanderbilt era; profiles of a gilded age. Scribner 1989 p163-74 il pors
Adams, Franklin P. (Franklin Pierce), 1881-1960, humorist
Biographical dictionary of American journalism; edited by Joseph P. McKerns. Greenwood Press 1989 p8-10 bibl
Adams, Gerry, Irish political leader
Fletcher, B. Interview with Sinn Fein President Gerry Adams. *Mon Rev* 41:16-26 My '89
Adams, Henry, 1838-1918, historian
Auchincloss, Louis. The Vanderbilt era; profiles of a gilded age. Scribner 1989 p163-74 il pors
Brogan, H. Faithful to his class. *N Y Times Book Rev* p22 N 19 '89
Delbanco, A. The seer of Lafayette Square. por *New Repub* 201:32-8 O 16 '89
Samuels, Ernest. Henry Adams. Belknap Press 1989 504p bibl
Adams, John, 1735-1826, president
Gelles, E. B. Gossip: an eighteenth-century case. *J Soc Hist* 22:667-83 Summ '89
Juvenile literature
Dwyer, Frank. John Adams. Chelsea House 1989 109p bibl il
Adams, John F. (John Franklin), 1919-1989, professor of insurance
Obituary
Natl Underwrit (Life Health Financ Serv Ed) 93:5 Mr 20 '89
Adams, Julius J., d. 1989, newspaper editor
Obituary
N Y Times Biogr Serv 20:741 Ag '89
Adams, Louisa Catherine, 1775-1852, president's wife
Juvenile literature
Lindsay, Rae. The presidents' first ladies. Watts 1989 p56-61 bibl il pors
Adams, Ralph E., d. 1989, seaman
Obituary
N Y Times Biogr Serv 20:402 My '89
Adams, Samuel, 1722-1803, statesman
Biographical dictionary of American journalism; edited by Joseph P. McKerns. Greenwood Press 1989 p10-11 bibl
Pencak, W. Samuel Adams and Shays's Rebellion. *N Engl Q* 62:63-74 Mr '89
Adams, Samuel Hopkins, 1871-1958, author and journalist
Adams, Samuel Hopkins. Grandfather stories. Syracuse Univ. Press 1989 312p
Biographical dictionary of American journalism; edited by Joseph P. McKerns. Greenwood Press 1989 p11-13 bibl
Adams-Ender, Clara, general
Cheers, D. M. Nurse Corps chief. il pors *Ebony* 44:64+ Je '89

Figure 7.3. Selected "Key to Periodical Abbreviations" from *Biography Index*. (Copyright 1990 by the H. W. Wilson Co. Material reproduced by permission of the publisher.)

Key to Periodical Abbreviations

19th Century Music — 19th Century Music

A

A + U — A + U
AB Bookman's Wkly — AB Bookman's Weekly
Academe — Academe
Accountancy — Accountancy
Ad Astra — Ad Astra
Advert Age — Advertising Age
AdWeek Mark Week — AdWeek's Marketing Week
Afterimage — Afterimage
Am Antiq — American Antiquity
Am Arch — The American Archivist
Am Art J — The American Art Journal
Am Artist — American Artist
Am Cinematogr — American Cinematographer
Am Craft — American Craft
Am Ethnol — American Ethnologist
Am Film — American Film
Am Health — American Health
Am Herit — American Heritage
Am Hist Illus — American History Illustrated
Am J Agric Econ — American Journal of Agricultural Economics
Am J Archaeol — American Journal of Archaeology
Am J Art Ther — American Journal of Art Therapy
Am J Econ Sociol — The American Journal of Economics and Sociology
Am J Orthopsychiatry — American Journal of Orthopsychiatry
Am J Psychol — The American Journal of Psychology
Am J Public Health — American Journal of Public Health
Am Jew Hist — American Jewish History
Am Libr — American Libraries
Am Music — American Music
Am Music Teach — The American Music Teacher
Am Photogr — American Photographer
Am Psychol — American Psychologist
Am Q — American Quarterly
Am Sch — The American Scholar
Am Visions — American Visions
Am West — American West
America — America
Americana — Americana
Américas — Américas
Annu Rev Biochem — Annual Review of Biochemistry
Annu Rev Plant Physiol Plant Mol Biol — Annual Review of Plant Physiology and Plant Molecular Biology
Antaeus — Antaeus
Antiques — Antiques
Antiques Collect Hobbies — Antiques & Collecting Hobbies
Apollo — Apollo (London, England)
Archaeology — Archaeology
Archit Aujourd'hui — L'Architecture d'Aujourd'hui
Archit Dig — Architectural Digest
Archit Rev — The Architectural Review
Architecture — Architecture
Archivo Esp Arte — Archivo Español de Arte
Art Am — Art in America
Art Antiqu — Art & Antiques
Art Dir — Art Direction
Art News — Art News
Arts Afr Noire — Arts d'Afrique Noire
Arts Rev — Arts Review (London, England)
Asian Aff — Asian Affairs (London, England)
Assoc Manage — Association Management
ASTM Stand News — ASTM Standardization News
Atlantic — The Atlantic
Audio — Audio
Audubon — Audubon
Automot News — Automotive News

B

Barrons — Barron's
Beijing Rev — Beijing Review
Bibliotekar' (U S S R) — Bibliotekar' (Moscow. Soviet Union)

Bicycling — Bicycling
Black Am Lit Forum — Black American Literature Forum
Black Enterp — Black Enterprise
Black Sch — The Black Scholar
Bookbird — Bookbird
Booklist — Booklist
Br J Criminol — The British Journal of Criminology
Br J Photogr — British Journal of Photography
Broadcasting — Broadcasting
Bull Am Meteorol Soc — Bulletin of the American Meteorological Society
Bull Am Sch Orient Res — Bulletin of the American Schools of Oriental Research
Bull At Sci — The Bulletin of the Atomic Scientists
Bull John Rylands Univ Libr Manchester — Bulletin of the John Rylands University Library of Manchester
Bull Med Libr Assoc — Bulletin of the Medical Library Association
Bull Res Humanit — Bulletin of Research in the Humanities
Burlington Mag — The Burlington Magazine
Bus Insur — Business Insurance
Bus Mark — Business Marketing
Bus Week — Business Week

C

Cah Cinema — Cahiers du Cinema
Can Archit — The Canadian Architect
Can Bus — Canadian Business
Can Hist Rev — Canadian Historical Review
Can J Hist — Canadian Journal of History
Car Driv — Car and Driver
Casabella — Casabella
Cathol Bibl Q — The Catholic Biblical Quarterly
Ceram Rev — Ceramic Review
Chain Store Age Exec — Chain Store Age Executive with Shopping Center Age
Change — Change
Changing Times — Changing Times
Channels — Channels (New York, N.Y.: 1986)
Chaucer Rev — The Chaucer Review
Chem Eng News — Chemical & Engineering News
Chem Rev — Chemical Reviews
Chem Week — Chemical Week
Child Today — Children Today
Christ Century — The Christian Century
Christ Crisis — Christianity and Crisis
Christ Today — Christianity Today
Chron Higher Educ — The Chronicle of Higher Education
Cineaste — Cineaste
Civ War Hist — Civil War History
Clarion — The Clarion
Clavier — Clavier
Columbia J Rev — Columbia Journalism Review
Columbia Libr Columns — Columbia Library Columns
Commentary — Commentary
Common Cause Mag — Common Cause Magazine
Commonweal — Commonweal
Commun ACM — Communications of the ACM
Community Jr Coll Libr — Community & Junior College Libraries
Comp Educ — Comparative Education
Comput Decis — Computer Decisions
Congr Q Wkly Rep — Congressional Quarterly Weekly Report
Connoisseur — Connoisseur
Conservationist — The Conservationist
Conservative Dig — Conservative Digest
Contemp Rev — Contemporary Review
Courier — The Courier (Unesco)
Creat Camera — Creative Camera
Ctry J — Country Journal
Curr Biogr — Current Biography
Cycle — Cycle

Figure 7.4. Selected "Checklist of Composite Books Analyzed" from *Biography Index*. (Copyright 1990 by the H. W. Wilson Co. Material reproduced by permission of the publisher.)

Checklist of Composite Books Analyzed

Works of collective biography (starred) are completely analyzed. Other books are analyzed for incidental biographical material only. Works of individual biography and autobiography are not included in this list, but will be found in the main alphabet under the names of the biographees.

† denotes juvenile literature.

A

*Auchincloss, Louis. The Vanderbilt era; profiles of a gilded age. Scribner 1989 214p il pors

B

* Biographical dictionary of American journalism; edited by Joseph P. McKerns. Greenwood Press 1989 820p bibl

C

Cannadine, David. The pleasures of the past. Norton 1989 338p il pors
Cox, Thomas R. The park builders; a history of state parks in the Pacific Northwest. University of Wash. Press 1988 248p bibl il pors maps

D

Dahl, Linda. Stormy weather; the music and lives of a century of jazzwomen. Limelight Eds. 1989 371p bibl il pors
Dictionary of the Russian Revolution; George Jackson, editor-in-chief; Robert Devlin, assistant editor. Greenwood Press 1989 704p bibl maps

G

Gardens and ghettos; the art of Jewish life in Italy; edited by Vivian B. Mann. University of Calif. Press 1989 354p bibl il pors
*Goldberg, Hillel. Between Berlin and Slobodka; Jewish transition figures from Eastern Europe. Ktav 1989 269p bibl
Gutin, Myra G. The president's partner; the first lady in the twentieth century. Greenwood Press 1989 195p bibl il por

H

*Healey, Charles J. Modern spiritual writers; their legacies of prayer. Alba House 1989 203p bibl

J

Jasen, David A. Tin Pan Alley; the composers, the songs, the performers and their times; the golden age of American popular music from 1886 to 1956. Fine, D.I. 1989 312p bibl il pors facsims

K

Kostelanetz, Richard. On innovative music(ian)s. Limelight Eds. 1989 319p

L

* Latin American writers; Carlos A. Solé, editor in chief; Maria Isabel Abreu, associate editor. Scribner 1989 1497p bibl
Lieven, D. C. B. Russia's rulers under the old regime. Yale Univ. Press 1989 407p bibl il pors
*†Lindsay, Rae. The presidents' first ladies. Watts 1989 288p bibl il pors
Lucie-Smith, Edward. Impressionist women. Harmony Bks. 1989 160p bibl il pors

M

*Mayeski, Marie Anne. Women: models of liberation. Sheed & Ward (Kansas City) 1988 240p bibl
*Meyer, Michael R. The Alexander complex; the dreams that drive the great businessmen. Times Bks. 1989 258p
Milton, Joyce. The yellow kids; foreign correspondents in the heyday of yellow journalism. Harper & Row 1989 412p bibl

P

*Perri, Colleen. Entrepreneurial women, Book II. Possibilities Pub. 1989 139p bibl il pors

R

* Reader's digest great biographies, v7; selected and condensed by the editors of Reader's digest. Reader's Digest Assn. 1989 570p il pors maps facsims autogs
* Reader's digest great biographies, v8; selected and condensed by the editors of Reader's digest. Reader's Digest Assn. 1989 605p il pors facsims
Roberts, Chalmers McGeagh. In the shadow of power; the story of the Washington post. Seven Locks Press 1989 539p bibl il
*Russell, Diana E. H. Lives of courage; women for a new South Africa. Basic Bks. 1989 375p bibl pors map

S

Smith, Lucinda. Women who write; from the past and the present to the future. Messner 1989 165p bibl pors

Figure 7.5. Selected "Index to Professions and Occupations" from *Biography Index*. (Copyright 1990 by the H. W. Wilson Co. Material reproduced by permission of the publisher.)

Index to Professions and Occupations

A

Abbesses
Héloïse, 1101-1164
Abbots
Marmion, Columba, 1858-1923
Abolitionists
Anthony, Susan Brownell, 1820-1906
Clay, Cassius Marcellus, 1810-1903
Douglass, Frederick, 1817?-1895
Garrison, William Lloyd, 1805-1879
Grimké, Sarah Moore, 1792-1873
Lovejoy, Elijah Parish, 1802-1837
Lundy, Benjamin, 1789-1839
Swisshelm, Jane Grey Cannon, 1815-1884
Abrasives industry
Farbstein, Burt
Accountants
See also
    Auditors
    Bookkeepers
Albano, James R., d. 1989
Couse, Philip Edward
Crumbley, D. Larry
Gluckman, Simon, d. 1989
Lowden, Gordon, 1927-
O'Toole, Thomas M.
Primoff, Bertram S., d. 1989
Wittenstein, Arthur, 1926-1989
Acoustic engineers
Cremer, Lothar, 1905-
Hamilton, Mark F.
Actors and actresses
See also
    Children as actors
    Chorus girls
    Comedians
    Entertainers
    Pantomimists
    Performance artists
Abraham, F. Murray
Alda, Alan
Allen, Woody
Alter, Tom
Anders, David
Andrews, Julie
Andrews, Nancy, d. 1989
Applegate, Christina
Arness, James
Arnette, Jeannetta
Ashcroft, Dame Peggy, 1907-
Attenborough, Richard
Aykroyd, Dan
Backus, Jim
Baker, Josephine, 1906-1975
Balaban, Bob
Ball, Lucille, 1911-1989
Banks, Jonathan
Barkin, Ellen
Béart, Emmanuelle
Bergen, Candice
Berle, Milton
Bernsen, Corbin
Bertinelli, Valerie, 1960?-
Birdsall, Jesse
Bisset, Jacqueline
Black, Shirley Temple, 1928-
Blake, Amanda, 1929-1989
Blanc, Mel
Bledsoe, Tempestt
Bond, Raleigh Verne, d. 1989
Bonnaire, Sandrine
Bostwick, Barry
Bowie, David
Bracco, Lorraine

Bragg, Bernard, 1928-
Branagh, Kenneth
Brandauer, Klaus Maria
Brooks, Avery
Brooks, Louise, 1906-1985
Brooks, Mel
Brosnan, Pierce
Brown, Tally, d. 1989
Brynner, Yul, d. 1985
Burke, Delta
Burnett, Carol
Burns, George, 1896-
Burnum Burnum
Burton, Richard, 1925-1984
Busch, Charles
Busey, Gary
Campbell, Mrs. Patrick, 1865-1940
Cannon, Dyan
Cantor, Eddie, 1892-1964
Carmine, Michael, d. 1989
Carney, Art
Carradine, Calista
Cassavetes, John
Chamberlain, Richard
Chaplin, Charlie, 1889-1977
Chapman, Graham
Cher, 1946-
Cherry, Eagle-Eye
Christopher, William
Cohan, George M., 1878-1942
Coleman, Gary
Connery, Sean
Cosby, Bill, 1937-
Coward, Noel
Cox, Courteney
Crosby, Bing, 1904-1977
Crystal, Billy
Culp, Robert
Curtis, Jamie Lee
Damian, Michael
Danson, Ted
Danza, Tony
Davis, Bette, 1908-1989
Davis, Geena
Davis, Sammy, Jr.
Day-Lewis, Daniel
De Santis, Joe, 1909-1989
Dean, James, 1931-1955
DeHaven, Gloria, 1925-
DeLuise, Peter
Dennehy, Brian
Desiderio, Robert
Dey, Susan
Dietrich, Marlene, 1904-
Dolenz, Ami
Doody, Alison
Dors, Diana
Douglas, Michael
Douglas, Suzzanne
Draper, Polly
Dryer, Fred, 1946-
Duffy, Julia
Dunaway, Faye
Eastwood, Clint
Eikenberry, Jill
Estevez, Emilio, 1963-
Evans, Peter, 1950-1989
Farmer, Gary
Fawcett, Farrah
Field, Kate, 1838-1896
Fonda, Bridget
Fonda, Jane, 1937-
Foster, Kimberly
Fox, Michael J.
Franklin, Hugh, d. 1986
French, Victor, d. 1989
Furst, Stephen

SELECTED BIOGRAPHICAL REFERENCE SOURCES

American Women 1935–1940: A Composite Biographical Dictionary. 2 vols. 1981.

Baker's Biographical Dictionary of Musicians. 7th ed. 1984.

Contemporary Designers. 1984.

The Continuum Dictionary of Women's Biography. 1989.

Dictionary of South African Biography. 4 vols. 1968.

Dictionary of Women Artists. 1985.

Directory of Medical Specialists. 23rd ed. 3 vols. 1987–1988. *Supplement.* 1988–1989.

Directory of the American Psychological Association. 1989.

The Europa Biographical Dictionary of British Women. 1983.

Great Lives from History. American Series. 5 vols. 1987.

International Encyclopedia of Women Composers. 2 vols. 1987.

International Who's Who in Music and Musicians' Directory. 11th ed. 1988.

International Who's Who of the Arab World. 1984.

Martindale-Hubbell Law Directory. 8 vols. 1931-.

Notable American Women 1607–1950. 3 vols. 1971.

Notable American Women: The Modern Period. 1980.

Notable Black American Women. 1990.

Reference Encyclopedia of the American Indian. 4th ed. 1986.

Who's Who Among Black Americans. 5th ed. 1988.

Who's Who in Entertainment. 1988.

Who's Who in Insurance. 1988.

Who's Who in Technology. 7 vols. 1986.

Women Anthropologists. 1988.

World Artists, 1950–1980. 1984.

REVIEW QUESTIONS
CHAPTER 7

1. Why are biographies important sources for research?

2. Name four possible steps (other than consulting the reference librarian) which you could take to find information in library sources about the lives of people.

3. What is the difference between a biographical dictionary and a biographical index?

4. What information about the person is useful in helping to select the appropriate biographical source?

5. What subject heading would be used to find a general biographical dictionary in the library catalog? How does this subject heading differ from one that might be used to find a biographical dictionary listing people in specific fields?

6. In addition to the alphabetical arrangement, biographical indexes and dictionaries sometimes have specialized indexes to aid in finding material about a person. Name three different kinds of these specialized indexes.

7. How does a retrospective biographical dictionary such as the *Dictionary of American History* differ from a current one such as *Who's Who in America*?

8. Select a biographical dictionary from among those listed in the Chapter that would be appropriate for finding information about each of the following: (Give the title.)

    a.   A popular American musician

    b.   A currently prominent political figure

    c.   A long critical article about Winston Churchill

    d.   Information about an individual who has contributed to the women's rights movement.

9. What types of sources are indexed in *Biography Index*?

(LAST)   (FIRST)

NAME _____

HOUR & DAY   _____

BIOGRAPHICAL DICTIONARY EXERCISE

Biographical dictionaries give information on the lives of individuals who are outstanding or well-known for their accomplishments. Using a biographical dictionary, look up information on the life of an individual in whom you are interested or one assigned by your instructor.

Name of person _____

When you have found your reference, note the following information:

1. Title of biographical dictionary used:

2. Call number of the biographical dictionary uscd:

3. Identify briefly the individual's:

    a.   Place of birth:

    b.   Date of birth, and death if not living:

    c.   Occupation or profession:

4. Write a bibliographic entry using the information you have found. (See textbook, Chapter 11, page 318, example.)

5. Write a short paragraph giving a few facts about the person's accomplishments.

Finding and Using
Indexes and Abstracts

8

A PREVIEW

Just as one may think of the library catalog as an index to its holdings, a large variety of indexes serve the same purpose for the contents of individual works. Effective and critical use of the library often depends on a mastery of these access tools. It is the goal of this chapter to de-mystify this subject by describing and analyzing the major indexes and their use.

An *index* is a guide to information; that is, it lists sources of information and tells where these may be found. The library catalog is an index because it lists the works contained in the library and tells where they may be found. However, it is not the only key to the collection. Other indexes analyze the contents of the individual works in the collection. They list topics and names in a book or series of books and give the pages on which the topics are treated. This kind of index is usually found at the end of the book or in the last volume of a multi-volume work. Another kind of index serves as a finding aid to the articles in periodicals, newspapers, and anthologies. This kind of index is usually separate from the works it indexes and lists the topics in broader terms than do indexes to the contents of individual books. A knowledge of all three of these finding aids is essential for effective use of the materials in the library. The library catalog is discussed in Chapter 5. The indexes found in individual works hardly need explanation since they are usually alphabetically arranged and are commonly placed at the end of the work. It is important, however, that these not be overlooked as a key to using any reference source. A basic knowledge of the indexes to the contents of periodicals, newspapers, and anthologies is necessary in order to take advantage of the wealth of information in each of these sources. These will be discussed in this chapter. The following types of finding aids will be covered with representative titles in each group.

1. Guides to periodical literature
   a. Periodical indexes
   b. Abstracts
   c. Citation indexes
2. Newspaper indexes
3. Indexes to book reviews
4. Indexes to literature appearing in anthologies or collections
5. Indexes to literary criticism

GUIDES TO PERIODICAL LITERATURE

Periodicals are literary works which are published at regular intervals. Periodicals, sometimes called ''serials'' by librarians, include magazines and journals. *Magazines* are periodicals which are designed to appeal to a broad segment of the population. They are characterized by relatively short articles written in non-technical language. The style of writing is easy to understand and concise. *Journals*, on the other hand, are intended for a much more limited readership. The articles are written by scholars or experts in the subject area. The vocabulary is often technical, and the style of writing is more complex than that found in popular magazines. Journal articles frequently represent the author's personal research. Bibliographies are standard for journal articles.

Periodical literature is valuable as a research medium for several reasons. Information appearing in periodicals constitutes the bulk of published information. There are thousands of periodicals and newspapers published regularly, each containing an abundance of articles on different topics. The material found in magazines, journals, and newspapers is the most recent information one can find. By locating an article written shortly after an event occurred, whether it be in the 19th century, the 1930s, or whatever, the library user will find contemporary opinion which reflects what people thought of the event at the time it occurred. Periodical literature reflects the constantly evolving nature of information. No matter when an event occurred, it is constantly being reexamined and new revelations brought forward. It is also possible to find comparative information for different periods. Sometimes periodical literature is the only information available—the topic may be too faddish ever to appear in a book. The findings of researchers and scholars are published in professional journals which supplement other types of literature in a particular field, such as medicine or education. There are times when a book or selections from books appear in magazines and journals before they are published in their final form.

The keys to locating periodical information are the indexes and abstracts which analyze the contents of periodicals. Although indexes to periodical literature have existed since the middle of the nineteenth century, the number of indexes to periodical literature has increased considerably over the past few years. The introduction of computers into information storage and retrieval has had an enormous impact on the quantity and quality of indexing services. Although many indexes and abstracts continue to be published in printed form, indexes in electronic format have become the norm. The information which is included in the index is put on magnetic tape or on CD-ROM. That information, called a *database*, can then be searched more quickly and more efficiently than the paper indexes. The electronic databases hold more information, they are up-dated frequently, and can be searched in ways not possible with a static paper index. Most online and CD-ROM databases are searchable by keyword, author, title, and subject. There are usually charges associated with online databases, but in most libraries CD-ROM databases may be used free-of-charge. Some libraries now include indexes to periodical literature in their online catalogs. Online databases and CD-ROM databases can be searched with keyword searching. (This method is discussed in more detail in Chapter 10.)

PERIODICAL INDEXES

Some indexes are general in coverage; that is, they include many subjects and index, for the most part, popular magazines. *The Readers' Guide to Periodical Literature* is an example of an index of this type. Other indexes deal principally with one subject area and index journals with scholarly articles. For example, *Applied Science and Technology Index* includes scholarly articles in the scientific and technological fields. Generally, each index includes different magazines and journals although there are some which overlap.

Most of the paper versions of periodical indexes are published monthly with an annual cumulation in which all of the articles included in the magazines and journals throughout the year are arranged in one alphabet. Indexes usually contain a section in the front of each issue and volume which lists alphabetically all the periodical titles indexed and gives the abbreviations used in the entries. There is also a "Key to the Abbreviations" used in the entries. Some indexes include a listing of the indexed periodicals with subscription information, including the publisher, address, and price.

Indexes on CD-ROM are usually updated monthly, although this may vary with the particular service. Many online databases are updated more frequently. The manuals supplied by the vendors indicate how often the databases are updated. The manuals which accompany CD-ROM indexes have instructions on how to use the database as well as giving some of the same information as found in the preliminary pages of the paper versions of the indexes. Many of the indexes listed in this chapter are on CD-ROM. Indexes listed as being on WILSONDISC are CD-ROM versions of the printed indexes.

Finding periodical information is a two-step operation. The first step is to locate the appropriate index(es). To locate articles in popular magazines, the user may select one of the general indexes listed in this chapter. The subject indexes and abstracts will lead to more scholarly and technical information. Many of these indexes are listed in this chapter. Subject indexes are also listed in guides to literature such as *Guide to Reference Books*. Abstracts and indexes may be located in the library catalog as a form subdivision following the subject.

For example:

COMPUTERS—INDEXES

COMPUTERS—ABSTRACTS

The reference librarian can also advise on the proper index to use. It is a good idea in doing a thorough search of the literature to use both general and subject indexes and abstracts. Once a user has found information it is then necessary to move to the second step of the process, which is to locate the periodical article in the library. To locate and read the articles cited in the entries of these indexes, the user must find the call numbers of the periodicals either in the library catalog or in the serials holding record. Figure 8.1 illustrates a periodical as it is listed in the online catalog.

Use of the various indexes and abstracts is relatively simple. Most contain the same basic information. If the researcher understands the arrangement of one, it is possible to use almost any of the other indexes, including those on

```
LOLA SEARCH REQUEST: T=DISCOVER
BIBLIOGRAPHIC RECORD -- NO. 2 OF 385 ENTRIES FOUND

Discover. v. 1- Oct. 1980- <Chicago, Time>
  v. ill. 28 cm.
  Monthly.
  "The newsmagazine of science."
 SUBJECT HEADINGS (Library of Congress; use s= ):
    Science--Periodicals.

LOCATION: MIDDLETON
CALL NUMBER: Q1 .D57
Current year and 2 previous years at Serials Desk
LIBRARY HAS:
  v.1 (1980)-
```

CD-ROM. The following explanation of *Readers' Guide to Periodical Literature* is provided to illustrate a typical index to periodicals. Knowing how to use *Readers' Guide* enables one to use other indexes more efficiently. Its arrangement and use are explained in detail below.

Frequency. Readers' Guide is published twice a month except February, July, and August when it appears monthly. The materials in the first issue of each month are cumulated (included in one alphabet) in the second issue of each month. The monthly issues cumulate every three months. The paperbound issues are replaced by a cumulative bound volume at the end of the year.

Arrangement. Each issue of *Readers' Guide* is divided into several important sections. These are: (1) a list of the periodicals indexed, (2) a list of other abbreviations used in the index, (3) the main body of the index consisting of subject and author entries, and (4) a listing of book reviews by authors with citations. (See Figures 8.2–8.5.) Earlier issues of *Readers' Guide* included book reviews in the main body of the entries under the author's name. Articles are listed alphabetically by subject and author. Title entries for dramas, operas, and ballets are treated as cross references.

In an author entry, the author's full name appears first in heavy print on a line by itself. The author entries contain the same information as the subject entries except that the author's name is not repeated after the title.

Figure 8.2. Selected "Periodicals Indexed" from *Reader's Guide to Periodical Literature*. (Copyright 1990 by the H. W. Wilson Company. Material reproduced by permission of the publisher.)

PERIODICALS INDEXED

All data as of latest issue received

*50 Plus. $15. m (ISSN 0163-2027) 50 Plus, 99 Garden St., Marion, OH 43302
Name changed to New Choices for the Best Years with December 1988

A

Ad Astra. $30. m (ISSN 1041-102X) National Space Society, 922 Pennsylvania Ave., S.E., Washington, DC 20003-2140
Continuation of: Space World
Aging. $5. q (ISSN 0002-0966) Superintendent of Documents, U.S. Government Printing Office, Washington, DC 20402
America. $28. w (except first Saturday of the year, and alternate Saturdays in Jl and Ag) (ISSN 0002-7049) America Press Inc., 106 W. 56th St., New York, NY 10019
American Artist. $24. m (ISSN 0002-7375) American Artist, 1 Color Court, Marion, OH 43305
American Craft. $40. bi-m (ISSN 0194-8008) Membership Dept., American Craft Council, P.O. Box 1308-CL, Fort Lee, NJ 07024
American Film. $20. m (except bi-m Ja/F, Jl/Ag) (ISSN 0361-4751) Membership Services, American Film, P.O. Box 2046, Marion, OH 43305
American Health. $14.95. m (except F, Ag) (ISSN 0730-7004) American Health: Fitness of Body and Mind, P.O. Box 3015, Harlan, IA 51537
*American Heritage. $24. 8 times a yr (ISSN 0002-8738) American Heritage Subscription Dept., Forbes Building, 60 Fifth Ave., New York, NY 10011
American History Illustrated. $20. bi-m (ISSN 0002-8770) American History Illustrated, Box 8200, Harrisburg, PA 17105
The American Scholar. $19. q (ISSN 0003-0937) The American Scholar, Editorial and Circulation Offices, 1811 Q St., N.W., Washington, DC 20009
The American Spectator. $30. m (ISSN 0148-8414) American Spectator, P.O. Box 10448, Arlington, VA 22210
American Visions. $18. bi-m (ISSN 0884-9390) American Visions, P.O. Box 53129, Boulder, CO 80322-3129
Americana. $14.97. bi-m (ISSN 0090-9114) Americana Subscription Office, 205 W. Center St., Marion, OH 43302
Américas. $42. bi-m (ISSN 0379-0940) Américas, Journals Div., CUA Press, 303 Administration Bldg., Catholic University of America, Washington, DC 20064
Antiques. $38. m (ISSN 0161-9284) The Magazine Antiques, Old Mill Rd., P.O. Box 1975, Marion, OH 43306
Antiques & Collecting Hobbies. $22. m (ISSN 0884-6294) Antiques & Collecting Hobbies, Circulation Dept., 1006 S. Michigan Ave., Chicago, IL 60605
Architectural Digest. $39.95. m (ISSN 0003-8520) Architectural Digest, P.O. Box 10040, Des Moines, IA 50350
Architectural Record. $42.50. m (semi-m Ap, S) (ISSN 0003-858X) Architectural Record, P.O. Box 2025, Mahopac, NY 10541
Art in America. $39.95. m (ISSN 0004-3214) Art in America, 542 Pacific Ave., Marion, OH 43306
Art News. $32.95. m (q Je-Ag) (ISSN 0004-3273) Art News, Subscription Service, P.O. Box 969, Farmingdale, NY 11737
Astronomy. $24. m (ISSN 0091-6358) Astronomy, 21027 Crossroads Circle, P.O. Box 1612, Waukesha, WI 53187
*The Atlantic. $14.95. m (ISSN 0276-9077) Atlantic Subscription Processing Center, Box 52661, Boulder, CO 80322
Audubon. $20. bi-m (ISSN 0097-7136) National Audubon Society, Membership Data Center, P.O. Box 2666, Boulder, CO 80322
Aviation Week & Space Technology. $80. w (ISSN 0005-2175) Aviation Week & Space Technology, P.O. Box 503, Hightstown, NJ 08520-9899

B

*Better Homes and Gardens. $14.97. m (ISSN 0006-0151) Better Homes and Gardens, P.O. Box 4536, Des Moines, IA 50336
Bicycling. $15.97. 10 times a yr (ISSN 0006-2073) Rodale Press, Inc., 33 E. Minor St., Emmaus, PA 18049
BioScience. $96.50. m (bi-m Jl, Ag) (ISSN 0006-3568) BioScience Circulation, AIBS, 730 11th St. N.W., Washington, DC 20001-4584
Black Enterprise. $15. m (ISSN 0006-4165) Black Enterprise, Circulation Service Center, P.O. Box 3009, Harlan, IA 51537-3009
The Bulletin of the Atomic Scientists. $30. m (except F, Ag) (ISSN 0096-3402) Bulletin of the Atomic Scientists, Circulation Dept., 6042 S. Kimbark Ave., Chicago, IL 60637
Business Week. $39.95. w (except 1 issue in Ja) (ISSN 0007-7135) Business Week, P.O. Box 430, Hightstown, NJ 08520
Byte. $29.95. m (except 2 issues in O) (ISSN 0360-5280) Byte Subscriber Service, P.O. Box 551, Hightstown, NJ 08520

C

Car and Driver. $16.98. m (ISSN 0008-6002) Car and Driver, P.O. Box 2770, Boulder, CO 80302
The Center Magazine. $25. bi-m (ISSN 0008-9125) Center Magazine, Box 4068, Santa Barbara, CA 93103
Continued by: New Perspectives Quarterly
Change. $40. bi-m (ISSN 0009-1383) Heldref Publications, 4000 Albemarle St., N.W., Washington, DC 20016
*Changing Times. $18. m (ISSN 0009-143X) Changing Times, The Kiplinger Magazine, Editors Park, MD 20782
Channels (New York, N.Y.: 1986). $65. m (bi-m Jl/Ag) (ISSN 0895-643X) Channels, Subscription Service Dept., P.O. Box 6438, Duluth, MN 55806
Children Today. $7.50. bi-m (ISSN 0361-4336) Superintendent of Documents, U.S. Government Printing Office, Washington, DC 20402
The Christian Century. $28. w (occasional bi-w issues) (ISSN 0009-5281) Christian Century, Subscription Service Dept., 5615 W. Cermak Rd., Cicero, IL 60650
Christianity Today. $24.95. semi-m (m Ja, My, Je, Jl, Ag, D) (ISSN 0009-5753) Christianity Today Subscription Services, 465 Gundersen Dr., Carol Stream, IL 60188
Commentary. $39. m (ISSN 0010-2601) American Jewish Committee, 165 E. 56th St., New York, NY 10022
Common Cause Magazine. $20. bi-m (ISSN 0271-9592) Common Cause Membership Dept., 2030 M St., N.W., Washington, DC 20036
Commonweal. $32. bi-w (m Christmas-New Year's and Jl, Ag) (ISSN 0010-3330) Commonweal Foundation, 15 Dutch St., New York, NY 10038
Compute!. $19.94. m (ISSN 0194-357X) Compute! Publications, Inc., P.O. Box 3245, Harlan, IA 51537
Congressional Digest. $28. m (bi-m Je-Jl, Ag-S) (ISSN 0010-5899) Congressional Digest Corp., 3231 P St., N.W., Washington, DC 20007
The Conservationist. $5. bi-m (ISSN 0010-650X) Conservationist Circulation Office, P.O. Box 1500, Latham, NY 12110
Conservative Digest. $18. bi-m (ISSN 0146-0978) Conservative Digest, P.O. Box 84905, Phoenix, AZ 85071
Ceased publication with September/October 1989
*Consumer Reports. $20. m (ISSN 0010-7174) Subscription Director, Consumer Reports, P.O. Box 53029, Boulder, CO 80322
*Consumers' Research Magazine. $18. m (ISSN 0095-2222) Circulation Dept., Consumers' Research Magazine, P.O. Box 642, Holmes, PA 19043
Country Journal. $16.95. bi-m (ISSN 0094-0526) Country Journal, P.O. Box 392, Mt. Morris, IL 61054

Figure 8.3.
''Abbreviations''used in
entries in *Reader's Guide
to Periodical Literature*.
(Copyright 1990 by the H.
W. Wilson Company.
Material reproduced by
permission of the
publisher.)

ABBREVIATIONS

+	continued on later pages of same issue	Ltd	Limited
		m	monthly
Ag	August	Mr	March
ann	annual	My	May
Ap	April		
Assn	Association	N	November
Aut	Autumn	no	number
Ave	Avenue		
		O	October
bi-m	bimonthly		
bi-w	biweekly	p	page
bibl	bibliography	por	portrait
bibl f	bibliographical footnotes	pt	part
bldg	building		
		q	quarterly
Co	Company		
cont	continued	rev	revised
Corp	Corporation		
		S	September
D	December	semi-m	semimonthly
Dept	Department	Spr	Spring
		Sr	Senior
ed	edited, edition, editor	St	Street
		Summ	Summer
F	February	supp	supplement
f	footnotes		
		tr	translated, translation, translator
il	illustration,-s		
Inc	Incorporated	v	volume
introd	introduction, introductory		
		w	weekly
Ja	January	Wint	Winter
Je	June		
Jl	July	yr	year
Jr	Junior		
jt auth	joint author		

Readers' Guide does not list articles by title although titles of plays, operas, and ballets are used as cross references. In older issues, cross references were included for titles of short stories. Plays are listed under the subject heading ''Dramas—Criticisms, plots, etc.'' as well as by author and title. Reviews of movies are listed under the subject heading ''Motion picture reviews.'' In the older indexes, movie reviews were listed under the subject heading ''Moving picture plays—Criticisms, plots, etc.'' Poems are listed by author only, but in older issues of the indexes they are listed by title.

The indexes contain many *see* and *see also* references which direct the reader to other names and subjects. A *see* reference refers the reader from a name, subject, or title that is not used to one that is used. A *see also* reference refers the reader to additional subject headings.

An example of a subject entry from *Readers' Guide* is shown in Figure 8.6. Figure 8.7 is an example of an entry from *InfoTrac*. It shows a typical entry from a periodical index on CD-ROM.

Figure 8.4.   Selected references from *Reader's Guide to Periodical Literature*. (Copyright 1990 by the H. W. Wilson Company. Material reproduced by permission of the publisher.)

Readers' Guide to Periodical Literature

FEBRUARY 1990

2 LIVE CREW (MUSICAL GROUP)
A rap album in the dock [obscenity case against Alexander, Ala. record store] N. Zeman. il *Newsweek* 114:72 O 16 '89
3-D ART
Making dimensional illustration. E. Rixford. il *American Artist* 53:70-2+ N '89
3-D CAMERAS
Testing
A born again Nimslo? [Nishika N8000] P. Kolonia. il *Popular Photography* 96:71-2 N '89
3-D OPTICAL STORAGE DEVICES
Multiplying computer memories into 3-D [work of Peter M. Rentzepis and Dimitri A. Parthenopoulos] I. Amato. *Science News* 136:151 S 2 '89
Three-dimensional optical storage memory. D. A. Parthenopoulos and P. M. Rentzepis. bibl f il *Science* 245:843-5 Ag 25 '89
8MM VIDEO CAMERAS See Video cameras
20 MOTT STREET RESTAURANT (NEW YORK, N.Y.) See New York (N.Y.)—Restaurants, nightclubs, bars, etc.
35MM CAMERAS See Cameras
35MM SINGLE-LENS REFLEX CAMERAS See Cameras, Single-lens reflex
44 (NEW YORK, N.Y.: RESTAURANT) See New York (N.Y.)—Restaurants, nightclubs, bars, etc.
150 WOOSTER STREET (NEW YORK, N.Y.: RESTAURANT) See New York (N.Y.)—Restaurants, nightclubs, bars, etc.
401(K) PLAN
Making hay with a 401(k). il *Money* 18 Money Guide:62 Fall '89
Managing your company plan. il *Fortune* 120 no10 Special Issue:48 Fall '89
Rules for borrowing from retirement plans. G. W. Padwe. il *Nation's Business* 77:92 N '89
737 AIRPLANES See Airplanes, Jet
747 AIRPLANES See Airplanes, Jet
777 AIRPLANES See Airplanes, Jet
800 TELEPHONE NUMBERS See Toll-free telephone service
900 TELEPHONE NUMBERS
Just call up and watch. M. Burgi. il *Channels (New York, N.Y.: 1986)* 9:92 N '89

A

A-BOMBS See Atomic bombs
A. L. WILLIAMS CORP.
The battalion that will press Primerica's sales attack. J. Friedman. il *Business Week* p91 D 4 '89
Ex-football coach Art Williams runs a winning insurance firm, but some people are crying foul. G. Stone. il pors *People Weekly* 32:161-2+ N 20 '89
A&W BRANDS INC.
Root beer gloat. E. Giltenan. il por *Forbes* 144:156+ D 11 '89
AAAS See American Association for the Advancement of Science
AAFLI See Asian American Free Labor Institute
AARNES, WILLIAM
Dishes [poem] *The American Scholar* 58:509-10 Aut '89
AARP See American Association of Retired Persons
ABA See American Booksellers Association
ABALONES
Mollusk teaches ceramics to scientists [rugged shell of the red abalone; research by Mehmet Sarikaya] I. Amato. *Science News* 136:383 D 9 '89
ABAS, BRYAN
Rocky Flats: a big mistake from day one. bibl f il *The Bulletin of the Atomic Scientists* 45:18-24 D '89

ABBADO, CLAUDIO
about
Abbado takes Berlin. N. Lebrecht. il por *Opera News* 54:16-17 D 23 '89
Abbado's Ravel: the piano concertos. R. Freed. il por *Stereo Review* 54:108 O '89
ABBEVILLE PRESS INC.
Abbeville announces new video series on wine. il *Publishers Weekly* 236:27-8 D 1 '89
ABBEY, EDWARD, 1927-1989
Hayduke lives! [fiction] il *The Mother Earth News* 120:57-9 N/D '89
about
Obituary
The Mother Earth News il por 120:56-7 N/D '89. D. Petersen
ABBOTT LABORATORIES
The slippery ladder at Abbott Labs [ouster of J. W. Schuler] J. F. Siler. il por *Business Week* p136-7 O 30 '89
ABBOUD, JOSEPH, 1950-
about
Joseph Abboud, down to earth. E. Stern. il pors *Gentlemen's Quarterly* 59:320-5+ O '89
ABBY PERKINS (FICTIONAL CHARACTER)
From mouseburger to sexpot on L.A. law. B. Davidson. il pors *TV Guide* 37:8-9+ N 11-17 '89
ABDOMINAL EXERCISES See Exercise
ABDUL, PAULA
about
All the right moves. D. Wild. il pors *Rolling Stone* p96-8+ N 30 '89
Paula Abdul. por *People Weekly* 32:76-7 D 25 '89-Ja 1 '90
Paula Abdul's double life. N. Malkin. por *Mademoiselle* 95:94+ N '89
ABDULLAH IBRAHIM
about
Abdullah Ibrahim's Ekaya. F. Bouchard. il por *Down Beat* 56:58-9 D '89
ABDUSSALAAM, MEENAH
about
New York mother throws two children out of window. il por *Jet* 77:18 O 23 '89
ABELL CLUSTER (GALAXIES) See Galaxies—Clusters
ABERCROMBIE, JOHN
about
Blindfold test. B. Milkowski. il por *Down Beat* 56:43 O '89
ABERCROMBIE, JOSEPHINE
about
Architecture: Quinlan Terry: a Palladian country house in Kentucky. C. Aslet. il por *Architectural Digest* 46:282-7 O '89
ABERNATHY, RALPH D.
about
Abernathy cuts book tour because of controversy. il pors *Jet* 77:14 N 13 '89
Abernathy takes a cheap shot. J. M. Wall. por *The Christian Century* 106:971-2 N 1 '89
A bitter battle erupts over the last hours of Martin Luther King. J. S. Kunen. il pors *People Weekly* 32:40-2 O 30 '89
Eyewitness statements on King's death dispute Abernathy's accounts. il pors *Jet* 77:57-9 N 6 '89
A fight among Dr. King's faithful. il por *Newsweek* 114:31 O 23 '89
On the humanity of saints. P. Marin. il *The Nation* 249:784-6 D 25 '89
Ralph Abernathy's book denounced for 'painful distortions' about King. il pors *Jet* 77:8-10 O 30 '89
Sexual charges and Martin Luther King. F. Bruning. il *Maclean's* 102:13 N 6 '89
Tattletale memoir. por *Time* 134:42 O 23
ABILITY
See also
Athletic ability
Creativity
Learning, Psychology of

Figure 8.5. Selected ''Book Reviews'' from *Reader's Guide to Periodical Literature*. (Copyright 1990 by the H. W. Wilson Company. Material reproduced by permission of the publisher.)

BOOK REVIEWS

THE 1990 BUICK LESABRE OWNER'S MANUAL.
The New York Times Book Review 94:18 D 24 '89.
N. Perrin
1990 CHEVROLET S-10 OWNER'S MANUAL.
The New York Times Book Review 94:18 D 24 '89.
N. Perrin
1990 YEARBOOK OF SCIENCE AND THE FUTURE.
Earth Science 42:33-4 Fall '89

A

ABERNATHY, R. And the walls came tumbling down.
1989
The New York Times Book Review 94:3 O 29 '89.
H. Hampton
ACADEMIC LABOR MARKETS AND CAREERS. 1988
Change 21:57-60 S/O '89. S. P. Dresch
ACKROYD, P. First light. 1989
National Review 41:53 O 13 '89. D. Bovenizer
ADAMS, A. After you've gone. 1989
The New York Times Book Review 94:27 O 8 '89.
R. Carlson
ADAMS, H. The letters of Henry Adams. 6v 1982
The New Republic 201:32-8 O 16 '89. A. Delbanco
ADAMS, H. Thomas Hart Benton. 1989
National Review 41:44-7 D 22 '89. S. Rodman
ADAMS, W. AND BROCK, J. W. Dangerous pursuits.
1989
The New York Times Book Review 94:28 D 17 '89.
M. A. Reichek
ADELMAN, K. L. The great universal embrace. 1989
The New York Times Book Review 94:28 N 19 '89.
L. Freedman
AESOP'S FABLES. ENGLISH & GREEK. The Medici
Aesop. 1989
The New York Times Book Review 94:9 O 29 '89.
D. J. R. Bruckner
AGNON, S. Y. Shira. 1989
The New Republic 201:42-6 N 20 '89. H. Halkin
The New York Times Book Review 94:6 D 24 '89.
G. Schulman
ALBERT, R. C. Damming the Delaware. 1987
Sierra 74:98+ N/D '89. J. Stiak
ALEXANDER, R. M. Dynamics of dinosaurs and other
extinct giants. 1989
Scientific American 261:126-7 O '89. P. Morrison
ALGAE AND HUMAN AFFAIRS. 1988
BioScience 39:817-18 D '89. L. B. Liddle
ALTER, R. The pleasures of reading. 1989
The New Leader 72:18-19 S 18 '89. L. Siegel
AMBROSE, S. E. Nixon; v2, The triumph of a politician,
1962-1972. 1990
National Review 41:46+ N 24 '89. D. J. Devine
The New York Times Book Review 94:1+ N 12 '89.
R. W. Apple
Time 134:100+ N 6 '89. L. I. Barrett
The Washington Monthly 21:58 O '89. T. Noah
ANDERSON, P. Busybodies. 1989
The New York Times Book Review 94:37 N 26 '89.
M. Orth
ANDO, T. Tadao Ando. 1989
Architectural Record 177:71 O '89. D. London
ANDRES, G. M. AND OTHERS. The art of Florence.
1987
Antiques 136:1286 D '89. A. Mayor
ANSA, T. M. Baby of the family. 1989
The New York Times Book Review 94:6 N 26 '89.
V. Sayers
APPLICATIONS OF PLANT CELL AND TISSUE CUL-
TURE. 1988
BioScience 39:645-6 O '89. E. G. Kirby, III
ARNSON, C. Crossroads. 1989
The New York Times Book Review 94:21 N 12 '89.
R. Caplan
ARONOWITZ, S. Science as power. 1988
Physics Today 42:96 N '89. R. N. Proctor
ASHBERY, J. Reported sightings. 1989
The New Republic 201:38-43 O 16 '89. J. Perl
ASHMORE, H. S. Unseasonable truths. 1989
Commonweal 116:710-11 D 15 '89. D. O'Brien
The New Yorker 65:142-6 O 23 '89. G. Steiner

Science 246:939 N 17 '89. J. D. Hoeveler, Jr.
ASPECTS OF DECAPOD CRUSTACEAN BIOLOGY.
1988
BioScience 39:816-17 D '89. L. H. Mantel
ATEEK, N. S. Justice, and only justice. 1989
Commonweal 116:712-13 D 15 '89. G. E. Irani
ATKINSON, R. The long gray line. 1989
Business Week p14+ O 23 '89. D. Griffiths
National Review 41:49-51 N 24 '89. B. Mitchell
The New York Times Book Review 94:18-19 O 22
'89. T. Buckley
Time 134:90+ O 30 '89. S. Kanfer
The Washington Monthly 21:46+ D '89. J. M. Fallows
AVERILL, L. J. Religious right, religious wrong. 1989
The Christian Century 106:1023-4 N 8 '89. E. Jorstad
AYRE, J. Northrop Frye.
Maclean's 102:65-6 D 11 '89. J. Bemrose

B

BABBAGE, C. The works of Charles Babbage. 11v 1989
Scientific American 261:128 N '89. P. Morrison
BAHN, P. G. AND VERTUT, J. Images of the Ice Age.
1988
Scientific American 261:125-6 O '89. P. Morrison
BAKER, P. R. Stanny. 1989
National Review 41:41-2 D 22 '89. J. P. Hart
BAKER, R. The good times. 1989
The Christian Century 106:1096-7 N 22 '89. R. Liefer
BALMER, R. H. Mine eyes have seen the glory. 1989
Commonweal 116:600-2 N 3 '89. M. Garbey
The New York Review of Books 36:20+ D 21 '89.
G. Wills
BALTHASAR, H. U. VON. Dare we hope "that all men
be saved?"; v1, Prolegomena.
America 161:432-3 D 9 '89. E. T. Oakes
BALTHASAR, H. U. VON. Theo-drama. 1988
America 161:432-3 D 9 '89. E. T. Oakes
BANKS, R. Affliction. 1989
The New York Review of Books 36:46-7 D 7 '89.
R. Towers
BARBER, R. W. AND BARKER, J. R. V. Tournaments.
1989
History Today 39:52 D '89. B. Stone
BARBOUR, K. Nancy. 1989
The New York Times Book Review 94:23 N 26 '89.
C. Olson
BARNARD, R. Death and the chaste apprentice. 1989
The New York Times Book Review 94:47 O 15 '89.
M. Cantwell
BARNES, J. A history of the world in 10½ chapters. 1989
The New Republic 201:40-3 D 4 '89. R. Locke
The New York Review of Books 36:7 O 26 '89. R.
M. Adams
BARR, A. H. Defining modern art. 1986
Art in America 77:39+ D '89. B. Wallis
BARRY, J. M. The ambition and the power. 1989
Business Week p16-18 N 27 '89. D. Harbrecht
National Review 41:41-2 D 31 '89. W. Allison
The New York Times Book Review 94:12 N 19 '89.
R. Dugger
BARTEL, P. C. The complete Gone with the wind trivia
book. 1989
The New York Times Book Review 94:7 D 10 '89.
D. Finkle
BARZUN, J. The culture we deserve. 1989
The American Spectator 22:41-4 O '89. J. Simon
BASALLA, G. The evolution of technology. 1988
The New York Review of Books 36:11-12 D 7 '89.
D. Joravsky
Science 245:991 S 1 '89. C. A. Dunlavy
BATESON, M. C. Composing a life. 1989
The New York Times Book Review 94:7-8 N 26 '89.
J. O'Reilly
BATRA, R. N. Regular economic cycles. 1989
The New York Times Book Review 94:31 O 29 '89.
W. N. Parker
BAWER, B. Diminishing fictions. 1988
The American Spectator 22:48 N '89. G. McCartney
BEAN, F. D. AND TIENDA, M. The Hispanic population
of the United States. 1987

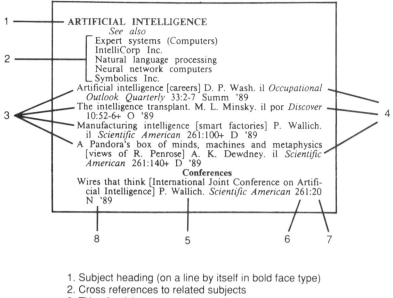

Figure 8.6. Subject entry. (*Reader's Guide to Periodical Literature.* Copyright 1990 by the H. W. Wilson Company. Material reproduced by permission of the publisher.)

1. Subject heading (on a line by itself in bold face type)
2. Cross references to related subjects
3. Title of articles
4. Title of magazines
5. Author of an article
6. Volume number of magazine
7. Page number of article in magazine
8. Date of magazine (month and year)

Figure 8.7. Subject entry from InfoTrac (Information Access Company, copyright 1990. Material reproduced by permission of the publisher.)

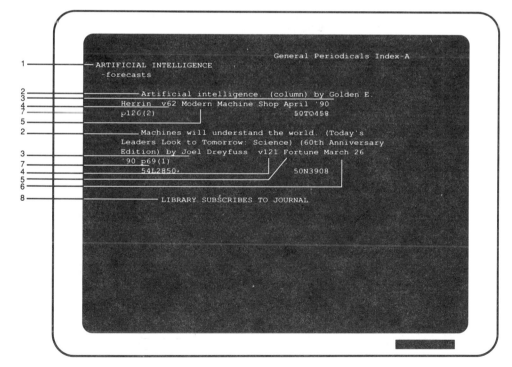

1. Subject heading with subdivision.
2. Title of article.
3. Author of article.
4. Volume number of magazine.
5. Title of magazine.
6. Date of magazine.
7. Page numbers in magazine where article is located.
8. Indicates that the library subscribes to that magazine.

ABSTRACTS

An abstract is a type of index which gives the location of the literature cited and includes a summary, or an abstract, of each item. Abstracts are important reference sources in that they index the literature in special subject fields. They are of value to both specialists and to non-specialists in the field. The specialist who is interested in finding the latest research on a particular topic should consult the abstracts in that subject area. The non-specialist will find them useful because the summary will tell them whether or not the literature is appropriate for their needs. Although the summaries in the different abstracts vary in length, there is usually sufficient information to determine the main ideas presented in the original work. Often, too, the summaries are less technical than the original work. Many of the subject fields are covered by abstracting services.

An excerpt from *Psychological Abstracts* is shown in Figures 8.8 and 8.9.

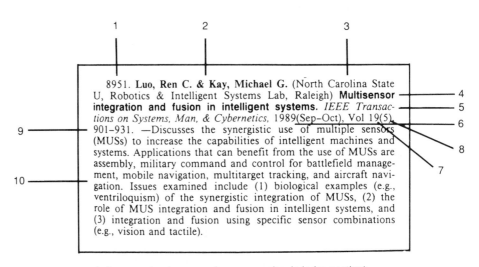

Figure 8.8. Excerpt from *Psychological Abstracts*. This citation is reprinted with permission of the American Psychological Association, publishers of *Psychological Abstracts* and *Psyc INFO Database* (Copyright 1990 by the American Psychological Association), *and may not be reproduced without their prior permission.*

1. Item number (use as reference number in index section)
2. Authors of article
3. University with which authors are affiliated
4. Title of article
5. Journal in which article appears
6. Date of journal
7. Volume number of Journal
8. Issue number
9. Inclusive pages
10. Summary of the article. *Psychological Abstracts*, 77, no. 4 (1990) 881

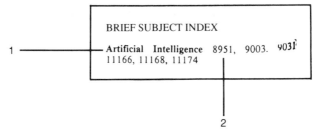

Figure 8.9. Excerpt from index to *Psychological Abstracts*. This citation is reprinted with permission of the American Psychological Association, publishers of *Psychological Abstracts* (Copyright 1990 by the American Psychological Association), and may not be reproduced without their prior permission.

1. Subject entry
2. Item numbers. *Psychological Abstracts*, 77 (1990), ii

CITATION INDEXES

Citation indexes list the works that are cited by authors in writing books, articles, theses and dissertations, conference proceedings, and the like. Although citation indexes are intended to list works cited, they usually include subject indexes so that they can be searched by subject as well as by author. The author indexes list the original author's work and the sources which they cited. Some citation indexes are: *Arts and Humanities Citation Index, Index to Book Reviews in the Sciences, Index to Scientific Proceedings, Index to Science Reviews, Index to Social Science and Humanities Proceedings, Social Sciences Citation Index,* and *Science Citation Index.*

ARTIFICIAL

ARTIFICIAL-INTELL.

LIBRARY - - - HSIEH CC
LINKAGE - - - GLOVER F
LITERATURE - HSIEH CC
LOGICAL-FO. ◆NILSSON N
◆SMOLIAR SW·
◆SOWA JF+

HSIEH CC
86 NEW ENGL J MED 315 587
SEE SCI FOR 5 ADDITIONAL CITATIONS
OLSEN GW   AM J PUB HE   79 1016 89

HSIEH CC
HALL W—SURVEY OF ARTIFICIAL-INTELLIGENCE AND EXPERT
SYSTEMS IN LIBRARY AND INFORMATION-SCIENCE
LITERATURE ◆ NOTE
INF TECH L   8(2):209-214   89   9R   AB933
COLUMBIA COLL LIB, CHICAGO, IL, USA
BARR A   81 HDB ARTIFICIAL INTEL   1   3
DOWNING D   86 DICT COMPUTER TERMS   14
HAFNER CD   78 INFORMATION RETRIEVA
HAWKINS DT   87 ONLINE   SEP   92
HUNT VD   86 ARTIF INTELL   152
MISHKOFF HC   85 UNDERSTANDING ARTIFI   11
MULVEHILL AM   79 STUDY DATA ORG TECHN
SMITH LC   76 INFORMATION PROCESSI   12 109
WINSTON PH   85 MANUFACTURING EN MAR   75

Figure 8.10. Selected references from the *SSCI*[R], *Social Sciences Citation Index,* 1989 Annual Index. (Reprinted with permission from the Permuterm Subject Index[TM] Copyright 1989 by the Institute for Scientific Information[R], Philadelphia, PA, USA.

Figure 8.11. Selected reference from the *SSCI*[R], *Social Sciences Citation Index,* 1989 Annual Index. Part 2, Citation Index. (Reprinted with permission from the Social Sciences Citation Index[R], Copyright 1989 by the Institute for Scientific Information[R], Philadelphia, PA, USA.

Figure 8.12. Selected reference from the *SSCI*[R], *Social Sciences Citation Index,* 1989 Annual. Part 4, Source Index. (Reprinted with permission from the Social Sciences Citation Index[R], Copyright 1989 by the Institute for Scientific Information[R], Philadelphia, PA, USA.

GENERAL INDEXES

InfoTrac. Los Altos, CA: Information Access, 1985-.

> *InfoTrac* is a periodical index on a CD-Rom disk which is updated monthly. It provides access to three databases—*InfoTrac, Government Publications Index*, and *LegalTrac.* This computer-run index includes citations to over half a million articles from more than 1,000 popular magazines and business and professional journals published since January 1982. The index to United States government documents provides access to about a quarter million documents published since 1979.

The Magazine Index. 1976 to date. Los Altos, CA: Information Access, 1976-.

> Periodical articles from popular American magazines arranged alphabetically by author and subject. Includes news reports, editorials on major issues, product evaluations, biographies, short stories, poetry, recipes and reviews. On microfilm.

Poole's Index to Periodical Literature 1802–1897. 7 vols. Boston: Houghton, 1882–1908.

> *Poole's* is a subject index to approximately 475 American and English magazines published during the 1800s. Entries include all information for locating the article except the date. Periodicals are listed alphabetically in the front with a chronological conspectus number which leads the reader by means of a table to the date.

Readers' Guide to Periodical Literature. 1900 to date. New York: H. W. Wilson, 1900-. (Also on WILSONDISC)

> *Readers' Guide* is probably the most widely used and well known of all the periodical indexes. It originally indexed about fifteen of the most popular magazines and now indexes more than 186 different periodicals. The magazines indexed are general in nature, covering all subject areas.

SUBJECT INDEXES, ABSTRACTS, AND CITATION INDEXES

Agriculture

Biological Abstracts. 1926 to date. Philadelphia: BioSciences Information Service, 1926-.

> Published semimonthly, this publication is a major index to the biological sciences. It has several sections useful to the researcher: "a major concept headings for abstracts," the section of abstracts listed by reference number under major subject headings, an author index, biosystematic index, generic index, and subject index. Instructions on how to use this index are located on the inside cover. Each abstract begins with the author, and includes the journal citation and title of the article. The abstract or description in brief of the article follows.

Biological and Agricultural Index. 1964 to date. New York: H. W. Wilson, 1964-. (Continues *Agricultural Index.* 1916–1964.) (Also on WILSONDISC)

A cumulative subject index to 226 English language periodicals in the fields of biology, agriculture, and related sciences such as botany, food science, forestry, soil science, and veterinary medicine. A list of book reviews is located in the back.

Art and Humanities

Art Index. 1933 to date. New York: H. W. Wilson, 1933-. (Also on WILSON-DISC)

Subject and author index to 227 journals, museum bulletins, domestic art publications, and foreign journals. Subject areas included are: painting, sculpture, architecture, ceramics, graphic arts, landscape architecture, archaeology, and other related subjects.

Arts and Humanities Citation Index. 1977 to date. Philadelphia: Institute for Scientific Information, 1976-.

Accesses about 6,900 journals in literature, poetry, plays, short stories, music, film, radio, dance, theater, etc.

Humanities Index. 1974 to date. New York: H. W. Wilson, 1974-. Continues *International Index.* 1907–1965, and *Social Sciences and Humanities Index.* 1965–1974. (Also on WILSONDISC)

Indexes, by author and subject, articles in more than 345 English language periodicals in the humanities: archaeology, classical studies, folklore, history, language and literature, theology, and related subjects. In recent issues book reviews are listed in a separate section in the back of the index under the author's name.

Biography

Biography Index. 1946 to date. New York: H. W. Wilson, 1947-. (Also on WILSONDISC)

Quarterly index to biographical material in books and about 2,700 different periodicals. Material is arranged: (1) by name of biographee and (2) by occupation or profession.

Business

ABI/Inform. Ann Arbor, MI: UMI, 1984-. (On CD-ROM)

Index to over 800 business and trade journals. Includes articles on business conditions, economics, managerial science and other business related topics. Allows keyword searching and several print options. Citations include abstracts. This CD-ROM version of the online database contains the current five years only.

Business Index. 1979 to date. Los Altos, CA: Information Access, 1979-.

A cumulative author/subject index on film to over 810 business periodicals. Also indexes articles in the *Wall Street Journal*, *Barron's*, the financial section of *The New York Times*, as well as articles relating to business appearing in over 1,100 general and legal periodicals. On microfilm.

Business Periodicals Index. 1958 to date. New York: H. W. Wilson, 1958-. Continues *Industrial Arts Index.* 1913–1957. (Also on WILSONDISC)

Indexes 344 magazines and journals in advertising, banking and finance, marketing, accounting, labor and management, insurance, and general business. Good source for information about an industry and about individual companies.

Education

CIJE, Current Index to Journals in Education. 1969 to date. Phoenix: Oryx, 1969-. (Also on ERIC CD-ROM)

Indexes 780 major educational and education related journals.

Education Index. 1929 to date. New York: H. W. Wilson, 1929-. Also on WILSONDISC)

A subject index to educational literature including 339 periodicals, pamphlets, reports, and books. Subjects include: counseling and personnel service, teaching methods and curriculum, special education and rehabilitation, educational research, and many others covering all aspects of education. Monthly with annual cumulations.

Public Affairs

PAIS Bulletin. 1915 to date. New York: Public Affairs Information Service, 1915-.

Especially strong in public administration, political science, history, economics, finance, and sociology. Indexes books, pamphlets, society publications, and government documents as well as periodicals. Published twice monthly, cumulates annually.

Science and Technology

Applied Science and Technology Index. 1958 to date. New York: H. W. Wilson, 1958-. Continues *Industrial Arts Index.* 1913–1957. (Also on WILSONDISC)

Indexes by subject articles from 335 scientific periodicals in the fields of aeronautics, automation, construction, electricity, engineering, and related subjects.

Chemical Abstracts. 1907 to date. Columbus, Ohio: American Chemical Society, 1907-.

Contains literature related to chemistry appearing in books, reports, annotated documents, and about 14,000 journals and conferences.

Engineering Index Monthly. 1984 to date. Baltimore: Engineering Index, Inc., 1984-. (Continues *Engineering Index.* 1884-1983.)

Issued monthly and cumulated annually. It contains abstracts of literature published in engineering journals, technical reports, monographs, conference proceedings. Annual volumes are divided into subject volumes and an author index volume. Title of article follows abstract number with bibliographic citation of article following.

General Science Index. 1978 to date. New York: H. W. Wilson, 1978-. (Also on WILSONDISC)

Cumulative subject/author index to 109 English language science periodicals. Subject fields indexed include: astronomy, atmospheric science, biology, botany, chemistry, earth science, environment and conservation, food and nutrition, genetics, mathematics, medicine and health, microbiology, oceanography, physics, physiology, psychology, and zoology.

SCI, Science Citation Index. 1961 to date. Philadelphia: Institute for Scientific Information, 1965-.

Published bimonthly with calendar year cumulations, it has three sections: a Source Index, the Permuterm Subject Index, and the Citation Index. The Source Index section lists all journals indexed with abbreviations used in the entries. To locate authors, use the Source Index; to find subjects, use the Permuterm Subject Index. The Source Index has the full information on the article—title of article, name of journal, volume, issue number, pages, and date. The Citation Index is used to locate authors' names cited in other publications. In order to locate the original author's source and the original citation, look directly below the author's name to find the information.

Social Sciences

Psychological Abstracts. 1927 to date. Arlington, VA: American Psychological Association, 1927-.

Includes summaries of journal articles, monographs, and reports on psychology and related studies listed under major classification categories with an author and subject index. Issued monthly

SSCI, Social Sciences Citation Index. 1966 to date. Philadelphia: Institute for Scientific Information, 1966-.

Indexes most recent significant journal literature in social, behavioral, and related sciences. Organized like *SCI*.

Social Sciences Index. 1974 to date. New York: H. W. Wilson, 1974-. Continues *International Index.* 1907–1961, and *Social Sciences and Humanities Index.* 1965–1974. (Also on WILSONDISC)

Gives author and subject entries for articles in more than 350 periodicals. Subjects covered include anthropology, area studies, economics, environmental science, geography, law and criminology, medical science, political science, psychology, public administration, sociology, and related subjects. Book reviews are in a separate section in the back.

Sociological Abstracts. 1952 to date. New York: Sociological Abstracts, 1952-.
Covers articles in all languages from journals concerned with sociology.

NEWSPAPER INDEXES

Newspaper indexes differ from periodical indexes in that they usually cover only one title. The exceptions to this are *DataTimes* and *NewsBank*. Periodical indexes give the library user references to many different publications, but the newspaper index gives access to the contents of only one newspaper. Usually newspaper indexes have only subject entries. As a rule the newspaper index does not give the exact title of an article which is often not too informative; instead, it gives a brief summary of the article. Newspapers are a good source for information on the local, state, national, and international levels. Most libraries subscribe to newspapers on a current and microfilm basis. Excerpts from newspaper indexes are shown in Figures 8.13, 8.14, 8.15, 8.16.

Figure 8.13. Selected reference from *The New York Times Index*, May 16–31, 1990, p. 33. (Copyright 1990 by The New York Times Company. Reprinted with permission.)

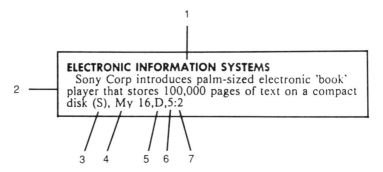

1. Primary subject heading
2. Brief summary of the newspaper article
3. Indicates that the article is short
4. Date of the article (year is found on the cover of the index)
5. D indicates the section of the newpaper in which the article is located
6. Page 5
7. Column 2

The following titles are examples of widely used newspaper indexes:

DataTimes. 1985 to date. Oklahoma City: DataTimes, 1985-.

    DataTimes is an online newspaper database access to several leading newspapers and newswires including the *Washington Post,* the *Dallas Morning News,* the *San Francisco Chronicle,* the Baton Rouge *State Times,* the Baton Rouge *Morning Advocate,* and others.

Index to the Christian Science Monitor International Daily Newspaper. 1959 to date. Boston: Christian Science Monitor, 1960-.

    Title of articles listed under subject with day, month, section, page, and column noted.

New York Times Index. 1913 to date. New York: New York Times Co., 1913-. The *Prior Series* published by Bowker covers the years 1851–1912.

    Subject index to *The New York Times* newspaper. Published twice monthly with annual cumulations. An excerpt from this index is shown in Figure 8.13.

NewsBank Index. Jan. 1982 to date. New Canaan, CT: Newsbank, Inc., 1982-.

This is an index to current events and issues from newspapers in over 100 cities. Topics are arranged alphabetically by name and subject. To find the correct *NewsBank* microfiche file, use the year, microfiche category, and microfiche number cited in the index. Excerpts from *NewsBank Index* are shown in Figures 8.14, 8.15, 8.16.

The Times Index (London). 1785 to date. Reading, England: Newspaper Archive Development, 1957-. Earlier issues are indexed under various titles.

Author and subject index not only to the daily *Times,* but also to the *Sunday Times,* the *Times Literary Supplement,* the *Times Educational Supplement,* and the *Times Higher Education Supplement.*

Times Picayune (New Orleans) Index. 1972 to date. Ann Arbor, MI: UMI, 1972-.

An easy to use alphabetical index to news articles, editorials, book reviews, obituaries, sports articles, business and financial news from one of the largest newspapers in the South and one of the oldest in the United States. Cites exact location of each article—date, page and column—of newspaper which is located on microfilm in libraries.

Wall Street Journal Index. 1957 to date. New York. Dow Jones, 1959 .

An index to a newspaper which emphasizes financial news.

The Washington Post Newspaper Index. 1971–78 to date. Ann Arbor, MI: UMI, 1978-.

Useful for coverage of news from the nation's capital. Originally part of the *Newspaper Index,* which also included the following newspapers: *The Chicago Tribune, The Detroit News, The Houston Post, The Los Angeles Times, The New Orleans Times Picayune,* and *The San Francisco Chronicle.*

Figure 8.14. Instructions from the *NewsBank Index*. (Copyright 1990. Material reproduced by permission of the publisher, NewsBank, Inc.)

———— How to Use NewsBank® ————

STEP 1.

Turn to your research topic in the **NewsBank Index,** which is arranged alphabetically by subject. An explanation of the index appears at the bottom of each left-hand index page. A key to the abbreviations for NewsBank's subject categories appears at the bottom of each right-hand page.

You may find a "See" reference, which will tell you that NewsBank has indexed this information under a different term.

EXAMPLE:

WELFARE
See **Public Aid (Welfare)**

You may also find a "See also" reference, which will suggest other headings where you can find related information.

EXAMPLE:

PUBLIC AID (WELFARE)
See also **Energy Assistance Programs; Food Assistance Programs; Medicaid; Medicare**

SAMPLE INDEX ENTRY ————————————————————————

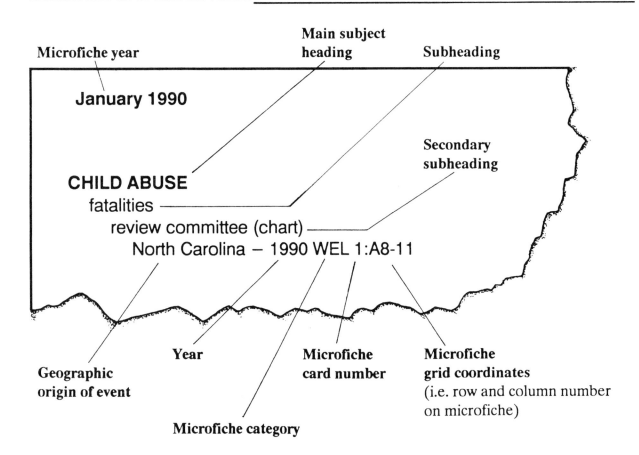

Figure 8.15. This page is from *NewsBank Index*. (Copyright May 1990. Material reproduced by permission of the publisher, NewsBank, Inc.)

STEP 2.

Go to the NewsBank microfiche files and select your microfiche by subject category, year, volume number, and microfiche number.

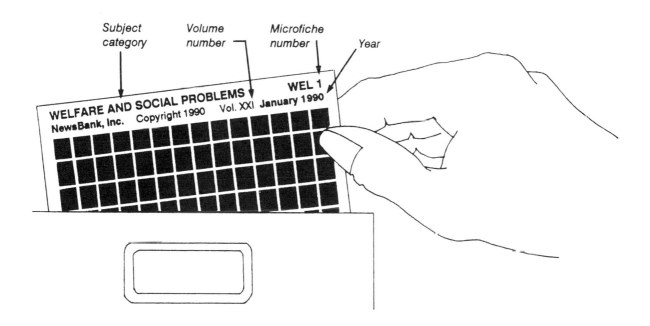

STEP 3.

Place the microfiche on a reader. The grid location — subject category, microfiche number, row letter and column number — will appear in the lower left corner of each frame. Locate your article on the grid as you would by using the coordinates on a road map. The article will appear in its original size on the screen.

Figure 8.16. This page is from *NewsBank Index*. (Copyright May 1990. Material reproduced by permission of the publisher, NewsBank, Inc.)

NewsBank® Can Be Cited as Follows

Since NewsBank gathers and reformats information first published elsewhere, the bibliographic citation needs to be in a special form. Following are two examples of citations:

1. *This example is derived from Eugene B. Fleischer, A Style Manual for Citing Microform and Nonprint Media (Chicago: American Library Association, 1978).*

Footnote:
    [10]Dan Chapman, "Panel Could Help Protect Children," <u>Winston-Salem</u> (North Carolina) <u>Journal</u>, January 14, 1990 (Located in <u>NewsBank</u> [Microform], Welfare and Social Problems, 1990, 1:A8-11, fiche).

Bibliography:
Chapman, Dan. "Panel Could Help Protect Children," <u>Winston-Salem</u> (North Carolina) <u>Journal</u>, January 14, 1990. Located in <u>NewsBank</u> [Microform], Welfare and Social Problems, 1990, 1:A8-11, fiche.

2. *This citation form was developed by the editors of the MLA Handbook for Writers of Research Papers, 2nd ed. (New York, 1984). This form will be included in future editions of the MLA Handbook. The editors do not provide a separate footnote example.*

Bibliography:
Chapman, Dan. "Panel Could Help Protect Children." <u>Winston-Salem Journal</u> [NC] 14 January 1990. NewsBank [Microform], Welfare and Social Problems, 1990, fiche 1, grids A8-11.

Figure 8.17.   Steps in locating periodical and newpaper articles.

How to Find Periodical and Newspaper Articles

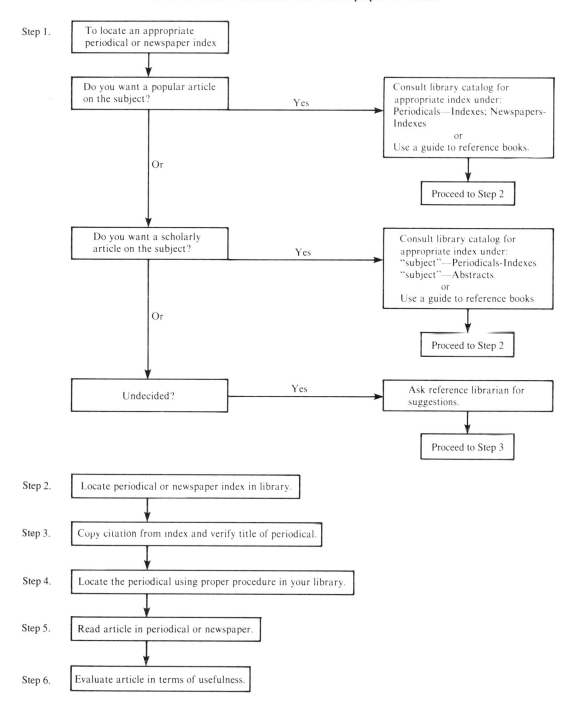

Step 1.   To locate an appropriate periodical or newspaper index

Do you want a popular article on the subject? — Yes → Consult library catalog for appropriate index under: Periodicals—Indexes; Newspapers-Indexes

or

Use a guide to reference books.

Proceed to Step 2

Or

Do you want a scholarly article on the subject? — Yes → Consult library catalog for appropriate index under: "subject"—Periodicals-Indexes "subject"—Abstracts.

or

Use a guide to reference books

Proceed to Step 2

Or

Undecided? — Yes → Ask reference librarian for suggestions.

Proceed to Step 3

Step 2.   Locate periodical or newspaper index in library.

Step 3.   Copy citation from index and verify title of periodical.

Step 4.   Locate the periodical using proper procedure in your library.

Step 5.   Read article in periodical or newspaper.

Step 6.   Evaluate article in terms of usefulness.

INDEXES TO BOOK REVIEWS

Reviews of most new books and of forthcoming books are published in newspapers and magazines. Written by critics and journalists, book reviews provide descriptions and critical evaluations of books. The success or failure of a book's sale frequently depends on the kind of review it receives. Indexes to book reviews are good sources to locate references to reviews of books appearing in periodicals and newspapers. Some of these indexes have excerpts from the reviews, while others only list the sources. References to book reviews can also be located through periodical and newspaper indexes.

The excerpt from *Book Review Digest* shown in Figure 8.18 illustrates a typical entry for an index to book reviews.

Figure 8.19 is taken from the Subject and Title Index of *Book Review Digest*. It shows the subject and title entry for the book shown in Figure 8.18. The list of periodicals indexed in *Book Review Digest* is shown in Figure 8.20.

Examples of some of the better known indexes to book reviews are listed below:

Book Review Digest. 1905 to date. New York: H. W. Wilson, 1905-. (On WILSONDISC)

> This index is organized in two sections. The first part is an alphabetical listing by authors of books. Each entry includes the title of the book, bibliographical information, and publisher's note. The publisher's note is followed by references to the reviews which appear in periodicals. Some of the references include excerpts from the book reviews. The second part is a subject and title index. A list of periodicals indexed is located in the front. Issued monthly with annual cumulation. Approximately 6,000 English-language books are reviewed. See Figures 8.18–8.20.

Book Review Index, a Master Cumulation, 1965–1984. 10 volumes. Ed. Gary C. Tarbert and Barbara Beach. Detroit: Gale, 1985; also 1985 *Update* volume.

> Authors listed in volumes 1 through 7; titles of books cited in volumes 8, 9, and 10. This index reviews 740,500 titles in 1,605,000 reviews.

Combined Retrospective Index to Book Reviews in Humanities Journals, 1802–1974. 10 volumes. Ed. Evan Ira Farber. Woodbridge, CT: Research Publications, 1983–1984.

> An author and title access to about 500,000 reviews from 150 humanities journals. Names of reviewers are also given. Volume 10 has a title index.

Combined Retrospective Index to Book Reviews in Scholarly Journals, 1886–1974. 15 volumes. Woodbridge, CT: Research Publications, 1979–1982.

> Lists titles alphabetically in "title volumes" which refer the user to the author volumes containing the reviews of the books.

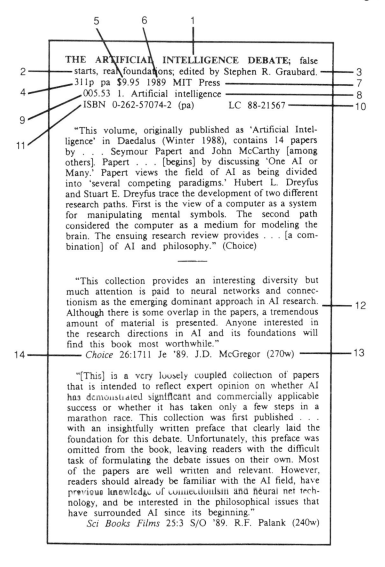

Figure 8.18. Selected references from the *Book Review Digest*. (Copyright 1990 by the H.W. Wilson Company. Material reproduced by permission of the publisher.)

1. Title of the book
2. Sub-title or explanatory title of the book
3. Editor of the book
4. Number of pages in the book
5. Price of the book
6. Date book was published
7. Publisher of the book
8. Main subject covered in the book
9. Dewey Decimal number
10. Library of Congress number
11. Indicates International Standard Book Number
12. Quotation or exerpt from a review which appeared in *Choice*
13. Author of the Review
14. Citation to a review which appeared in *Choice,* volume 26, page 1711, June 1989. The review has 270 words.

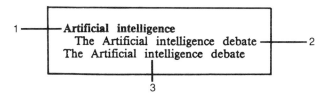

1. Subject heading
2. Title of the book
3. Title entry for book

Figure 8.19. Excerpt from *Subject and Title Index to Book Review Digest*. (Copyright 1990 by the H.W. Wilson Company. Material reproduced by permission of the publisher.)

Figure 8.20. ''Abbreviations of Periodicals'' used in *Book Review Digest* entries. (Copyright 1990 by the H.W. Wilson Company. Material reproduced by permission of the publisher.)

ABBREVIATIONS OF PERIODICALS

For full information consult the List of Periodicals

A

Am Book Rev — American Book Review
Am Hist Rev — The American Historical Review
Am J Sociol — American Journal of Sociology
Am Lit — American Literature
Am Q — American Quarterly
Am Sch — The American Scholar
America — America
Ann Am Acad Polit Soc Sci — The Annals of the American
   Academy of Political and Social Science
Antioch Rev — The Antioch Review
Appraisal — Appraisal
Archaeology — Archaeology
Art Am — Art in America
Atlantic — The Atlantic

B

Booklist — Booklist
Books Relig — Books & Religion
Books Young People — Books for Young People
Bull At Sci — The Bulletin of the Atomic Scientists
Bull Cent Child Books — Bulletin of the Center for
   Children's Books
Bus Hist Rev — Business History Review
Bus Horiz — Business Horizons

C

Can Forum — The Canadian Forum
Can Hist Rev — Canadian Historical Review
Can Lit — Canadian Literature
Choice — Choice
Christ Century — The Christian Century
Christ Sci Monit — The Christian Science Monitor (Eastern
   edition)
Christ Today — Christianity Today
Classical Rev — The Classical Review
Classical World — The Classical World
Columbia J Rev — Columbia Journalism Review
Commentary — Commentary
Commonweal — Commonweal
Contemp Sociol — Contemporary Sociology

E

Economist — The Economist
Educ Stud (AESA) — Educational Studies (American
   Educational Studies Association)
Encounter — Encounter (London, England)
Engl Hist Rev — The English Historical Review
Ethics — Ethics

F

Film Q — Film Quarterly

G

Grow Point — Growing Point

H

Harv Educ Rev — Harvard Educational Review
Hist Today — History Today
History — History
Horn Book — The Horn Book

I

Interracial Books Child Bull — Interracial Books for
Children Bulletin

J

J Am Acad Relig — Journal of the American Academy
of Religion
J Am Hist — The Journal of American History
J Econ Lit — The Journal of Economic Literature
J Marriage Fam — Journal of Marriage and the Family
J Relig — The Journal of Religion

K

Kenyon Rev — The Kenyon Review

L

Libr J — Library Journal
London Rev Books — London Review of Books

M

Middle East J — The Middle East Journal
Mon Labor Rev — Monthly Labor Review
Ms — Ms.

N

N Engl Q — The New England Quarterly
N Y Rev Books — The New York Review of Books
N Y Times Book Rev — The New York Times Book
   Review
Nat Hist — Natural History
Nation — The Nation
Natl Rev — National Review
New Leader — The New Leader
New Repub — The New Republic
New Sci — New Scientist
New Statesman Soc — New Statesman & Society
New Yorker — The New Yorker
Newsweek — Newsweek
Notes — Notes

P

Parameters — Parameters (Carlisle Barracks, Pa.)
Phi Delta Kappan — Phi Delta Kappan
Poetry — Poetry (Modern Poetry Association)
Polit Sci Q — Political Science Quarterly
Psychol Today — Psychology Today

Q

Quill Quire — Quill & Quire

R

Readings — Readings
Relig Educ — Religious Education
Rev Am Hist — Reviews in American History

S

San Francisco Rev Books — San Francisco Review of
   Books
Sci Am — Scientific American
Sci Books Films — Science Books & Films
Sewanee Rev — The Sewanee Review
Sight Sound — Sight & Sound
SLJ — School Library Journal
Small Press — Small Press
Smithsonian — Smithsonian
Society — Society

Science Fiction Book Review Index, 1923–1973. Ed. Halbert W. Hall. Detroit: Gale, 1975.

Science Fiction Book Review Index provides access to book reviews in science fiction and fantasy magazines; also includes nonfiction magazines which had science fiction book reviews. Provides a research aid for studying fiction writers and their works.

Science Fiction Book Review Index, 1974–1979. Detroit: Gale, 1981.

Continues *Science Fiction Book Review Index,* 1923- 1973. Kept up-to-date with annual supplements.

Technical Book Review Index. 1917 to date. Pittsburgh: Carnegie Library, 1917–1929. 5 vols. New York: Special Libraries Association, 1935-.

Topical arrangement of reviews which appear in scientific and technical journals. Entries give brief quotations from the reviews.

INDEXES TO LITERATURE IN COLLECTIONS (ANTHOLOGIES)

Selected literary works of varied authorship have been placed together in one collection since the Greeks compiled the first *Greek Anthology* during the first and second centuries B.C. This first anthology is a collection of over 6,000 short poems and epigrams by some 320 authors. These works, considered the "flowers of literature," were given the name anthology, which means "a garland of flowers" or "gathered flowers." The practice of gathering the best work into a collection has resulted in much of the world's great literature being included in anthologies.

In modern times the term anthology refers to any collection of varied literary compositions. Works placed together in anthologies include poems, stories, essays, plays, and speeches. Anthologies can also include works from a period of history or works devoted to a particular subject or theme. Most anthologies include works of varied authorship, but it is not uncommon to have representative works of one author selected by an editor and collected in an anthology.

The outstanding characteristic of an anthology is the inclusion under one title of many different titles of shorter works. The titles of anthologies which a library owns, quite naturally, are listed in the catalog. The titles of the shorter works found in the anthology, however, are not usually included in the catalog. For example, the title, *Ten Modern Masters: An Anthology of the Short Story,* would be listed in the catalog; the short story, "I'm a Fool," which is included in *Ten Modern Masters,* ordinarily would not be listed.

The excerpts in Figures 8.21 and 8.22 are from the *Essay and General Literature Index* to illustrate essays in collections (anthologies).

To analyze, or list, the contents of anthologies in the library catalog is costly and time consuming. Instead, most libraries subscribe to various indexes which analyze the contents of literature in collections. Some of these indexes are described below.

Figure 8.21. Subject entry from *Essay and General Literature Index 1985–1989*. (Copyright 1990 by the H.W. Wilson Company. Material reproduced by permission of the publisher.)

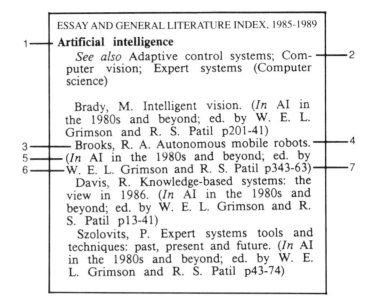

ESSAY AND GENERAL LITERATURE INDEX, 1985-1989

1 — **Artificial intelligence**
See also Adaptive control systems; Computer vision; Expert systems (Computer science) — 2

Brady, M. Intelligent vision. (*In* AI in the 1980s and beyond; ed. by W. E. L. Grimson and R. S. Patil p201-41)
3 — Brooks, R. A. Autonomous mobile robots. — 4
5 — (*In* AI in the 1980s and beyond; ed. by
6 — W. E. L. Grimson and R. S. Patil p343-63) — 7
Davis, R. Knowledge-based systems: the view in 1986. (*In* AI in the 1980s and beyond; ed. by W. E. L. Grimson and R. S. Patil p13-41)
Szolovits, P. Expert systems tools and techniques: past, present and future. (*In* AI in the 1980s and beyond; ed. by W. E. L. Grimson and R. S. Patil p43-74)

1. Subject entry
2. Cross references to other subject headings
3. Author of article on artificial intelligence in collection
4. Title of article in collection
5. Title of book in which articles appear
6. Editors of *AI in the 1980's*
7. Pages on which article, "Autonomous mobile robots" appears in the book

AI in the 1980s and beyond; an MIT survey; edited by W. Eric L. Grimson and Ramesh S. Patil. MIT Press 1987 374p (MIT Press series in artificial intelligence) ISBN 0-262-07106-1 LC 87-3241

Based on a conference held January 21-23, 1986 at the Massachusetts Institute of Technology; sponsored by the Artificial Intelligence Laboratory, the Laboratory for Computer Science, and the Seminar Office of the Center for Advanced Engineering Study at MIT

Figure 8.22. Selected references from "List of Books Indexed." Excerpt from *Essay and General Literature Index.* (Copyright 1990 by the H.W. Wilson Company. Material reproduced by permission of the publisher.)

Essays

Essay and General Literature Index, 1900/1933 to date. New York: H. W. Wilson, 1900/1933-. (On WILSONDISC)

An alphabetical author, subject, and sometimes title index to thousands of essays and chapters found in books. Particularly strong in the fields of the humanities and the social sciences but covers other disciplines as well. It is an excellent source for a criticism of an author's work.

Plays

Keller, Dean H. *Index to Plays in Periodicals.* Rev. and expanded ed. Metuchen, N.J.: Scarecrow, 1979.

Indexes about 10,000 plays located in 267 periodicals in one volume.

Ottemiller's Index to Plays in Collections, an Author and Title Index Appearing in Collections Published between 1900 and Early 1985. Rev. and enlarged by John M. Connor and Billie M. Connor. 7th ed. Metuchen, N. J.: Scarecrow, 1988.

Index to full-length plays appearing in books published in England and the United States. It is divided into three sections: (1) author index with titles and dates of performance, (2) list of collections analyzed with key to symbols, and (3) title index.

Play Index. 1949/52 to date. New York: H. W. Wilson, 1949- .

The key index to 26,000 plays published from 1949 to 1986 in six volumes. The volume for 1983–1987 is an index to 3,964 plays. It is divided into two parts: Part I lists plays under authors' names and anthologies in which found. Part II includes the cast analysis by number of male and female characters needed. Part III lists anthologies with full bibliographic information. Part IV includes a Directory of Publishers and Distributors.

Poetry

American Poetry Index: An Author and Title Index to Poetry by Americans in Single Author Collections. Vol. 1, 1981–1982. Vol. 2, 1983. Vol. 3, 1984. New York: Grander Book Co., 1983.

An alphabetical index to authors and titles of over 10,000 poems published in 190 collections which are located by number after author's name in main index.

Caskey, Jefferson D., Comp. *Index to Poetry in Popular Periodicals, 1955–1959.* Westport, CT: Greenwood, 1984.

Indexes 7,400 poems by title appearing in American periodicals from 1955 1959. Also includes a first-line index, author index, and subject index.

————. *Index to Poetry in Popular Periodicals, 1960–1964.* Westport, CT: Greenwood, 1988.

The Columbia Granger's Index to Poetry. 9th ed. New York: Columbia University Press, 1990.

Continues *Granger's Index to Poetry, 1970–1981.* Indexes over 100,000 poems appearing in over 400 anthologies.

Granger, Edith. *Granger's Index to Poetry, 1970–1981.* Ed. William James Smith. 7th ed., completely rev. and enl., indexing anthologies published through December 31, 1981. New York: Columbia University Press, 1982.

First published in 1904, this is considered the standard index to poetry. Each edition enlarges on the previous one, omitting some anthologies, adding new ones. Later editions arranged by sections as follows: (1) title and first-line index, (2) author index, and (3) subject index.

Short Stories

Short Story Index, an Index to 60,000 Stories in 4,320 Collections, 1900–1949. New York: H. W. Wilson, 1953-. *Supplements*: 1950–1954, 1955–1958, 1959–1963, 1964–1968, 1969–1973, 1974–1978, 1979, 1980, 1981, 1982, 1983, 1984-1988. New York: H. W. Wilson, 1956–1989.

Author, title, subject index to short stories appearing in collections. The 1984–1988 volume indexes 21,400 stories published in 1,250 recent collections.

Speeches

Mitchell, Charity. *Speech Index: An Index to Collections of World Famous Orations and Speeches for Various Occasions. Supplement, 1966–1980.* Metuchen, NJ: Scarecrow, 1982.

Alphabetical arrangement of speeches by author, subject, and type of speech.

Sutton, Roberta Briggs. *Speech Index; an Index to 259 Collections of World Famous Orations and Speeches for Various Occasions.* 4th ed. Rev. and enl. New York: Scarecrow, 1966.

INDEXES TO LITERARY CRITICISM

Works of literary criticism contain articles or essays which evaluate or judge, describe, analyze, and compare an author's novel, poem, play, short story, or other literary work.

The following is an excerpt from *Twentieth Century Short Story Explication* demonstrating how to locate criticisms of the short story, ''Ad Astra,'' by William Faulkner.

Figure 8.23. Author entry. (From *Twentieth Century Short Story Explication, Supplement III.* Copyright 1987 by the Shoe String Press. Material reproduced by permission of the publisher.)

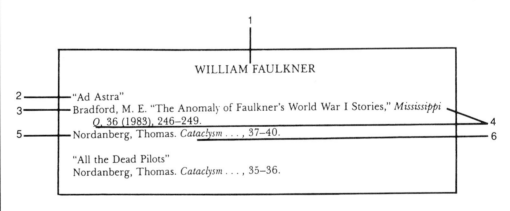

1. Author of short story "Ad Astra"
2. Title of short story
3. Author of periodical article about short story
4. Title of periodical , volume, date, and pages where article appears
5. Author of book in which criticism of story appears
6. Title of book in which criticism of story appears, including pages for locating information

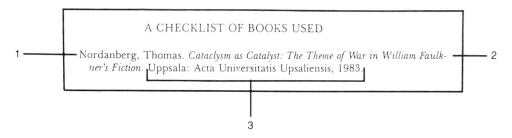

A CHECKLIST OF BOOKS USED

1 ——————— Nordanberg, Thomas. *Cataclysm as Catalyst: The Theme of War in William Faulkner's Fiction.* Uppsala: Acta Universitatis Upsaliensis, 1983. ——————— 2

3

1. Author of book in which criticisms appear about William Faulkner's works
2. Title of book in which articles appear
3. Imprint of book

The following list of publications is useful in searching for commentaries, criticisms, interpretations, and explanatory information about literature of all kinds—novels, plays, poetry, and short stories. Some of the guides are limited to literature of a specific nationality, while others are international in their coverage. Both the titles and the annotations indicate in some measure the scope of the guide.

General

Essay and General Literature Index. 1900 to date. New York: H. W. Wilson, 1900/1933-. (Also on WILSONDISC)

As noted earlier, this is an excellent source for criticism of all types of literature.

Magill, Frank Northern. *Magill's Bibliography of Literary Criticism; Selected Sources for the Study of More than 2,500 Outstanding Works of Western Literature.* 4 vols. Englewood Cliffs, NJ: Salem, 1979.

Criticisms in books, parts of books, and periodicals of poetry, drama, and fiction.

Novels

Abernethy, Peter L., Christian J. W. Kloesel, and Jeffry R. Smitten. *English Novel Explication. Supplement I.* Hamden, CT: Shoe String, 1976. *Supplement II,* 1981. *Supplement III,* 1987.

This work supplements and updates the Palmer and Dyson guide. Extends *English Novel Explication* series to 1985.

Adelman, Irving, and Rita Dworkin. *The Contemporary Novel, a Checklist of Critical Literature on the British and American Novel since 1945.* Metuchen, NJ: Scarecrow, 1972.

A selective survey of critical articles and essays of contemporary British and American novels in periodicals and books. Abbreviations used for periodicals listed in front before main entries and a bibliography of books analyzed is found in the back.

Bell, Inglis Freeman, and Donald Baird. *The English Novel 1578–1956: A Checklist of Twentieth-Century Criticisms.* Denver: Allan Swallow, 1958.

References to critical articles in books and periodicals. Arranged alphabetically by novelists and their individual works. Key to abbreviations of books and periodicals indexed included in the back.

Gerstenberger, Donna, and George Hendrick. *The American Novel, a Checklist of Twentieth Century Criticism on Novels Written Since 1789.* 2 vols. Denver: Allan Swallow, 1961–1970. Vol 1, *The American Novel 1789–1959.* Vol. 2, *Criticisms Written 1960–1968.*

Criticisms are listed under major authors by titles of works. Includes citations from books and periodicals.

Kearney, E. I., and L. S. Fitzgerald. *The Continental Novel, a Checklist of Criticism in English 1967–1980.* Metuchen, NJ: Scarecrow, 1988.

Critical entries are organized under the following categories: the French novel, the Spanish and Portuguese novel, the Italian novel, the German novel, the Scandinavian novel, and the Russian and East European novel.

Palmer, Helen H., and Anne Jane Dyson. *English Novel Explication: Criticisms to 1972.* Hamden, CT: Shoe String, 1973.

Cites criticisms found in books and periodicals in English and foreign languages from 1958 to 1972.

Plays (Drama)

Breed, Paul F., and Florence M. Snideman. *Dramatic Criticism Index: a Bibliography of Commentaries on Playwrights from Ibsen to the Avante-Garde.* Detroit: Gale, 1972.

Includes critical articles from over 200 periodicals and 630 books. Main entries under authors. Includes a title and a critic index.

Eddleman, Floyd Eugene. *American Drama Criticism: Interpretations 1890–1977.* 2nd ed. Hamden, CT: Shoe String, 1979. *Supplement I,* 1984.

Palmer, Helen H., and Anne Jane Dyson. *American Drama Criticism Interpretations, 1890–1965, Inclusive of American Drama, since the First Play Produced in America.* Hamden, CT: Shoe String, 1967. *Supplement I,* 1970. *Supplement II,* 1976. Comp. Floyd Eugene Eddleman.

Lists critical articles of American plays located in periodicals, books, and monographs. Arrangement is alphabetical by playwright.

Palmer, Helen H. *European Drama Criticism 1900–1975.* 2nd ed. Hamden, CT: Shoe String, 1977.

A source book to critical writings of representative European plays in selected books and periodicals. Information is organized in three parts: (1) alphabetical list of playwrights with critical articles which appear in periodicals and books, (2) a list of books used as sources and a list of periodicals searched, and (3) an author-title index.

Poetry

Alexander, Harriet Semmes, comp. *American and British Poetry: A Guide to the Criticism Published Between 1925–1978.* Athens, OH: Swallow Press/Ohio University Press, 1984.

Indexes criticisms located in 170 journals and 500 books published between 1925–1978.

Cline, Gloria Stark, and Jeffrey A. Baker. *An Index to Criticisms of British and American Poetry.* Metuchen, NJ: Scarecrow, 1973.

Cites critical articles on poetry published in periodicals and books between 1960 and 1970. List of abbreviations of periodicals used in entries and a bibliography of books cited are found in the back of this work.

Kuntz, Joseph M., and Nancy C. Martinez. *Poetry Explication: A Checklist of Interpretation since 1925 of British and American Poems, Past and Present.* 3rd ed. Boston: G. K. Hall, 1980.

Lists interpretations found in selected anthologies and periodicals, incorporating checklists of 1950 and 1962. A bibliography of poetry explication printed during the period 1925–1977.

Shields, Ellen F. *Contemporary English Poetry: An Annotated Bibliography of Criticism to 1980.* New York: Garland, 1984.

Short Stories

Walker, Warren S. *Twentieth-Century Short Story Explication: Interpretations 1900–1975 of Short Fiction since 1800.* 3rd ed. Hamden, CT: Shoe String, 1977. *Supplement I*, 1980. *Supplement II*, 1984. *Supplement III*, 1987.

Analyses of short stories appearing in books, periodicals, and monographs.

SELECTED SUBJECT PERIODICAL INDEXES

Aerospace

Aerospace Medicine and Biology: A Continuing Bibliography. 1964 to date. 1964-.

International Aerospace Abstracts. 1961 to date. 1961-.

Scientific and Technical Aerospace Reports (STAR Index). 1963 to date. 1963-.

Agriculture

Abstracts on Tropical Agriculture. 1975 to date. 1975-.

Agris/Agrindex. 1975 to date. 1975-.

Animal Breeding Abstracts. 1933 to date. 1934-.

Bibliography of Agriculture. 1942 to date. 1942-. (Also on AGRICOLA CD-Rom)

Fertilizer Abstracts. 1968 to date. 1968-.

Field Crop Abstracts. 1948 to date. 1948-.

International Bibliography of Rice Research. 1951 to date. 1951-.

Review of Applied Entomology. 1913–1989.

Soils and Fertilizers. 1938 to date. 1938-.

World Agricultural Economics and Rural Sociology Abstracts. 1959 to date. 1959-.

Anthropology

Abstracts in Anthropology. 1970 to date. 1970-.

Anthropological Index to Current Periodicals in the Library of Mankind. 1963 to date. 1963-.

Anthropological Literature: An Index to Periodical Articles & Essays. 1979 to date. 1979-.

International Bibliography of Social and Cultural Anthropology. 1955 to date. 1955-.

Aquatic Sciences
Aquatic Sciences and Fisheries Abstracts. 1971–1977.
    (Continues *Aquatic Biology Abstracts.* 1969–1971, and *Current Bibliography for Aquatic Sciences and Fisheries.* 1958–1971.)

Archaeology
Art and Archaeology Technical Abstracts. 1966 to date. 1966 -.

Architecture
The Architectural Index. 1950 to date. 1950-.
Architectural Periodicals Index. 1972 to date. 1972-.
Avery Index to Architectural Periodicals. 1973.
Building Industry Technology. 1977 to date. 1977-.
Geodex System/A Retrieval System for Architectural Literature. 1977 to date. 1977-.

Art/Interior Design
Art Bibliographies, Modern. 1968 to date. 1968-.
Art in Life. 1965.
Art in Time. 1970.
Arts and Humanities Citation Index. 1977 to date. 1977-.
Design Index. 1982 to date. 1982-.
Illustration Index (Greer), 1963–1971. 1973.
Index to Art Periodicals. 1962.
RILA; International Repertory of the Literature of Art. 1975 to date. 1975-.

Astronomy
Astronomy and Astrophysics Abstracts. 1969 to date. 1969-.

Biography
Biography Index. 1946 to date. 1946-.
Index to Artistic Biography. 1973 to date. 1973-.

Biology
Biological Abstracts. 1926 to date. 1926-.
Bioresearch Index. 1967 to date. 1967-. (Continues *Bioresearch Titles.* nos. 1–12, 1965/66.)

Business
ABI/Inform. 1971 to date. 1971-. (Online and on CD-ROM)
Accountants' Index. 1921 to date. 1921-.
Accounting Articles. 1963 to date. 1963-.
Business Index. 1979 to date. 1979-.
Business Periodicals Index. 1958 to date. 1958-. (Continues *Industrial Arts Index.* 1913–1957.)
Consumers Index to Product Evaluations and Information Sources. 1973 to date. 1973-.
Index of Economic Articles, in Journals and Collective Volumes. 1966 to date. 1966-. (Continues *Index of Economic Journals.* 1886–1965.)
Key to Economic Science and Managerial Sciences. 1976 to date. 1976-. (Continues *Economic Abstracts.* 1953–1975.)
Personnel Management Abstracts. 1955 to date. 1955-.

Predicasts F & S Index: Europe. 1978 to date. 1978-.

Predicasts F & S Index: International. 1968 to date. 1968-.

Predicasts F & S Index: United States. 1979 to date. 1979-. (Continues *F & S Index of Corporations and Industries.* 1960–1978.)

Chemistry and Physics

Chemical Abstracts. 1907 to date. 1907-.

Electrical and Electronics Abstracts. 1966 to date. 1966-. (Continues *Science Abstracts.* 1898-.)

Physics Abstracts. 1941 to date. 1941-. (Continues *Science Abstracts.* 1898-.)

Criminology

Abstracts on Criminology and Penology. 1969–1979. (Continues *Excerpta Criminologica.* 1961–1968.)

Criminal Justice Abstracts. 1977 to date. 1977-. (Continues *Crime and Delinquency Literature.* 1968–1977.)

Criminal Justice Periodical Index. 1975 to date. 1975-.

Criminology and Penology Abstracts. 1980 to date. 1980-. (Continues *Abstracts on Criminology and Penology.* 1969–1979.)

Criminology Index. 1945–1972. 1975.

Index to Minorities and Criminal Justice: An Index to Periodicals and Books Relating to Minorities and Criminal Justice. 1981.

Police Science Abstracts. 1980 to date. 1980-. (Continues *Abstracts on Police Science.* 1973–1979.)

Ecology and Environment

Abstracts on Health Effects of Environmental Pollutants. 1972 to date. 1972-.

Chicorel Index to Environment and Ecology. 1975 to date. 1975-.

Ecological Abstracts. 1974 to date. 1974-.

Ecology Abstracts. 1980 to date. 1980-. (Continues *Applied Ecology Abstracts.* 1975–1979.)

Environment Index. 1971 to date. 1971-.

HydroAbstracts. 1980 to date. 1980-. (Continues *Selected Water Resources Abstracts.* 1968–1979.)

MER (Man, Environment Reference) Environmental Abstracts. 1974 to date. 1974-.

Pollution Abstracts. 1970 to date. 1970-.

Education

British Education Index. 1954 to date. 1954-.

Business Education Index. 1940 to date. 1940-.

Child Development Abstracts and Bibliography. 1927 to date. 1927-.

Current Index to Journals in Education. (CIJE). 1969 to date. 1969-. (Also on ERIC CD-Rom)

Developmental Disabilities Abstracts. 1977 to date. 1977-. (Continues *Mental Retardation and Developmental Disabilities Abstracts*)

Education Index. 1929 to date. 1929-.

Educational Administration Abstracts. 1969 to date. 1969-.

Exceptional Child Education Abstracts. 1969 to date. 1969-.

Higher Education Abstracts. 1984/85 to date. 1984/85-. (Continues *College Student Personnel Abstracts.* 1965/66–1983/84.)

Language Teaching. 1982 to date. 1982-. (Continues *Language Teaching Abstracts.* 1968–1974; *Language Teaching and Linguistics Abstracts.* 1975–1981.)

Resources in Education (ERIC). 1975 to date. 1975-. (Continues *Research in Education.* 1966–1974.)

State Education Journal Index. 1963/64 to date. 1963/64-.

Energy

The Energy Index. 1970/73 to date. 1970/73-.
Energy Information Abstracts. 1976 to date. 1976-.
Energy Research Abstracts. 1976 to date. 1976-. (Continues *ERDA*)
Energy Review. 1977 to date. 1977-.
Renewable Energy Bulletin. 1974 to date. 1974-.
Solar Energy Index. 1980.

Engineering

Computer and Control Abstracts. 1966 to date. 1966-.
Engineering Monthly Index. 1984 to date. 1984-.
Metals Abstracts. 1968 to date. 1968-.

Ethnology

Abstracts of Popular Culture. 1977/78–1982.
African Abstracts. 1950–1972. 1972.
Index to Black Periodicals. 1984 to date. 1984-. (Continues *Index to Periodical Articles By and About Blacks.* 1973- 1983.
Index to Literature on the American Indian. 1970–1973.
Index to Selected Periodicals Received in the Haller Q. Brown Library. 1950–1959.

Food Science and Technology

Food Science and Technology Abstracts. 1969 to date. 1969-.
Nutrition Abstracts and Reviews. 1931/32 to date. 1932-.

Forestry

Forestry Abstracts. 1939/40 to date. 1940-.

Genealogy

American Genealogical-Biographical Index. 1952 to date. 1952-.
Genealogical Periodical Annual Index. 1962 to date. 1962-.
An Index to Genealogical Periodical Literature. 1960–1977. 1979.

Genetics

Genetics Abstracts. 1968/69 to date. 1969-.

Geography

Bibliographie Geographique Internationale. 1891 to date. 1891-.
Current Geographical Publications. 1938–1978.
Geographical Abstracts. 1966–1971. 1986 to date. 1986-. (Continues *Geo Abstracts.* 1972–1985.)
A Guide to Geographic Periodicals. 1972.
A Tri-Index to Geography Periodicals. 1971.

Geology

Abstracts of North American Geology. 1966–1971. (Continues *GeoScience Abstracts.* 1959–1966.) Supersedes *Geological Abstracts.*
Bibliography and Index of Geology. 1969 to date. 1969-. (Continues *Bibliography and Index of Geology Exclusive of North America*)
Offshore Abstracts. 1974 to date. 1974-.
Petroleum Abstracts. 1961 to date. 1961-.

Health, Physical Education, and Recreation

Abstracts of Health Care Management Studies. 1978 to date. 1978-. (Continues *Abstracts of Hospital Management Studies.* 1964–1977.)
Abstracts on Hygiene and Communicable Diseases. 1981 to date. 1981-. (Continues *Abstracts on Hygiene* 1926–1980.)
Completed Research in Health, Physical Education, Recreation, and Dance. 1980 to date. 1980-. (Continues *Completed Research in Health, Physical Education, and Recreation.* 1959–1979.)
HPESR Abstracts. 1966/67 to date. 1967-.
Index and Abstracts of Foreign Physical Education Literature. 1955–1975.
Physical Education Index. 1978 to date. 1978-.

History

America: History and Life. 1964 to date. 1964-.
Combined Retrospective Index to Journals in History. 1838–1974. 1977.
Historical Abstracts. 1955 to date. 1955-.
Writings on American History. 1902 to date. 1904-.

Horticulture

Horticultural Abstracts. 1931 to date. 1931-.

Human Resources

Human Resources Abstracts. 1973 to date. 1973-. (Continues *Poverty and Human Resources Abstracts.* 1965–1972. 1972.)

Language and Literature

Abstracts of English Studies. 1958 to date. 1958-.
American Literature Abstracts. 1967–1972.
British Humanities Index. 1962 to date. 1962-. (Continues *Subject Index to Periodicals* 1920–1961.)
Humanities Index. 1974/75 to date. 1974/75-. (Continues *International Index.* 1907–1965 and *Social Sciences and Humanities Index.* 1965–1974.)
Internationale Bibliographie der Zeitschriftenliteratur. 1963–64 to date. 1965-.
LLBA, Linguistics and Language Abstracts. 1985 to date. 1985-. (Continues *Language and Language Behavior Abstracts.* 1967–1984.)
MLA Abstracts of Articles in Scholarly Journals. 1971 to date. 1971-.
MLA International Bibliography of Books and Articles on the Modern Languages and Literatures. 1921 to date. 1921-. (Also on WILSONDISC)

Latin America

Hispanic American Periodicals Index. 1975 to date. 1975-.
Index to Latin American Periodical Literature. 1929–1960. 8 vols. 1962. First Supplement. 1961–1965. 2 vols. 1968.
Index to Latin American Periodicals. 1961–1970. 1972.

Law
Index to Legal Periodicals. 1908 to date. 1908-. (Also on WILSONDISC)
Index to Periodical Articles Related to Law. 1958 to date. 1958-.

Library Science
Information Science Abstracts. 1969 to date. 1969-. (Continues *Documentation Abstracts.* 1966–1968.)
Library Literature. 1921/32 to date. 1934-. (Also on WILSONDISC)

Mathematics
Mathematical Reviews. 1940 to date. 1940-.

Medicine
Allergy Abstracts. 1937 to date. 1937-.
Birth Defects, Abstracts of Selected Articles. 1964–1970.
Current Awareness in Biological Sciences. 1983 to date. 1983-. (Continues *International Abstracts of Biological Sciences.* 1956–1982.)
Dental Abstracts. 1956 to date. 1956-.
Index Medicus. 1960 to date. 1960-.
Mental Retardation and Developmental Disability Abstracts. 1974 to date. 1974- (Continues *Mental Retardation Abstracts.* 1964–1973.)

Medieval Studies
International Guide to Medieval Studies. 1961–1973.

Meteorology
Meteorological and Geoastrophysical Abstracts. 1960 to date. 1960-. (Continues *Meteorological Abstracts and Bibliography.* 1950–1959.

Microbiology
Current Advances in Microbiology. 1984 to date. 1984–.
Microbiological Abstracts. 1965 to date. 1965-.

Military Science
Air University Library Index to Military Periodicals. 1963 to date. 1963-. (Continues *Air University Periodical Index.* 1949–1962.

Motion Pictures
Film Literature Index. 1973 to date. 1973-.
Film Review Digest. 1976 to date. 1976-.
International Index to Film Periodicals. 1972 to date. 1972-.
New York Times Film Reviews. 1913 to date. 1913-.
Retrospective Index to Film Periodicals. 1930–1971.

Music
Guide to the Musical Arts. 1953–1956. 1957.
Music Article Guide. 1966 to date. 1966-.
The Music Index. 1949 to date. 1949-.
Music Psychology Index. 1976 to date. 1976-. (Continues *Music Therapy Index.*)
Popular Music Periodicals Index. 1973–1976.
RILM Abstracts of Music Literature. 1967 to date. 1967-.

Mycology

Abstracts of Mycology. 1967 to date. 1967-.
Review of Plant Pathology. 1970 to date. 1970-. (Continues *Review of Applied Mycology.* 1922–1969.)

Nursing

Health Services Research. 1966 to date. 1966-.
Hospital Literature Index. 1957 to date. 1957-.
International Nursing Index. 1966 to date. 1966-.
Nursing and Allied Health. 1977 to date. 1977-. (Continues *Cumulative Index to Nursing and Allied Health Literature.* 1956–1976.)
Nursing Studies Index. 1970 to date. 1970-.

Oceanography

Oceanic Abstracts. 1972 to date. 1972-. (Continues *Oceanic Coordinate Index.* 1965–1967 and *Oceanic Citation Journal with Abstracts.* 1968–1971.)
Oceanographic Index. 1946–1971. 1971–1976.

Philosophy

Philosopher's Index. 1967 to date. 1967-.

Political Science

ABC Pol Sci, Advance Bibliography of Contents: Political Science and Government. 1969 to date. 1969-.
C.R.I.S.: the Combined Retrospective Index to Articles in Political Science, 1886–1974. 1977/1978.
International Bibliography of Political Science. 1953 to date. 1953-.
International Political Science Abstracts. 1951 to date. 1951-.

Population

Population Index. 1935 to date. 1935-.

Psychology

Psychological Abstracts. 1927 to date. 1927-.

Religion

Abstracts Islamica. 1926 to date. 1926-.
Catholic Periodical and Literature Index. 1967/68 to date. 1967/68-. (Continues *Catholic Periodical Index.* 1930–1966.)
Christian Periodical Index. 1958 to date. 1958-.
Guide to Social Science and Religion in Periodical Literature. 1970 to date. 1970-. (Continues *Guide to Religious and Semi-religious Periodicals.* 1964–1969.)
Index to Jewish Periodicals. 1963 to date. 1963-.
Quarterly Index Islamicus. 1977 to date. 1977-.
Religion Index One: Periodicals. 1978 to date. 1978-. (Continues *Index to Religious Periodical Literature.* 1949–1977.)
Religious and Theological Abstracts. 1958 to date. 1958-.
Southern Baptist Periodical Index. 1965–1984.

Science

Applied Mechanics Reviews. 1948 to date. 1948-.

Applied Science and Technology Index. 1958 to date. 1958-. (Continues *Industrial Arts Index.* 1913–1957.)

Computer Abstracts. 1957 to date. 1957-.

Current Contents: Agriculture, Biology and Environmental Science. 1973 to date. 1973-. (Continues *Current Contents: Agricultural, Food and Veterinary Sciences.*)

Current Technology Index. 1980 to date. 1980-.

General Science Index. 1978 to date. 1978-.

INIS Atomindex. 1970 to date. 1970-. (Continues *Nuclear Science Abstracts.* 1948–1970.)

Index to Scientific and Technical Proceedings. 1978 to date. 1978-.

Pollution Abstracts. 1970 to date. 1970-.

Science Citation Index. 1961 to date. 1961-.

Social Science

Social Sciences Citation Index. 1972 to date. 1973-.

Social Sciences Index. 1974 to date. 1974-. (Continues *International Index.* 1907–1965 and *Social Sciences and Humanities Index.* 1965–1974.)

Sociology

Index to Sociology Readers. 2 vols. 1960–1965.

International Bibliography of Sociology. 1952 to date. 1952-.

Sage Family Studies Abstracts. 1979 to date. 1979-.

Sage Urban Studies Abstracts. 1973 to date. 1973-.

Social Work Research and Abstracts. 1978 to date. 1978-. (Continues *Abstracts for Social Work.* 1965–1977.)

Sociological Abstracts. 1952 to date. 1952-.

World Agricultural Economics and Rural Sociology Abstracts. 1959 to date. 1959-.

Speech

DSH (Deafness, Speech, and Hearing) Abstracts. 1960 to date. 1960-.

Index to Journals in Communication Studies. 1975 to date. 1975-.

Speech Abstracts. 1970 to date. 1971-.

Speech Communication Abstracts. 1975–1978.

Statistics

American Statistics Index. 1973 to date. 1973-.

Statistical Reference Index. 1981 to date. 1981-.

Statistical Theory and Methods Abstracts. 1959 to date. 1959-.

Textiles

World Textile Abstracts. 1969 to date. 1969-. (Continues *Textile Abstracts.*)

Theater

Cumulated Dramatic Index. 1909–1949. 1965.

Guide to Dance Periodicals. 1931–1962. 1948–1963.

Guide to the Performing Arts. 1957 to date. 1960-.

Index to Plays in Periodicals. 1979.

The New York Times Theater Reviews. 1920/26–1970/71. 1971-.
Theater/Drama Abstracts. 1974 to date. 1974-. (Continues *Theatre/Drama/Speech Index*)

Traffic
Guide to Safety Literature. 1958 to date. 1958-.
Highway Safety Literature. 1973 to date. 1973-.

Urban Affairs
Housing and Planning References. 1965–1983. (Continues *Housing References.* 1961–1964.)
Land Use Planning Abstracts. 1974 to date. 1974-.
Project Reference File. 1971 to date. 1971-.
Urban Affairs Abstracts. 1971 to date. 1971-.
Urban Mass Transportation Abstracts. 1972 to date. 1972-.

Virology
Virology Abstracts. 1967 to date. 1967-.

Vocational Education
T & D Abstracts. 1975 to date. 1975-. (Continues *CIRF Abstracts.* 1961–1974.)

Women
Resources in Women's Educational Equity. 1977 to date. 1977-.
Women Studies Abstracts. 1972 to date. 1972-.

Zoology
Keyword Index to Wildlife Research. 1974 to date. 1974-.
Wildlife Review. 1952 to date. 1952-.
Zoological Record. 1864 to date. 1864-.

REVIEW QUESTIONS
CHAPTER 8

1. Give three reasons why periodical materials are important sources for research.

2. List the different kinds of indexes.

3. What is the difference in scope between a periodical index and a newspaper index?

4. How does an abstract differ from a periodical index?

5. Which type of index indexes only articles in books?

6. Most periodical indexes are issued cumulatively. What does this mean?

7. What is the difference between a book review and a literary criticism?

8. Can book reviews be located through periodical indexes? Justify your answer.

9. What is the purpose of a citation index?

10. How does one locate periodical articles in the library after the information has been found in an index?

PERIODICAL INDEX PRACTICE SHEET

ARTHRITIS
    See also
    Lyme disease
                Therapy
    Arthritis relief [use of hydroxychloroquine and sul-
    fasalazine to slow rheumatoid arthritis] il *Prevention
    (Emmaus, Pa.)* 41:8+ O '89
    Arthritis: what works [excerpt] D. Sobel and A. C. Klein.
    il *Good Housekeeping* 209:138-9+ O '89
    For arthritis, try fitness. il *Prevention (Emmaus, Pa.)*
    41:10+ S '89
ARTHROPODS, FOSSIL
    The early radiation and relationships of the major ar-
    thropod groups. D. E. G. Briggs and R. A. Fortey.
    bibl f il *Science* 246:241-3 O 13 '89
ARTHUR, PAUL
    The place is the thing. il *USA Today (Periodical)* 118:93
    N '89
    Voices from the underground. il *USA Today (Periodical)*
    118:33 S '89
ARTHURIAN ROMANCES
              Adaptations
    A Connecticut Yankee in hell [work of M. Twain] J.
    Kaplan. il *American Heritage* 40:97-102+ N '89
    Crossway's crossover novelist [S. Lawhead's Arthurian
    saga] B. Summer. il por *Publishers Weekly* 236:28+
    O 6 '89
ARTICLES FOR PERIODICALS *See* Periodical articles
ARTIFACTS, INDIAN (AMERICAN) *See* Indians of North
    America—Antiquities
ARTIFACTS, PROTECTION OF *See* Cultural property—
    Protection
ARTIFICIAL BODY PARTS *See* Prosthesis
ARTIFICIAL BONE *See* Bone, Artificial
ARTIFICIAL CHROMOSOMES *See* Chromosomes, Artifi-
    cial
ARTIFICIAL FERTILIZATION IN VITRO *See* Fertiliza-
    tion in vitro
ARTIFICIAL FOOD *See* Food, Artificial
ARTIFICIAL FUR *See* Fur, Artificial
ARTIFICIAL INSEMINATION
        See also
    Ova—Transplantation
ARTIFICIAL INSEMINATION, HUMAN
        See also
    Surrogate mothers
    Single mothers by choice. J. Seligmann. il *Newsweek*
    114 Special Issue:40+ Wint '89/Spr '90
ARTIFICIAL INTELLIGENCE
        See also
    Expert systems (Computers)
    IntelliCorp Inc.
    Natural language processing
    Neural network computers
    Symbolics Inc.
    Artificial intelligence [careers] D. P. Wash. il *Occupational
    Outlook Quarterly* 33:2-7 Summ '89
    The intelligence transplant. M. L. Minsky. il por *Discover*
    10:52-6+ O '89
    Manufacturing intelligence [smart factories] P. Wallich.
    il *Scientific American* 261:100+ D '89
    A Pandora's box of minds, machines and metaphysics
    [views of R. Penrose] A. K. Dewdney. il *Scientific
    American* 261:140+ D '89
             Conferences
    Wires that think [International Joint Conference on Artifi-
    cial Intelligence] P. Wallich. *Scientific American* 261:20
    N '89

Figure 8.25. Entries from *Readers' Guide to Periodical Literature.* (Copyright 1990 by the H. W. Wilson Company. Material reproduced by permission of the publisher.)

Answer the following questions based upon the entries taken from *Readers' Guide to Periodical Literature*. You will need to consult the front section of *Reader's Guide* for the "Key to Abbreviations" and the "Titles of the Periodicals" used in the entries.

1. What subject do you use to locate additional information on arthritis? _____

2. Who wrote the article on fossil anthropods? _____

3. Did the authors include a list of sources in the article? _____

   If so, what indicates this? _____

4. List some author entries: _____

5. In which magazines can you locate some articles on adaptations of Arthurian romances? _____

   _____

6. How many of the articles are illustrated? _____

7. To locate articles in popular magazines on artificial chromosomes, what subject would you use in

   Readers' Guide? _____

8. Which periodicals contain articles on arthritis? _____

9. In which periodicals can you locate articles on artificial intelligence? _____

10. What do you consult in your library to locate call numbers of magazines and journals? _____

11. What does the 8+ mean in the first entry under the subject "Arthritis"? _____

12. Who wrote the article on surrogate mothers? _____

13. To read this article, what search strategy would you use in your library? _____

_____

14. To locate periodical articles on Indian artifacts, which subject would you find it under in *Readers' Guide*? _____

15. Arrange the last entry in correct bibliographical form:

ESSAY AND GENERAL LITERATURE INDEX EXERCISE

The Essay and General Literature Index is an index to materials in anthologies. Consult the index for information on your topic or another subject you may select. After you have found your reference, answer the following questions:

1. What was the call number of the *Essay and General Literature Index?*

2. Give the date of the volume used.

3. Complete subject heading under which you located your topic.

4. Analyze the reference you located by giving the following information:

   a.   Author of the article

   b.   Title of the article

   c.   Did the book have an author or an editor? Circle one or the other and record the name.

   d.   Name of the book in which the article appears

e. Pages in the book in which the article appears

f. Place, publisher, and copyright or publication date of the book

5. Does the library own the book? If so, what is the call number?

6. Write a bibliographic reference to the article you have found. Use the form in the textbook p. 317, I.J. for citing an essay in a collection or an anthology.

7. Would this book be a good reference for your topic? Justify your answer. (Use back of sheet if necessary.)

BOOK REVIEW EXERCISE

Locate a review of a book on a topic on which you are doing research or a book you have read recently. Book reviews may be obtained from *Book Review Digest, Book Review Index* or any other book review source. Choose one of the reviews listed and answer the following questions:

1. Name and date of the book review source used

2. Call number of the book review source

3. Analyze one reference you found by giving the following information:

    a. Author of book selected

    b. Title of the book

    c. Author of review (If unsigned, mark NA.)

    d. Source in which the review appears:

        (1) Complete title of the magazine or journal _____

        (2) Volume _____

        (3) Pages _____

        (4) Date _____

        (5) No. of Words in review _____

4. Call number of the magazine or journal in which the review appears

5. How many other references to reviews were given?

6. Write a bibliographic reference to the review using one of the forms given in the textbook pp.320–321, III.G, H, or I.

7. Read the complete review. Is this a book which you would find useful when doing research on your topic? Justify your answer.

LITERARY CRITICISM EXERCISE

Using an index to literary criticism, locate a reference to a criticism of a novel, poem, play, or short story that you have read. Locate the criticism, read it, and complete the answer sheet below:

1. Title of the index used:

2. Procedures used to locate the index:

3. Author of the literary work you selected:

4. Title of the literary work you selected:

5. Author and title of the source in which the criticism appears:

6. Place, publisher, and date of the source if a book; if a periodical, give the date and volume of the periodical and the pages on which it appears:

7. Call number of the book or periodical in which the criticism appears:

8. Write a bibliographical citation for the criticism you found:

9. Do you agree or disagree with the critic's assessment of the work? Justify your answer.

PERIODICAL INDEX EXERCISE

Locate two different periodical indexes or abstracts which have references to articles on your topic. Consult the flow-chart on page 225 for help in locating materials. Give the following information:

First periodical index:

1. Method used to find the index

2. Entry used in library catalog to locate information (if applicable)

3. Call number of index

4. Title of Index

5. What are the subjects covered in the index?

6. How is the index arranged? (alphabetically or by broad topics?)

7. Subject heading used in index for an article on your topic

8. Citation to the article as it appeared in index

9. Over each part of the above citation label these parts:

   (1) author   (2) title of article   (3) title of journal

   (4) volume   (5) date of issue   (6) pages of article

   (Use numbers to label each.)

10. Full title of periodical

11. Call number of periodical

12. Is the issue of the periodical cited in question 8 available in your library? If so, where is it located?

Bibliographic Citation:

Second periodical index:

1. Method used to find the index

2. Entry used in library catalog to locate information (if applicable)

3. Call number of index

4. Title of index

5. What are the subjects covered in the index?

6. How is the index arranged? (alphabetically or by broad topics?)

7. Subject heading used in index for an article on your topic

8. Citation to the article as it appeared in index

9. Over each part of the above citation label these parts:

    (1) author   (2) title of article   (3) title of journal

    (4) volume   (5) date of issue   (6) pages of article

    (Use numbers to label each.)

10. Full title of periodical

11. Call number of periodical

12. Is the issue of the periodical cited in question 8 available in your library? If so, where is it located?

Bibliographic Citation:

Guide to
Government Publications

A PREVIEW

Government publications constitute a major component of the library's resources, and virtually any information search can be enhanced by their use. This chapter provides a guide to the kinds of information available from international, federal, state, and local governmental units.

In the United States it is an elementary—but all important— principle that the operations of government are to be open to scrutiny and criticism by citizens This kind of uninhibited criticism makes it possible for citizens to participate in government and to contribute to the advancement of society. Indeed, the American political system, and to a large extent, the education system, rests on the widespread acceptance of ready and fair access to information about government and information produced by government. It is this principle which has led local, state, national, and even international governing bodies to produce large quantities of all sorts of information. In fact, in the United States, government agencies are the most prolific suppliers of information. The amount of information produced each year by the various levels of government is thought to be twice that of commercial publishers. The Federal government alone produces more than 20,000 different publications each year. Add to that the publications of various city, county, state, and international agencies and the result is an enormous body of literature.

Aside from the intrinsic value of contributing to an informed citizenry, government publications have a number of distinctive characteristics which add to their value as reference sources.

1. *Volume and diversity.* As we can infer from the discussion above, government publications provide a large amount of information covering a broad spectrum of subjects. Since the government is necessarily responsive to public needs, the subjects covered in government publications range from those that are useful only to scholars and specialists in a field to those which are of interest to the masses.

2. *Ready availability.* Because the government is not in the publishing business for profit, government publications are inexpensive or, in many cases, free of charge. One can write or call government agencies to acquire many of the publications. However, this is usually not necessary since most government publications can be found in libraries. It is common practice

for governmental bodies to place their publications in libraries in order to make government information available to all citizens.

3. *Primary sources of information.* Much of the information disseminated by the government is considered to be a primary source. Statistics, for example, which are gathered first-hand fit into this category. The decennial census published by the U.S. Bureau of the Census is the result of an actual door-to-door count of U.S. citizens.

4. *Free of bias.* The individuals who work for government agencies are not supposed to represent a particular viewpoint, a particular political party, or a special interest group; as a result, government information is generally considered to be objective.

5. *Up-to-date information.* Since the government is the primary source for much of the information which appears in non-government publications, information from a government source is often more current than that in a non-government publication.

6. *Only source of information on many topics.* Much of the information available from governmental agencies is not available from any other source. For example, the Federal government is the sole provider of information on the amounts of toxic air releases by various industries; the state government is the unique source for expenditures on state services.

Even with all its advantages and its ready availability government publications are frequently overlooked as a source of information, primarily because potential users are unaware of their existence. Government publications are frequently kept in a separate area in the library although they may be cataloged along with the other materials in the library's general collection. This chapter is designed to serve as a guide for locating government publications. The emphasis is on U.S. Federal government publications, which are more numerous than those of the other entities; there are brief introductions to local, state, and United Nations documents.

UNITED STATES GOVERNMENT PUBLICATIONS

The Federal government is the single largest producer of information in the world. The information sources from the United States government are as varied as they are numerous. They come in all sizes and shapes—from one-page leaflets to works of several thousand pages and many volumes. They vary in scope from highly technical scientific research reports to popular pamphlets on such topics as diets for weight loss and caring for pets. Included in government publications are all the official documents such as laws, regulations, court decisions, presidential documents, treaties, congressional proceedings, military records, and census reports. The government issues a large number of reference books including indexes, abstracts, bibliographies, directories, atlases, handbooks, yearbooks, and almanacs. Approximately 1200 government periodicals are published on a regular basis.

The format of government information is almost as varied as its scope. While many government publications are available in traditional paper format, a large volume of the information is issued on microfiche and other audio/visual media. Audio/visual materials available from the Federal government include film, video and cassette tapes, photographs, maps, charts, and posters. The Federal government has been a leader in utilizing new technologies to produce, store, and retrieve information. The Library of Congress, a government agency, was the first library in the world to institute an automated catalog system; online databases such as that from the National Library of Medicine have been available since the early 1970s. Much of the information coming from the Federal government is now in electronic format—either online, on magnetic tapes, or on CD-ROM.

Depository Libraries

Most United States government publications are issued by the Government Printing Office (GPO) which was established in 1861. Prior to that time the official documents of the U.S. government were printed by private firms. Consequently, we have historical documents published by authority of the Federal government dating back to the Continental Congress. The GPO publishes all the official documents of the legislative, executive, and judicial branches of the Federal government—the congressional debates, laws, executive orders, annual reports, court decisions, regulations, reports, and special studies.

In 1895, Congress enacted legislation which provided for the free distribution of documents to designated libraries and institutions. The libraries receiving documents free of charge from the GPO are called depository libraries. Today there are over 1300 depository libraries in the United States. Of these, about 50 are regional depository libraries which receive all the publications distributed by GPO. Other libraries are selective depositories, so designated because they can choose the items which they wish to receive. The depository library provides the facilities for housing documents and the staff needed to administer the collections. The only other obligations of the depository library are to assure that the materials are cared for according to guidelines established by the GPO and to make the documents available to all citizens.

Library users should inquire whether there is a depository library at their institution or in the area in order to take advantage of the full spectrum of U.S. government publications.

Finding Government Documents

Most depository libraries house documents in a separate area arranged by Superintendent of Documents (SuDocs) number. The SuDocs system is an alphanumeric system based on the agency which issues the document. (For a full explanation of the SuDocs classification system, see Chapter 4.) Even though documents are shelved in a separate area, it is not unusual to find them listed in the online catalog with other library materials. However, most online catalogs contain only records of items cataloged since 1976 when GPO began creating machine readable catalog (MARC) records. Figure 9.1 illustrates how to locate documents which are shelved by SuDocs number.

Finding Aids—General

To locate government publications which are shelved by the SuDocs call number and are *not* listed in the library catalog, one must consult one of the finding aids available with the collection. The major finding aid for government publications is the *Monthly Catalog of United States Government Publications* (Washington: GPO, 1895-). The *Monthly Catalog* is the comprehensive index to government publications. It is issued each month, and has semiannual, annual, and quinquennial indexes. The bibliographic entries are arranged alphabetically by issuing agency in the main body of the catalog. Each issue contains separate

Figure 9.1. Instructions for locating a U. S. Government publication.

How to find a U.S. Government Publication

As a Federal Depository Library, we receive many publications issued by agencies of the U.S. Government. These publications, which may include books, maps, posters, pamphlets, and periodicals, contain information on careers, business opportunities, space exploration, health and nutrition, energy, and many other subjects.

Federal Government publications in this collection are arranged by the Superintendent of Documents classification number. Publications are grouped together by issuing agency.* To ensure that you find all of the materials available on a particular subject, be sure to check the indexes recommended by the librarian.

The example below shows how the Superintendent of Documents classification number C 61.34:987 is constructed for the publication *U.S. Industrial Outlook:*

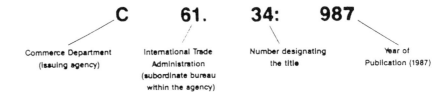

C	**61.**	**34:**	**987**
Commerce Department (Issuing agency)	International Trade Administration (subordinate bureau within the agency)	Number designating the title	Year of Publication (1987)

Here are the prefixes from the Superintendent of Documents classification numbers for some other agencies that you may be interested in:

A	Agriculture Department
C 3.	Census Bureau (Commerce Department)
D	Defense Department
E	Energy Department
ED	Education Department
GA	General Accounting Office
GS	General Services Administration
HE	Health and Human Services Department
I	Interior Department
I 19.	U.S. Geological Survey (Interior Department)
J	Justice Department
Ju	Judiciary
L	Labor Department
LC	Library of Congress
NAS	National Aeronautics and Space Administration
S	State Department
SI	Smithsonian Institution
T 22.	Internal Revenue Service (Treasury Department)
X, Y	Congress
Y 4.	Congressional Committees .

indexes for subjects, titles, title keywords, authors, series reports, contract numbers, stock numbers, and SuDocs numbers. Figure 9.2 shows an entry from the *Monthly Catalog's* subject index found at the end of the catalog. The bibliographic entry for the publication listed in the index entry is shown in Figure 9.3.

Since 1976, the Government Printing Office has been creating the *Monthly Catalog* from the same MARC records. Prior to this, the bibliographic entries in

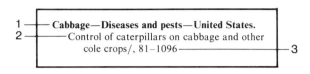

1 — **Cabbage—Diseases and pests—United States.**
2 — Control of caterpillars on cabbage and other cole crops/, 81–1096 — 3

Figure 9.2. Excerpt from subject index in *Monthly Catalog.*

Explanation:

1. Subject heading.
2. Title of document.
3. Entry number (refers to location of entry in the main body of the catalog).

Figure 9.3. Monthly Catalog of United States Government Publications.

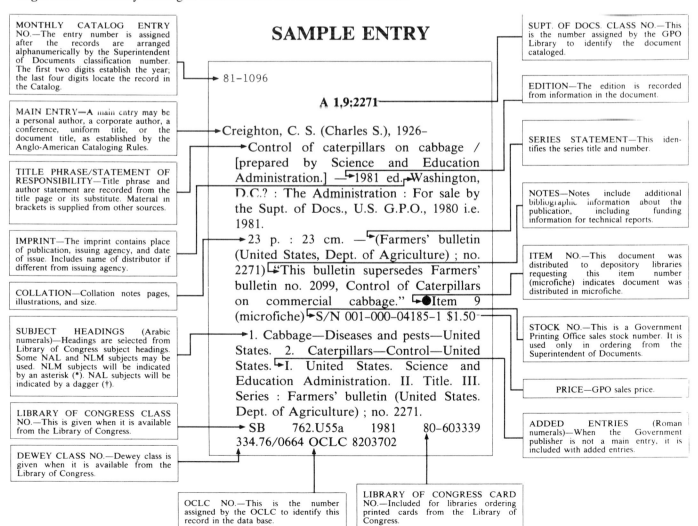

SAMPLE ENTRY

MONTHLY CATALOG ENTRY NO.—The entry number is assigned after the records are arranged alphanumerically by the Superintendent of Documents classification number. The first two digits establish the year; the last four digits locate the record in the Catalog.

MAIN ENTRY—A main entry may be a personal author, a corporate author, a conference, uniform title, or the document title, as established by the Anglo-American Cataloging Rules.

TITLE PHRASE/STATEMENT OF RESPONSIBILITY—Title phrase and author statement are recorded from the title page or its substitute. Material in brackets is supplied from other sources.

IMPRINT—The imprint contains place of publication, issuing agency, and date of issue. Includes name of distributor if different from issuing agency.

COLLATION—Collation notes pages, illustrations, and size.

SUBJECT HEADINGS (Arabic numerals)—Headings are selected from Library of Congress subject headings. Some NAL and NLM subjects may be used. NLM subjects will be indicated by an asterisk (*). NAL subjects will be indicated by a dagger (†).

LIBRARY OF CONGRESS CLASS NO.—This is given when it is available from the Library of Congress.

DEWEY CLASS NO.—Dewey class is given when it is available from the Library of Congress.

SUPT. OF DOCS. CLASS NO.—This is the number assigned by the GPO Library to identify the document cataloged.

EDITION—The edition is recorded from information in the document.

SERIES STATEMENT—This identifies the series title and number.

NOTES—Notes include additional bibliographic information about the publication, including funding information for technical reports.

ITEM NO.—This document was distributed to depository libraries requesting this item number (microfiche) indicates document was distributed in microfiche.

STOCK NO.—This is a Government Printing Office sales stock number. It is used only in ordering from the Superintendent of Documents.

PRICE—GPO sales price.

ADDED ENTRIES (Roman numerals)—When the Government publisher is not a main entry, it is included with added entries.

81–1096

A 1,9:2271

Creighton, C. S. (Charles S.), 1926-
Control of caterpillars on cabbage / [prepared by Science and Education Administration.] —1981 ed. Washington, D.C.? : The Administration : For sale by the Supt. of Docs., U.S. G.P.O., 1980 i.e. 1981.
23 p. : 23 cm. —(Farmers' bulletin (United States, Dept. of Agriculture) ; no. 2271) "This bulletin supersedes Farmers' bulletin no. 2099, Control of Caterpillars on commercial cabbage." Item 9 (microfiche) S/N 001-000-04185-1 $1.50
1. Cabbage—Diseases and pests—United States. 2. Caterpillars—Control—United States. I. United States. Science and Education Administration. II. Title. III. Series : Farmers' bulletin (United States. Dept. of Agriculture) ; no. 2271.
SB 762.U55a 1981 80-603339
334.76/0664 OCLC 8203702

OCLC NO.—This is the number assigned by the OCLC to identify this record in the data base.

LIBRARY OF CONGRESS CARD NO.—Included for libraries ordering printed cards from the Library of Congress.

the *Monthly Catalog* contained less detail than in the post-1976 editions. Usually there was only a subject/corporate author index. Figures 9.4 and 9.5 are examples of an index entry and a bibliographic record from a pre-1976 *Monthly Catalog*.

To locate government documents by using the *Monthly Catalog*, one would proceed as follows:

1. Select the appropriate year for the information.
2. Look in the index section under the appropriate heading to find the entry number.
3. Locate the entry number in the bibliographic section of the catalog.
4. Copy all pertinent information: author, title, issuing agency, date, and call number.
5. Locate the document by its *SuDocs* call number on the depository library shelf, or give the call number to a library page if the documents stacks are closed.

Figure 9.4.   Subject index.

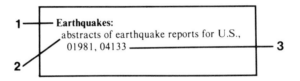

Explanation:

1. Subject heading.
2. Title of document.
3. Entry number.

Figure 9.5.   Main entry section of the catalog.

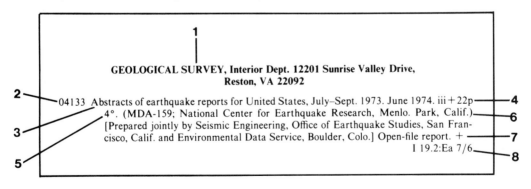

Explanation:

1. Issuing agency.
2. Entry number.
3. Title.
4. Pagination (3 preliminary pages + 22 pages of text).
5. Code number describing its size.
6. Imprint.
7. + indicates that the item is distributed by the issuing agency.
8. Superintendent of Documents call number or SuDocs number.

The edition of the *Monthly Catalog* described below is available on microfilm. It comes with its own viewing machines.

Government Documents Catalog Subscription. Pomona, CA: Autographics, 1976-. Microfilm. Updated monthly.

Gives author/title records in one section and subjects in another. Each entry gives full bibliographic information. The microfilm reader has large format print and is easy to use.

The *Monthly Catalog* from 1976 to date, is available online through DIALOG and BRS. (See Chapter 10.) The advantage of searching the online database is that it is possible to locate documents by combining terms and searching keywords in a way that is not possible in the printed or microfilm versions. The online database is more up-to-date than the printed or microfilm editions of the *Monthly Catalog*.

CD-ROM versions of the *Monthly Catalog* are available from several vendors including Autographics, Inc.; Information Access Co.; Marcive, Inc.; and Silverplatter. The Autographics and Marcive versions include the records since 1976 and offer the same advantages of keyword searching as the online databases. The *InfoTrac* database (Information Access Co.) available on CD-ROM provides a subject access only and includes the records from 1979 to the present. Figures 9.6–9.8 show a keyword search in the Marcive version of the Monthly Catalog on CD-ROM.

The catalog records from the Government Printing Office are entered into the OCLC database and can be retrieved by libraries which have access to OCLC bibliographic utilities. Government publications in the OCLC database are searchable by author, title, and SuDocs number.

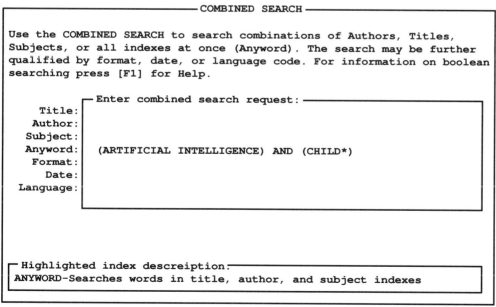

```
─────────────────── COMBINED SEARCH ───────────────────

Use the COMBINED SEARCH to search combinations of Authors, Titles,
Subjects, or all indexes at once (Anyword). The search may be further
qualified by format, date, or language code. For information on boolean
searching press [F1] for Help.

               ┌─ Enter combined search request: ──────────
     Title:    │
    Author:    │
   Subject:    │
   Anyword:    │  (ARTIFICIAL INTELLIGENCE) AND (CHILD*)
    Format:    │
      Date:    │
  Language:    │
               │
               │
               └──────────────────────────────────────────

┌─ Highlighted index descreiption:──────────────────────
│ ANYWORD-Searches words in title, author, and subject indexes
└───────────────────────────────────────────────────────

-Change Index [ENTER]-Search
WAITING FOR INPUT
```

Figure 9.6. Keyword search combining artificial intelligence and child* (truncation for children, etc.) Reprinted from the GPO CAT/PAC CD-ROM database, courtesy of Marcive, Inc. San Antonio, TX 78265.

Figure 9.7.   Results of
search in Figure 9.6.

```
┌─ COMBINED SEARCH: ANY-(ARTIFICIAL INTELLIGENCE) AND (CHILD*) ──┐
│                    ─── TITLE LIST ───                          │
│                                                                │
│                                                                │
│  SEARCHING FOR:            WORD    PREVIOUS      RESULT         │
│     ARTIFICIAL             525                                  │
│     INTELLIGENCE           1609      525           45           │
│     CHILD                  1496                                 │
│     CHILD                   0       1496          1496          │
│     CHILDBEARING            0         6             6           │
│     CHILDBIRTH              6        39            43           │
│     CHILDCARE              43         1            44           │
│     CHILDCRAFT             44         1            45           │
│     CHILDERN               45         1            46           │
│     CHILDERS               46        16            62           │
│     CHILDERSBURG           62         2            64           │
│     CHILDHOOD            1496       164          1620           │
│     CHILDLESSNESS          64         2            66           │
│     CHILDREARING           66         1            67           │
│     CHILDREN                                                    │
│                                                                │
└────────────────────────────────────────────────────────────────┘
```

```
-Move highlight [ENTER]-Select PgUp,PgDn-Page Home-Beginning End-End
 F1-Help F2-Jump F5-Browse F6-Save F7-Print F9-Back F10- Main menu
PROCESSING REQUEST
```

Most of the finding aids listed in Figures 9.7 and 9.8, except the GPO issued version of the Monthly Catalog, contain only the records for documents
cataloged since 1976. For access to retrospective documents listed in the *Monthly Catalog* one should consult:

*Cumulative Subject Index to the Monthly Catalog of the U.S. Government Publi-
cations, 1900–1971.* Comp. William Buchanan and Edna M. Kanely. 15
vols. Washington: Carrollton, 1973.

> This publication cites the document under the subject, then gives the
> year and page (or entry number) of the *Monthly Catalog* in which it is
> found.

Other general finding aids are:

Andriot, John L. *Guide to U.S. Government Publications.* McLean, VA: Documents Index, 1959-. Annual.

> A list of all the GPO serial publications. Published as *Guide to U.S.
> Government Serials and Periodicals* from 1959 until 1972. Beginning in
> 1973 the name changed to present title and the contents were revised and
> enlarged. The main body of the work is an annotated list of classes. Includes
> agency and title indexes and an Agency Class Chronology.

*List of Classes of United States Government Publications Available for Selection
by Depository Libraries.* Washington: GPO, 1953-. Semiannual.

> Provides a listing by classification number of documents currently avail-
> able. Useful as a finding tool for series. Includes an alphabetical listing of
> government authors and a list of discontinued documents.

Publications Reference File (PRF). Washington: GPO, Current. Bimonthly.
(Microfiche)

> An index on microfiche to the publications currently available for sale
> from the GPO. Used to identify current government publications. Informa-

Figure 9.8.   Record display from search in Figure 9.6.

```
┌─COMBINED SEARCH: ANY-(ARTIFICIAL INTELLIGENCE) AND (CHILD*) ──────┐
├─TITLE:Final report: artificial intelligence applications in special educa┘
│──────────────── CATALOG RECORD DISPLAY ───────────────
    LOCATION/CALL #: ED 1.310/2: 284402
            AUTHOR: Hofmeister, Alan M.
             TITLE: Final report: artificial intelligence applications in
                    special education: how feasible? / principal investigator
                    Alan M. Hofmeister, co-principal investigator Joseph M.
                    Ferrara.
  PUBLICATION INFO: [Logan, Utah] : Utah State University, [1986]
     PHYSICAL DESC: iii, 144 leaves : ill. ; 28 cm
              NOTE: "Funded by Special Education Programs, U.S. Department of
                    Education."
              NOTE: Distributed to depository libraries in microfiche.
              NOTE: "June 1986."
              NOTE: Includes bibliographical references.
              NOTE: "Grant #G008400650."
           SUBJECT: Artificial intelligence - Educational applications.
           SUBJECT: Handicapped children - United States - Identification -
                    Data processing.
```

```
-Scroll  PgUp,PgDn-Page  --Previous record  +-Next record
F1-Help F6-Save F7-Print F9-Back F10- Main menu
WAITING FOR INPUT
```

tion can be searched by title, keyword, subject, agency, SuDocs class number, or GPO stock number.

Finding Aids—Special Types of Government Publications

The numerous bibliographic tools which access government publications attest to the complexity of accessing the myriad of information which the Federal government produces. The following is a selected list of finding aids for special types of publications:

American Statistics Index: A Comprehensive Guide and Index to the Statistical Publications of the U.S. Government. (ASI/Index). Washington: Congressional Information Service, 1973-. Monthly with annual cumulations.

Comprehensive index to statistics which appear in publications of the Federal government. Published in two volumes—an index volume listing subjects and titles alphabetically and an abstract volume arranged by issuing agency. Available online through DIALOG. CD-ROM version also available. (Figure 9.9–9.10 show excerpts from the ASI/Index.)

Congressional Information Services Index to Publications of the United States Congress. (CIS/Index). Washington: Congressional Information Service, 1970-.

A basic guide to Congressional actions. Part I provides brief abstracts of committee hearings, committee prints, House and Senate documents and reported bills, public laws, and miscellaneous publications of the U.S. Congress. Part II is a subject, name, and title index. Available online through DIALOG. CD-ROM version also available.

Government Reports Announcements and Index. Washington: National Technical Information Service, 1970-. Bimonthly.

The spectrum of government documents includes a large number of publications which do not come under the aegis of the Federal depository system. These include all the research by private contractors which is funded by Federal agencies. The National Technical Information Service (NTIS) serves as a clearinghouse for government funded research as well as for many other nondepository publications by Federal agencies. The *Government Reports Announcements and Index* (GRAI) is a guide to government research available through NTIS. The reports are arranged by subject fields which are primarily scientific, but there is a subject field for the "Behavioral and Social Sciences." The indexes are by keywords, personal authors, corporate authors, contract/grant numbers, and NTIS order/report numbers. There is a CD-ROM version of the GRAI database. It is also available online from DIALOG and BRS.

U.S. Dept. of Energy. Technical Information Center. *Energy Research Abstracts.* Oak Ridge, Tenn.: 1976-. Semimonthly.

An index with abstracts to the scientific and technical reports, journal articles, conference papers, proceedings, patents, etc. from the DOE or its contractors. Includes reports from foreign sources. Available online through DIALOG.

Government Periodicals

There are several ways to locate titles of United States government periodicals. Prior to 1976, the February issue of the *Monthly Catalog* listed government periodicals alphabetically by title. Since 1976 periodicals are listed in *The Monthly Catalog, Serial Supplement*, 1976-. Periodical titles are also found in Andriot's *Guide to U.S. Government Publications*. To find articles in government periodicals, the library user should consult:

Index to U.S. Government Periodicals, a Computer-Generated Guide to 180 Selected Titles by Author and Subject. Chicago: Infordata International, 1970-. Quarterly with annual cumulations.

An author/subject guide to articles in selected periodicals published by the U.S. government. The list of periodicals indexed includes SuDocs call numbers. Available online through DIALOG.

Retrospective Indexes

Some useful indexes available to find the older publications of the Congress and other governmental agencies are listed below in chronological order by the beginning date of coverage.

Poore, Ben Perley. *A Descriptive Catalogue of the Government Publications of the United States, September 5, 1775–March 4, 1881.* Washington: GPO, 1885. (48th Cong. 2nd sess. Misc. S. doc. 67.)

First attempt to compile a list of all government publications. Arrangement is chronological.

CIS/U.S. Serial Set Index, 1789–1969. Washington: Congressional Information Service, 1975.

Indexes House and Senate documents and reports which are published in the *Serial Set* and the *American State Papers*. The *Serial Set* is a compilation of Congressional reports and documents beginning in 1817. Prior to

1817, Congressional reports and documents were published as the *American State Papers.*

Cumulative Title Index to United States Public Documents, 1789–1976. Comp. Daniel W. Lester, Sandra K. Faull, and Lorraine E. Lester. 16 vols. Arlington, Va.: United States Historical Documents Institute, 1979–1983.

An alphabetical listing of the titles of publications in the Public Documents Library of the Government Printing Office.

Greely, Adolphus Washington. *Public Documents of the First to the Fourteenth Congress, Supplemented by a List of All Official Journals, Documents, and Reports of the First Fourteen Congresses 1789–1817, Papers Relating to Early Congressional Documents.* Washington: GPO, 1900. (56th Cong. 1st sess. S. doc. 428.)

Arranged chronologically by Congress followed by a name index. Does not have subject access.

U.S. Superintendent of Documents. *Checklist of United States Public Documents 1789–1909. Congressional: to Close of 60th Congress. Departmental: to Close of Calendar Year 1909. Vol. 1. List of Congressional and Departmental Publications.* 3rd ed. rev. and enl. Washington: GPO, 1911.

A reproduction of the shelf list of the Public Documents Library. Arranged in three sections: Congressional publications by serial number, department publications by SuDocs classification number, and miscellaneous publications by classification number.

———. *Tables and Annotated Index to the Congressional Series of United States Public Documents.* Washington: GPO, 1902.

Lists publications of the 15th to the 52nd Congresses, 1817–1893. Gives Congressional series in one section and subject/name index in the second section.

Ames, John Griffith. *Comprehensive Index to the Publications of the United States Government, 1881–1893.* 2nd ed. Washington: GPO, 1905. (58th cong. 2nd sess. H. doc. 754.)

Ames' index was intended to pickup where Poore's left off. It is alphabetically arranged by subject and has a personal name index at the end of volume 2.

U.S. Superintendent of Documents. *Catalog to the Public Documents of the 53rd to 76th Congress and All Departments of the Government of the United States for the Period from March 4, 1893 to Dec. 31, 1940.* 25 vols. Washington: GPO, 1896–1945.

An author/subject index to government documents for the period covered. Includes proclamations, executive orders, and periodicals.

———. *Index to the Reports and Documents of the 54th Congress, 1st Session to 72nd Congress, 2nd Session, December 2, 1895-March 4, 1933, with Numerical Lists and Schedule of Volumes.* 43 vols. Washington: GPO, 1897–1933.

An alphabetical listing by subject of congressional documents and reports.

Figure 9.9. Reprinted from *American Statistics Index, 1989, Annua*l, Index Voulme, through the courtesy of Congressional Information Service, Bethesda, MD.

Index by Subjects and Names

Fed Govt computer systems with sensitive info, and plans submitted to oversight agencies, by agency, 1989, GAO rpt, 26125-34

Computer software
see Computer industry and products

Computer use
Air Force fiscal mgmt system operations and techniques, quarterly rpt, 3602-1

Air traffic control and airway facilities staff, by selected employment and demographic characteristics, FY88, annual rpt, 7504-41

Banks in Fed Reserve System, expenses and operations itemized by service, office, and district, 1988, annual rpt, 9364-11

County Business Patterns, 1987: employment, establishments, and payroll, by SIC 2- to 4-digit industry and county, annual State rpt series, 2326-8

DOD Ada computer programming language implementation and use, costs and technical issues, FY82-89, GAO rpt, 26125-32

DOD in-house commercial activities work-years, by service branch, State, and installation, FY88, annual rpt, 3544-25

Earnings, annual average percent changes for selected occupational groups, selected MSAs, monthly rpt, 6782-1.1

Education in science, methods, materials, and factors affecting elementary and secondary student proficiency, views of students, teachers, and administrators, 1983-85 surveys, 4828-37.1

Education statistics, detailed data on elementary and secondary education, 1920s-88 and projected to 1997, annual rpt, 4824-1.1

Employment and occupation of householder, by occupation of spouse, race, and family composition, 1988, annual Current Population Rpt, 2546-1.437

Employment, earnings, and hours, by SIC 1- to 4-digit industry, monthly 1983-Feb 1989, annual rpt, 6744-4

Employment in nonmanufacturing industries, by detailed occupation and SIC 2-digit industry, 1987, triennial rpt, 6748-60

Employment, unemployment, and labor force characteristics, by region and census div, 1988, annual rpt, 6744-7.1

Fed Govt computer systems security training activities, by agency, 1988, GAO rpt, 26125-31

Fed Govt standards for data recording, processing, and transfer, and for purchase and use of computer systems, series, 2216-2

Fed Reserve System, Board of Governors, and district banks financial statements, performance, and fiscal services, 1987-89, annual rpt, 9364-10

Financial instns financial and operating statements by deposit size, Fed Reserve functional cost analysis, 1988, annual rpt, 9364-6

Industry finances and operations, by SIC 2- to 4-digit industry, forecast 1989 and trends from 1950s, annual rpt, 2044-28

Manufacturing high technology use and plans, with data by technology, selected industry, and firm and market characteristics, 1988 survey, 2508-1

Multinatl US firms and foreign affiliates finances and operations, by industry of parent firm and affiliate, world area, and country, preliminary 1987, annual rpt, 2704-5

Occupational injury and illness rates, by SIC 2- to 4-digit industry, 1987, annual rpt, 6844-1

Police agencies employment, spending, and operations, FY87, 6066-25.20

Police dept operations, staff, and expenses, for large cities by population size, 1987, 6066-19.51

Schools (elementary and secondary) computer use, by grade level, 1989 edition, annual rpt, 4824-2.30

Science and engineering employment, by nonmanufacturing industry and field, 1987, triennial rpt, 9627-31

SEC staffing, pay, and turnover by occupation and city, with proposed fee revenues to improve work conditions, 1989 hearing, 21368-116

Service industries census, 1987: establishments, receipts, employment, and payroll, by SIC 2- to 4-digit kind of business, MSA, county, and city, State rpt series, 2391-1

Service industries receipts, by SIC 2- to 4-digit kind of business, 1988, annual rpt, 2413-8

Statistical Abstract of US, social, political, and economic data, 1790-2025, comprehensive annual compilation, 2324-1.1

Stock market crash of 1987, market performance, foreign futures market activity, and computer-aided trading impacts on price variability, 1980s-88, hearings, 25168-70

Tax (income) return processing, IRS workload forecasts, compliance, and enforcement, data compilation, 1989 annual rpt, 8304-1

Tax (income) returns of partnerships, income statement items by industry group, 1986, annual article, 8302-2.903

Tax (income) returns of sole proprietorships, income statement items, by industry group, 1987, annual article, 8302-2.904; 8302-2.921

Tax (income) withholding and related documents filed, by type and IRS service center, 1988 and projected 1989-96, annual rpt, 8304-22

Wages and workers in computer and data processing services by occupation and sex, and benefits, by selected MSA, 1987 survey, 6787-6.236

Wages for 4 occupational groups, relative pay levels in 61 MSAs, 1988, annual rpt, 6785-8

Young adults computer use, by selected characteristics, 1984, annual rpt, 4824-2.30

see also Automation
see also Computer networks
see also Computer sciences
see also Economic and econometric models

COMSAT
see Communications Satellite Corp.

Concentration, business
see Economic concentration and diversification

Conferences

Concord, Calif.
see also under By City in the "Index by Categories"

Concrete
see Cement and concrete

Condemnation of property
see Property condemnation

Condominiums and cooperatives
American Housing Survey: unit and households detailed characteristics, and unit and neighborhood quality, MSA rpt series, 2485-6

American Housing Survey: unit and households detailed characteristics, and unit and neighborhood quality, 1985, biennial rpt, 2485-12

Housing and households summary characteristics, 1985 and trends, biennial chartbook, 2486-1.7

Market absorption rate and characteristics, 1987 and trends from 1970, annual Current Housing Rpt, 2484-2

Market absorption rates for condominiums, and completions by sales price, quarterly rpt, 2482-2

Mortgage insurance programs of HUD, finances and lending activity by program, FY88, annual rpt, 5004-8

Mortgages by lender type and related to neighborhood characteristics, for Boston, Mass, 1982-87, article, 9373-1.915

Mortgages FHA-insured for 1-family units, by loan type and mortgage characteristics, quarterly rpt, 5142-45

New condominium units completed and absorption rates, by size and price class, preliminary 1988, annual Current Housing Rpt, 2484-3

New condominium units completed, by size, price, and location, 1984-88, annual rpt, 2384-1.7

New condominiums, by intended use, units per structure, tenure, and region, monthly rpt, annual tables, 2382-1

Services provided by Residential Community Assns, and RCAs relations with local govts, 1988 conf, 10048-75

Tax (income) returns of corporations, income and tax items by asset size and detailed industry, 1986, annual rpt, 8304-4; 8304-21

Confectionery products
see Candy and confectionery products

Conference Board
"Marketer's Guide to Discretionary Income", 2308-54

Conferences
AIDS health care and epidemiological research, methodological issues, 1988 conf, 4188-61

AIDS health care services research status, needs, methods, and impacts on public health policy and funding, with data for selected cities, 1989 conf papers, 4188-59

AIDS prevention, prevalence, and treatment, 1988 conf papers, 4042-3.905

Air traffic and other aviation activity forecasts of FAA, 1989 annual conf, 7504-58

Alcohol use and abuse among minority groups, and related problems, by selected characteristics, 1985 conf papers, 4488-13

Figure 9.10. Reprinted from *American Statistics Index, 1989, Annual*, Index Volume, through the courtesy of Congressional Information Service, Bethesda, MD.

United States Congress   **25248-108**

25168
SENATE AGRICULTURE,
NUTRITION, AND FORESTRY
COMMITTEE
Special and
Irregular Publications

25168-69   OVERSIGHT OF
                       CONSERVATION
                       PROGRAMS
                       Mar. 24, 1988. ix + 770 p.
                       S. Hrg. 100-757.
                       •Item 1032-C; 1032-D.
                       GPO $21.00.
                       CIS/Index (89) S161-1.
                       ASI/MF/10
                       S/N 552-070-04739-5.
                       °Y4.Ag8/3:S.hrg.100-757.
                       MC 89-3761.   LC 88-602872.

Hearing held Mar. 1988 before the *Subcommittee on Conservation and Forestry* to evaluate implementation of Food Security Act conservation provisions, including soil conservation programs requiring farmers to develop conservation plans for highly erodible land as a condition of USDA assistance; wetlands conservation programs restricting eligibility for Federal farm program benefits of farmers using certain converted wetlands for crop production; and conservation reserve program (CRP), providing incentives for farmers to remove highly erodible croplands from production.

Insertions from USDA and Interior Dept officials include scattered charts and tables showing CRP itemized costs, and impacts on agricultural finance and credit expenditures, highly erodible acreage and other land use, and average crop yield and farm prices by crop; and waterfowl breeding population and area, by wetland habitat type and region; nationwide with some detailed data for North Dakota, 1980s with trends from 1950s.

The following insertions include additional statistical material:

a. North Carolina Farm Bureau Federation prepared statement. Includes 2 tables showing acres of highly erodible cropland, wetland, and uncultivated agricultural land and wetland with potential for conversion to cropland, by State (except Alaska), 1982. (p. 48-54)

b. Soil Conservation Service prepared statement. Includes 2 tables showing number of farms and tracts, for highly erodible land, and land with conservation plans, by State; and contract funds of State conservationists transferred to State Cooperative Extension Services, for conservation education and information activities in selected States; FY88. (p. 74-95)

c. Wildlife Habitat Charitable Trust prepared statement. Includes 2 charts and 15 tables showing modeling estimates of crop yield, production costs, and fertilizer and pesticide use, under conventional and experimental crop management systems, often by crop and type of crop management system, 1986. (p. 524-603)

25168-70   OVERSIGHT HEARINGS:
                       Matters Relating to the
                       October 19 Market Break
                       1988. v + 515 p.
                       S. Hrg. 100-763.
                       •Item 1032-C; 1032-D.
                       GPO $14.00.
                       CIS/Index (89) S161-5.
                       ASI/MF/8
                       S/N 552-070-04738-7.
                       °Y4.Ag8/3:S.hrg.100-763.
                       MC 89-3764.   LC 88-602891.

Hearings held Mar.-Apr. 1988 to examine policy issues involved in Oct. 1987 stock market decline. Focuses on actions undertaken and planned by regulatory agencies and self-regulatory organizations to improve the operations of securities and futures markets, and provide for a coordinated response in the event of future market disorder.

The following submissions include statistical material:

a. Report by Chicago Board of Trade includes 1 chart and 8 tables showing government bond and selected stock index futures and options contracts trading volume on foreign futures exchanges, by exchange, various periods 1982-Mar. 1988; and percent of Dow Jones Industrial stocks not trading, by time of day, Oct. 19-21, 1987. (p. 320-373)

b. Grossman, Sanford J. (Princeton University), "Report on Program Trading: An Analysis of Interday Relationships" Includes 3 charts and 7 tables showing input data and correlations and regression results relating indicators of stock price variability to indicators of program (computer-initiated) trading intensity, daily Jan.-Oct. 1987. (p. 478-515)

25168-71   EFFECT OF THE DROUGHT
                       ON FOOD PRICES
                       Oct. 5, 1988. iii + 70 p.
                       S. Hrg. 100-929.
                       •Item 1032-C; 1032-D.
                       GPO $2.25.
                       CIS/Index (89) S161-13.
                       ASI/MF/3
                       S/N 552-070-05443-0.
                       °Y4.Ag8/3:S.hrg.100-929.
                       MC 89-9476.   LC 89-601331.

Hearing held Oct. 1988 to examine the impact of the 1988 drought on food prices.

Prepared statements from GAO and a private consumer assn include 9 charts and 3 tables showing monthly retail prices, percent distribution of surveyed supermarkets by price action (increase, decrease, no change), and median price increase and decrease, for 8-17 food items; and percent distribution of supermarkets, by price action, for 16 cities; 1988.

25248
SENATE BANKING,
HOUSING, AND URBAN
AFFAIRS COMMITTEE
Special and
Irregular Publications

25248-107 REPORT OF THE NATIONAL
                        HOUSING TASK FORCE
                        Apr. 1988. v + 371 p.
                        S. Hrg. 100-689.
                        •Item 1035-C; 1035-D.
                        GPO $11.00.
                        CIS/Index (88) S241-28.
                        ASI/MF/6
                        S/N 552-070-04494-9.
                        °Y4.B22/3:S.hrg.100-689.
                        MC 88-17649.
                                            LC 89-602639.

Hearings held Apr. 1988 before the *Subcommittee on Housing and Urban Affairs* to examine findings and recommendations of the National Housing Task Force regarding national housing policies impacting low- and moderate-income housing affordability and availability.

The following insertions include statistical material:

a. National Assn of Homebuilders prepared statement. Includes 5 charts and tables showing homeownership rates, by region and age of homeowner; selected years 1973-87. (p. 67-81)

b. Mortgage Insurance Companies of America response to Subcommittee questions. Includes text statistics and 2 tables showing foreclosure rates for all and conventional home mortgage loans, 1980-87. (p. 122-124)

c. Harvard University Joint Center for Housing Studies, "State of the Nation's Housing, 1988" Includes 11 charts and 21 tables showing house prices, homeownership rates, monthly housing costs, and urban and rural households living in inadequate housing, variously by age and marital status of household head, tenure, household income and composition, and region, various periods 1967-87. (p. 231-259)

d. Mellman and Lazarus, "Survey of Attitudes Toward Hunger and Homelessness in America, Jan. 8-19, 1988" Presents results of a nationwide survey of 1,000 persons, covering attitudes toward Federal assistance to hungry and homeless, by political party/ideology, sex, education, and age. Includes 7 charts, 10 tables, and facsimile questionnaire with tabulated responses. (p. 260-277)

25248-108 NEW DIRECTIONS FOR
                        DEALING WITH THE
                        INTERNATIONAL DEBT
                        PROBLEM
                        Aug. 1988. v + 246 p.
                        S. Hrg. 100-856.
                        •Item 1035-C; 1035-D.
                        GPO $7.50.
                        CIS/Index (89) S241-6.
                        ASI/MF/5
                        S/N 552-070-05063-9.
                        °Y4.B22/3:S.hrg.100-856.
                        MC 89-7039.   LC 88-603396.

———. *Numerical Lists and Schedule of Volumes of the Reports and Documents of the 73rd Congress—to Date.* Washington: GPO, 1934-.

Listing of Congressional documents and reports in numerical sequence. Gives *Serial Set* number.

STATE GOVERNMENT PUBLICATIONS

The individual state governments have a similar mission as the Federal government to keep their citizens informed. Although state governments publish information on a more limited scope than the national government, they, too, are prolific publishers of information. Each state provides descriptions of its governmental activities, reports of special developments in industry and economics, maps, laws, and statistics on education, crime, health, employment, business, etc. The information found in state documents is especially useful because of its timeliness. Statistics on employment, housing construction, crime, and health, for example, are gathered by the states and published in state documents before they appear in Federal documents.

Most states do not have funds to provide widespread distribution of their publications. Rather, certain libraries are designated as depository libraries for state documents and automatically receive the State's publications. The way that depository collections are organized varies among libraries. Some libraries keep their documents in a separate state collection with other special materials on the state, others house them as a separate collection within the government documents department. Still other libraries integrate state documents with their general collection.

The access to state documents varies among libraries. Many states publish checklists and bibliographies listing currently available publications. A few libraries catalog state documents along with other library materials. Even so, it is difficult to identify and use state publications. For that reason, in most libraries with state documents collections, a librarian with special training and experience in state documents is usually available to assist patrons in locating information on the state level.

LOCAL GOVERNMENT PUBLICATIONS

In the United States there are many local units of government—towns, cities, counties, and special districts. Although information about local governmental units appears in publications of the Federal government as well as in commercial publications, most of the key information is produced by the local governmental units. Publications from local governments include records of their activities such as charters, laws, regulations, financial reports, city plans, maps, statistics, budgets, decisions, etc. Local publications are an important primary source of information. These documents usually are not widely distributed, making them difficult to locate and access. One way to get information from local governments is to request it directly from the local agency. Another way is through the library. Libraries, especially college and university libraries, often serve as depositories for local documents. The way local documents are handled varies among libraries. Some catalog local documents along with the other materials in the library, others keep them in separate collections which may or may not be cataloged. Since there are no quick and easy guides to local government publications, one should ask the librarian for assistance when seeking local documents or information about a local governmental unit. The librarian can direct users to the appropriate source.

UNITED NATIONS PUBLICATIONS

The United Nations issues an enormous quantity of documents in mimeographed, offset, and printed form. The primary purpose of United Nations documents is to serve the immediate needs of the delegates to the United Nations. However, the publications of the United Nations and its allied agencies, such as the World Health Organization (WHO) and the United Nations Education, Scientific, and Cultural Organization (UNESCO), are of great value because they deal with all the important issues in international affairs. They provide an enormous amount of statistics and other types of information gathered from all over the globe on all facets of human endeavors. They document world problems such as hunger, illiteracy, and human rights.

The publications of the United Nations and its allied agencies may or may not be listed in the main catalog along with the other resources of a library. In either case they may be shelved in a separate collection. Libraries which serve as depository libraries for United Nations documents usually keep the publications in a separate collection shelved by the series symbol which is assigned by the United Nations. The series symbol numbers are composed of capital letters in combination with numerical notations. The elements in the numbers are separated by slash marks. For example, the 1985 *Report on the World Social Situation* has the call number ST/ESA/165. The first part of the notation *ST* stands for the United Nations Secretariat; *ESA* stands for the Department of International and Social Affairs, *165* is the series number designation. United Nations documents filed by UN series symbol numbers must be accessed by finding aids which are produced by the United Nations. The following indexes serve as guides to United Nations publications for the periods indicated:

Checklist of United Nations Documents. New York: United Nations, 1946–1949.

> A complete list of the United Nations documents issued by the UN organization from 1946 through 1949.

United Nations Documents Index. (UNDI). New York: United Nations, 1950–1973.

> Lists all the documents received by the Documents Index Unit for the time indicated.

United Nations Documents Index. (UNDEX). New York: United Nations, 1970–1978.

> Two separate indexes, one by subjects, the other by countries. Each entry gives subject or country, type of document, and series symbol.

UNDOC: Current Index. 1979-to date. New York: United Nations, 1979-.

> Each issue contains a checklist of documents and publications; lists of official records, sales publications, documents republished in the *Official Records*, language tables; and subject, author, and title indexes.

REVIEW QUESTIONS
CHAPTER 9

1. Why is the government such a prolific producer of information?

2. Name four characteristics of government information which adds to its value as a reference source.

3. Discuss the ways in which U.S. Government publications vary (a) in scope and (b) in format.

4. What are U.S. depository libraries?

   Why were they established?

5. Which classification system is used to classify U.S. government publications in many academic libraries?

6. What is the purpose of the *Monthly Catalog*?

   How is it arranged?

7. How does one locate articles which appear in U.S. government periodicals?

8. What kind of information is one likely to find among the publications of state governments?

9. What is meant by ''local government'' publications? What is the value of these publications?

10. Why are publications of the United Nations and its allied agencies important sources of information?

11. Is there a depository for U.S. documents at your school?

    If so, what type depository is it?

U.S. GOVERNMENT PUBLICATIONS EXERCISE

Information on a great variety of topics is included among the publications of the U.S. Government. Use one of the finding aids listed below to locate information on a topic which interests you or a topic which your instructor assigns.

Finding Aids:

Monthly Catalog (either the GPO edition or one of the microfilm or CD-ROM versions)
American Statistics Index
Congressional Information Service Index
Guide to U.S. Government Periodicals

Complete the following information:

TOPIC:

1. Name of finding aid used and date.

     Subject heading used in index and entry number of abstract if applicable.

2. Analyze the reference you find by giving the following information:

   a.   Author

   b.   Title

c.   No. of pages in the document

d.   Publication date

e.   Agency which issued document

f.   SuDocs call number

3. Write a brief annotation for the publication, in which you summarize its content and comment on its usefulness.

4. Make a bibliographic citation to the document. Study carefully the citations found in the textbook on pages 323–326 and then use the appropriate citation for a model.

Introduction to
Online Databases

10

A PREVIEW

One of the ways that libraries have taken advantage of the electronic age is to provide online databases to library users. This chapter analyzes the availability and use of this technology. A major goal of this chapter is to acquaint library users with the kinds of information available in online databases and to help them make wise decisions in developing online research strategies. The search techniques discussed in this chapter will also be helpful in conducting other searches in electronic format such as online catalogs and databases on CD-ROM.

The purpose of this chapter is to introduce the reader to the possibilities of acquiring information through an online search. *Online search* is a term used to describe a search in which a computer is used to retrieve information from databases which are stored in the mainframe computer of a data center located at a distance from where the search originates. Many users may access the data at the same time. The computer data center also arranges for the telecommunications services between the database user and the data center. Computer data centers do not usually produce the databases themselves; rather, they acquire them from organizations or businesses to whom they pay a lease and/or royalty fee. Thus, the computer data center is known as a *vendor*. Some producers of databases permit direct access to their databases, but most market their product to vendors. Examples of database producers who provide direct access to their databases are H. W. Wilson Co., producer of *WILSONLINE;* the National Library of Medicine, producer of *MEDLINE;* Datatek Corporation, producer of *DataTimes;* and Dun and Bradstreet, producers of *DUNSPRINT.* The major vendors of online services are:

1. DIALOG (Lockheed Information Systems)
2. BRS (Information Technologies, Inc.)
3. ORBIT (System Development Corporation—SDC)
4. INFOLINE (Pergamon Press)
5. LEXIS (Mead Data Central)

All of these vendors provide access to numerous databases. For example, Dialog offers about 300 databases while BRS provides approximately 100. Some of the

KEY TERMS

Online Databases
Computer Data Centers
(Vendors)
Kinds of Information Available
in Online Database
Indexes and Abstracts
Full Text
Aggregate Data
Directory information
Steps in Conducting an
Online Search
Boolean Searching
Advantages of Online
Searching
Disadvantages of Online
Searching

same databases are available through both services. Each system uses a different command language to instruct the computer to perform an online search.

Online databases are available on a wide variety of subjects in the areas of science, social science, and humanities. The kinds of information available in online databases include: (1) *indexes and abstracts* which give citations to periodical articles, books, government reports, statistics, patents, research reports, conference proceedings, and dissertations; (2) the *full-text* of newspapers and periodicals, court cases, encyclopedias, research reports, etc; (3) *aggregate data,* such as statistics in ''raw form'' which can be manipulated to suit the needs of the researcher; and (4) *directories* which can be accessed to provide information in varying formats such as company size, geographical locations, type of business, etc.

Libraries subscribe to the database services in order to provide access to the search services for its patrons. The search is carried out by means of a terminal or microcomputer equipped with a modem located in the subscribing library. (See Figure 10.1) The computer is linked by telephone to the computer data center of one of the vendors such as DIALOG or BRS. A reference librarian who has been trained in search techniques arranges a search interview to prepare a search strategy with the patron desiring the search. The search strategy consists of determining what information is desired, the keywords or subject terms to be used, databases to be searched, dates, etc. Many databases have a

Figure 10.1. Searcher conducting online search.

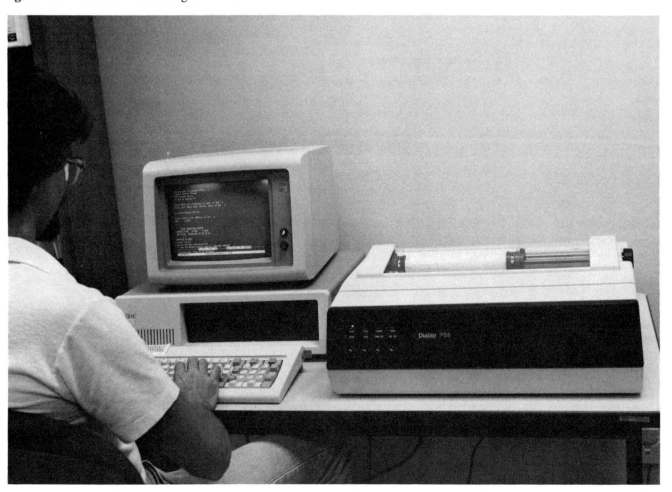

thesaurus listing the subject terms or controlled vocabulary for the database. The search strategy is then entered into the computer. Within seconds the computer responds with the number of citations it has located meeting the search strategy criteria. The searcher may request citations only, citations with abstracts, specially formatted reports, or the full-text or articles, depending on what is available in the database. The results of the search may then be printed online or offline. Online printouts are generated immediately and printed on a local printer. Offline printouts are requested while the computer is linked to the vendor's information system; these are then printed by the vendor and sent by mail or other delivery service to the library.

Online searching involves both direct and indirect costs; the direct costs include the fees charged by the vendor for use of the database, telecommunications charges, and printing costs; indirect costs include expenses for equipment, staff time, staff training, and searching aids. While most libraries do not charge the user for indirect costs, they usually charge the person or organization requesting the search for direct costs. The cost of an online search varies according to the database used, the connect time (time spent online), and the number of citations printed. Connect time charges for DIALOG databases range from about $25 an hour to $300 an hour; the average hourly charge is between $60 and $80. Online citations range from $.10 per citation to about $5.00. Full-text retrieval costs more.

In some libraries, it is possible for end-users (persons who use the information) to conduct their own online searching. Many libraries provide instruction for end-user searching. *BRS BRKTHRU* and *BRS AFTERDARK* have easy to follow menu-driven programs designed to be used by persons without extensive computer searching experience. Other vendors offer similar programs.

An online search can be divided into the following steps:

1. Preparing the search strategy, which consists of:
   a. determining the broad topic to be searched;
   b. selecting the best databases to use;
   c. finding the search terms to be used by consulting the appropriate thesauri, dictionaries, or paper indexes;
   d. narrowing the search by combining search terms.
2. Connecting the library computer to the vendor service.
3. Connecting to the database(s) as planned in Step 1.
4. Executing the search by typing the commands on the terminal's keyboard.
5. Printing the results online or requesting an offline printout.
6. Disconnecting from the vendor service.

Online searching is a powerful research tool. Yet, in many ways it can be compared to searching printed indexes, abstracts, and library catalogs. Researchers recognize the importance of being able to interpret the elements in an index, abstract, or library catalog. It is just as important to know what kind of information is in a database and how to interpret the results retrieved from an online search. The individual entries in databases are called records. A typical record in a bibliographic database has many of the same elements as an entry in an index or abstract. The elements are divided into *fields* each of which is labeled. A typical record might contain the following fields: database accession number (unique number assigned to that record in the database), author, title, issuing source or publisher, date, language, subjects (frequently called descriptors), and abstract.

One key to successful online searching is the use of Boolean logic which employs the terms *and, or,* or *not* to combine words and phrases. The example below is presented to illustrate how Boolean logic is used in online searching.

The searcher wanted to find out all the information in the database that shows how artificial intelligence is used to write poetry or music.

Step 1. The searcher asked for all the records containing the term "artificial intelligence." The computer responded by displaying the number of records (sets) which met the search criteria:

set 1   574   documents found [with]   artificial intelligence

Next the searcher asked for music *or* poetry. The results were:

set 2   6946   documents found [with]   music
set 3   3958   documents found [with]   poetry
set 4   10573   documents found [with] music *or* poetry

The searcher then asked the computer to combine set 1 (artificial intelligence) *and* set 4 (music or poetry). The results were:

set 6   617   documents [with] set 1 and set 4.

The diagram below illustrates how the logic works.

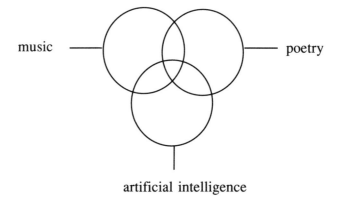

The advantages of online searching are enumerated below:

1. It saves valuable research time. It takes minutes or even seconds to search an entire database or several databases. To search the same indexes in paper copy might take hours or even longer.
2. Online searching is usually more successful than searching a printed source because it permits the searcher to link words and terms in a way that can never be done manually. For example, to find information on using computers to teach library skills to college students, it is possible to search for the terms "computer assisted instruction," "library skills," and "college or university." It is also possible to exclude terms in the same search request. By putting in *not* "elementary or secondary," the search could ex-

clude any records that might pertain to library skills for elementary or secondary students.

3. Online searching is more flexible than searching printed indexes and abstracts because it is possible to search for words regardless of where they appear in the record. This is called *free test searching.*

4. It is possible to truncate or shorten terms so that all the variations of a term can be located. For example, using the term "colleg" would retrieve "college," "colleges," "collegial," and "collegiate."

5. Online searching provides access to many more databases than are available in the library. Even the largest libraries do not receive all the information that is available through online databases. Some databases are available only online.

6. The information available online is more current than that found in printed sources. Online databases are updated frequently; some databases are updated daily.

7. Searches can be updated easily; it is even possible to save the search statements in the computer so that the information is automatically updated.

8. Acquiring a printout, either online or offline, is more convenient than hand copying citations from an index or abstract.

While the advantages of online searching far outweigh the disadvantages, there are some disadvantages which must be taken into consideration:

1. Because online searching is expensive, it may be out of reach for many library users.

2. Sometimes the "logic" in database searching does not work. For example, a search for articles on apricots retrieved articles on the fruit as well as on a computer named "Apricot." This kind of result is called a "false hit" or "false drop."

3. Information printed prior to the 1960s is not usually included in online databases and in many cases the information does not go beyond the last two or three years.

Because online searching is expensive, a user should determine whether a topic is suitable for online searching or whether it should be searched manually. For example, a search for studies showing the effects of advertising on consumer preferences would yield a number of bibliographic citations in an online search. On the other hand, to find out how much money was spent in the United States on advertising each year, one should consult a statistical reference book. To find articles written in the 1950s relating to fraudulent advertising, one should consult a printed index from that period.

SELECTED LIST OF ONLINE DATABASES

The following list provides a small sample from among the hundreds of databases which can be found in the appropriate vendor catalogs. The list below is divided into broad subject categories, but one must keep in mind that many databases lend themselves to interdisciplinary searching. Each entry contains the name of the database, the producer, and the beginning date of coverage. The name of the vendor (either Dialog or BRS) is indicated except for those databases which are distributed by the producer. Many of the titles listed here are also available in printed format and may have been listed elsewhere in this book.

General Databases

Dissertation Abstracts. University Microfilms International. 1861—. DIALOG, BRS.

> The complete list of all American dissertations accepted since 1861. Also includes many Canadian dissertations.

GPO Monthly Catalog. U.S. Government Printing Office. 1976—. DIALOG, BRS.

> Indexes the publications of the Government Printing Office. Information covers many disciplines and areas of interest. Record includes the Superintendent of Documents call number.

Magazine Index. Information Access. 1959–1970, 1973—. DIALOG, BRS.

> Indexes over 435 popular magazines. Covers a wide spectrum of topics such as current affairs, business, consumer information, sports, science, health, etc.

National Newspaper Index. Information Access. 1979—. DIALOG, BRS.

> Index to the *Christian Science Monitor,* the *New York Times,* and the *Wall Street Journal.* Also contains selected references from the *Washington Post* and the *Los Angeles Times.*

Subject Databases

Agriculture and Food Science

Agricola. U.S. Department of Agriculture. 1970—. DIALOG, BRS.

> The database of the National Library of Agriculture. Covers all aspects of agriculture. Some abstracts are included.

Biological and Agricultural Index. H. W. Wilson. 1983—. WILSONLINE.

> Covers agriculture as well as biological and some medical topics.

CRIS (Current Research Information System). U.S. Department of Agriculture. Currently active or recently completed. DIALOG.

> Valuable for current research in farming, food and nutrition, health, agricultural economics, and other consumer related fields. Includes abstracts.

Food Science and Technology Abstracts. International Food Information Service. 1969—. DIALOG.

> Access to research and new developments in food science and related disciplines such as agriculture, chemistry, and biochemistry.

Arts and Humanities

America: History and Life. ABC-CLIO. 1964—. DIALOG.

> Extensive coverage of U.S. and Canadian history and current affairs. Indexes over 2,000 journals as well as books and dissertations.

Art Literature International (RILA). RILA, J. Paul Getty Trust. 1973—. DIALOG.

Abstracts and indexes current publications in art history.

Arts and Humanities Citation Index. Institute for Scientific Information. 1980—. BRS.

Bibliographic citations, including a complete list of cited references to the literature in the arts and humanities. Covers archaeology, architecture, art, dance, music, religion, theology, and other related disciplines.

MLA Bibliography. Modern Language Association. 1968—. DIALOG.

Index to books and journal articles in languages, literature, and linguistics.

Philosopher's Index. Philosophy Documentation Center. 1940—. DIALOG.

Indexes articles from the major philosophical journals. Contains lengthy abstracts.

Religion Index. American Theological Library Association. 1975—. DIALOG, BRS.

Covers approximately 200 journals in religion and theology. Emphasis on American and English language journals, but some non-English journals included.

Business and Economics

ABI/Inform. Data Courier. 1971—. DIALOG, BRS.

Indexes the major journals in business administration, economics, management, real estate, and other business related fields.

Business Periodicals Index. H. W. Wilson. 1982—. WILSONLINE.

Index to periodicals in advertising, banking, finance, marketing, management, insurance, and general business.

Economic Literature Index. American Economic Association. 1969—. DIALOG.

Indexes the literature in approximately 260 economics journals. Also includes some monographs. Some entries include abstracts.

Management Contents. Information Access. 1974—. DIALOG, BRS.

Covers approximately 120 U.S. and international journals plus proceedings, business course materials, and research reports. Subject fields include accounting, marketing, operations research, and public administration.

PTS F & S Indexes. Predicasts, 1972— DIALOG.

Company, product, and industry information. Coverage is international. Other Predicasts databases include: *PTS International Forecasts,* 1971—; *PTS Marketing and Advertising,* 1984—; *PTS Prompt,* 1972—; and *PTS U.S. Forecasts,* 1971—.

Trade and Industry Index. Information Access. 1981—. DIALOG, BRS.

Selective coverage of business information from about 1200 newspapers and periodicals. Also includes some trade journals. Provides access to *Area Business Databank* which includes many local and regional journals and periodicals.

Computers

Business Software Database. Data Courier. Current. DIALOG, BRS.

Directory of software which includes machine specifications, names and addresses of producers, price, and date of release. Also includes textual description of software.

Computer Database. Information Access. 1983—. DIALOG.

Covers approximately 500 publications in the computer field. Abstracts are medium length, but useful.

Microcomputer Index. Databases Services. 1981—. DIALOG.

Subject and abstract guide to about 50 microcomputer journals. Includes abstracts.

Criminal Justice

Criminal Justice Periodical Index. University Microfilms International. 1975—. DIALOG.

Covers about 100 journals, newsletters, and law reports dealing with crime and law enforcement.

NCJRS. National Institute of Justice/National Criminal Justice Reference Service. 1972—. DIALOG.

Contains references to periodical articles, research reports, books and unpublished materials from private sources as well as from local, state, and national governments.

Education

ERIC. National Institute of Education, 1966—. DIALOG, BRS.

The most comprehensive database available in the field of education. It includes citations to journals, books, government publications, and unpublished reports. Provides lengthy abstracts.

Education Index. H. W. Wilson. 1983—. WILSONLINE.

Environment, Energy, and Natural Resources

DOE Energy. U.S. Department of Energy. 1974—. DIALOG and direct from DOE.

Extensive coverage of energy reports from the U.S. and some international sources. Covers all types of energy sources: fossil, renewable, synthetic, nuclear. Energy related topics in the field of chemistry and physics are also included.

Energyline. EIC/Intelligence. 1971—. DIALOG.

Not as extensive as *DOE Energy,* but it contains some important energy information that is not included in that database.

Enviroline. EIC/Intelligence. 1971—. DIALOG.

The most extensive source of environmental information. Includes abstracts.

Environmental Bibliography. Environmental Studies Institute. 1973—. DIALOG.

Covers pollution, waste management, and other ecological and environmental related topics. Database does not include abstracts.

Law and Public Affairs

Legal Resources Index. Information Access. 1980—. DIALOG, BRS.

Covers both legal periodicals and law related articles appearing in general periodicals.

LEXIS. Mead Data Central. Dates vary. Available only through Mead.

U.S. Supreme Court decisions, lower court cases, and a host of other databases in the legal field, much of which is full-text. A companion service, *NEXIS,* provides full-text coverage of several major media services.

Mathematics, Chemistry and Physics

CA Search. Chemical Abstracts Service. 1967—. DIALOG, BRS, also direct from CAS.

The most comprehensive database in the field of chemistry. Also useful for physics, biochemistry, and related subjects. Abstracts provided.

MathSci. American Mathematical Society. 1973—. DIALOG, BRS.

Includes information relating to mathematics, statistics, physics, and computer science.

Medicine and Biological Science

Biosis Previews. BioSciences Information Service. 1969—. DIALOG, BRS.

Extensive coverage of biomedicine, biochemistry, pharmacology, microbiology, virology, and other biological and medical topics.

Embase. Excerpta Medica. 1974—. DIALOG, BRS.

Contains information on drugs, pharmaceuticals, hospital management, and public health. Includes abstracts.

International Pharmaceutical Abstracts. American Society of Hospital Pharmacists. 1970—. DIALOG, BRS.

Information on the drug and cosmetic industries. Includes abstracts.

Medline. National Library of Medicine. 1966—. DIALOG BRS, also direct from NLM.

Designed primarily for the medical professional, it is also useful to lay persons interested in medical-related topics.

Science and Technology

Applied Science and Technology Index. H. W. Wilson. 1983—. WILSONLINE.

Covers industrial arts, computer technology, fuels, robotics, and other subjects related to technology.

Compendex. Engineering Information. 1970—. DIALOG, BRS.

> The major index for engineering. Covers approximately 4,500 journals and engineering related government reports and monographs. Contains lengthy abstracts.

GEOREF. American Geological Institute. 1785—(North American), 1967—(Worldwide). DIALOG.

> Comprehensive coverage of more than 4,500 international journals, books, proceedings, dissertations, and maps in geology and geography.

Inspec. Institution of Electrical Engineers. 1969—. DIALOG, BRS.

> Index to journals in electrical engineering, physics, computers, electronics, and the like. Lengthy abstracts.

NTIS. National Technical Information Service. 1964—. DIALOG, BRS.

> Index to all government sponsored research. Covers a broad range of topics in the physical, behavioral, information, and social sciences. Informative abstracts.

SCISearch. Institute for Scientific Information. 1974—. DIALOG.

> Claims to include over 90% of the world's literature in pure and applied sciences. Includes medicine, agriculture, aquaculture, engineering, and physical science. Covers over 3000 U.S. and international journals. Provides the references to sources that cited the work.

TRIS (Transportation Research). U.S. Department of Transportation. 1969—. DIALOG.

> Index to information on all aspects of transportation: air, highway, rail, and maritime. Includes information on regulations, traffic control, environmental factors, communications, etc.

Social Sciences

CENDATA. U.S. Bureau of the Census. Current. DIALOG.

> Selected statistical data on a wide range of topics from the U.S. Bureau of the Census. Include press releases from the U.S. Bureau of the Census.

Family Resources Database. National Council on Family Relations. 1966—. DIALOG, BRS.

> Includes topics related to family life: marriage, divorce, lifestyles, counselling, sexual attitudes and behavior, and alcohol and drug abuse. Abstracts are informative.

PsycINFO. American Psychological Association. 1967—. DIALOG, BRS.

> Comprehensive coverage of the psychological literature. International in scope. Indexes 1300 journals, technical reports, dissertations, and books.

PAIS International. Public Affairs Information Service. 1976—. DIALOG, BRS.

> Covers a wide range of disciplines in the social sciences: governmental affairs, public administration, political science, law, economics, foreign affairs, etc. Indexes books, government reports, and periodicals.

Social SCISearch. Institute for Scientific Information. 1972—. DIALOG, BRS.

Covers all the areas of the social sciences: history, economics, political science, sociology, urban planning, criminology, social welfare, etc. Does not provide abstracts, nor does it have descriptors. Includes references to citations in other sources.

Sociological Abstracts. Sociological Abstracts, Inc. 1963—. DIALOG, BRS.

References the literature appearing in over 1200 journals, books, conference proceedings, and other sociological sources. Includes lengthy abstracts.

U.S. Political Science Documents. NASA Industrial Applications Center. 1975—. DIALOG.

Indexes the major political science journals in the U.S. Includes foreign policy, public affairs, economics, political theory, political behavior, law, and other areas related to political science.

REVIEW QUESTIONS
CHAPTER 10

1. What is an online search?

2. What is a vendor?

3. How is an online search carried out?

4. What is the difference between an online printout and an offline printout?

5. What costs are involved in online searching?

6. Name the steps involved in conducting an online search.

7. How is Boolean logic applied on online searching?

8. Name the "fields" found in a typical record in an online database.

9. What are the advantages of online searching in comparison with manual searching?

10. What are the disadvantages of online searching?

Preparing the
Research Paper

A PREVIEW

One of the ways that a student learns to locate, evaluate, and use library resources is through the term paper assignment. The goal of this chapter is to provide the student not only with clear and precise technical counsel as to planning, researching and documenting a research paper, but to provide a concrete illustration of and model for this process. It is hoped that the advice given in this chapter will sharpen the student's ability to make critical judgments in selecting and using library sources.

Library research fills a variety of information needs from finding out telephone numbers to engaging in complicated investigations of the origin of the universe. For the college student library research is an integral part of the learning process. Generally speaking, education is characterized by two kinds of learning: (1) passive learning, involving exposure to "facts" with an emphasis on memorization and (2) active learning in which there is a discovery of new facts and an expansion of knowledge. In active learning, the student engages in seeking answers and unravelling problems which arise out of exposure to facts. It is anticipated that the college student will learn much more than "spoonfed" facts. At a minimum, undergraduate students are expected to prepare themselves for living by learning how to locate and use information. Graduate students are expected to prepare themselves to become participants in the creation of new knowledge. Teachers seeking to develop their students' skills will usually rely on some type of formal research project. The most common type of research project is the research paper, usually a formal essay requiring library research. The research paper offers the student an opportunity to examine issues, locate material relevant to an issue, digest, analyze, evaluate, and present the information with conclusions and interpretations.

Before undertaking a research project, the student should have some knowledge of library resources. The earlier chapters of this book are designed to guide the student through the library. Bewilderment at having to write a research paper should be considerably lessened by knowing something about the library's organization and how its resources can be used effectively. This chapter will focus on the techniques and the mechanics of preparing a research paper.

It is helpful to approach the research paper assignment as a series of stages or steps. Seven rather obvious steps are:

1. selecting a topic
2. formulating a thesis
3. preparing an outline
4. preparing the search strategy and gathering information
5. taking notes
6. writing the text of the paper
7. documenting the sources

The remainder of this chapter will provide guidance in each of the steps.

SELECTING A TOPIC

Sometimes the initial step in the preparation of a research paper is the most challenging one. The selection of a topic is also the most crucial one in determining the success of the research paper. If the instructor assigns a topic, the student need only determine how to proceed with the research. In most cases, however, students must choose their own topics.

There are several overriding principles to consider in choosing a research topic:

1. *Interest of the researcher.* It is important to select a topic that will arouse the researcher's curiosity and stir the imagination. The research process involves not only finding information, but also discerning from the abundance of available information that which is most relevant and which most nearly answers the questions which are the focus of the research. If the research is to be worthwhile, the researcher must conduct a diligent investigation to uncover all the information. Lack of curiosity obviously mitigates against a successful search. Suggestions for topics can be gleaned from reading articles in newspapers and magazines. The *New York Times, Wall Street Journal, Newsweek,* or *Time* are good sources for timely topics. For topics in a specific subject area one should consult subject oriented periodicals such as *Business Week, Psychology Today, Scientific American, FBI Law Enforcement Bulletin,* etc. One way to locate a periodical in a subject field is to browse in the periodical section of the library. Encyclopedias, handbooks, and bibliographies are also helpful for finding topics.

2. *Researcher's understanding of the topic.* Although research involves examining and using the ideas of others, the researcher must also project one's own thought and imagination. For this reason, it is important to have a basic understanding of the terminology in the field of study. If most of the research involves language that is highly technical and beyond the researchers level of understanding, the research will be unrewarding.

3. *Manageability of the topic.* The topic should be appropriate for the length of the paper which has been assigned. A study on "Civil Rights" would be much too broad for a ten-page research paper. "Civil Rights of American Indians Living on Indian Reservations" would be more suitable. In order to narrow an overly broad subject, the student should conduct a preliminary library search. A general encyclopedia is a good source to consult in this initial step. Although the encyclopedia gives a broad overview of a topic, it also provides ideas for the subject's narrower aspects. In the article on the Supreme Court of the United States in *The New Encyclopaedia Britannica,*

one can find references to the court's historical development, its procedures, and its landmark decisions. From the article the reader should be able to find one specific aspect of the court worthy of further investigation and narrow enough to cover in ten pages.

4. *Availability of research materials.* Again, a general encyclopedia might serve as a guide. The bibliography provided at the end of the article indicates the availability of research materials. A quick search in the library catalog or in a periodical index will also help to determine whether sufficient materials are available in the library.

FORMULATING A THESIS

After the student has become somewhat familiar with the topic selected, the second step is to determine the *thesis* of the paper. What is the purpose of the paper? What will be the focus? What is to be proven or shown in the paper? The thesis statement is a concise statement of the paper's purpose and the approach to be used. The *search strategy*, or process to be used in locating information, is determined by the thesis since the information located must support the paper's thesis. Some preliminary reading from one or two sources such as an encyclopedia article or a periodical article is probably sufficient to help formulate the thesis statement.

PREPARING THE OUTLINE

The third step is to prepare a working outline that includes all the facets of the topic to be investigated. The same preliminary sources used as a guide to narrow the topic and formulate the thesis statement are also helpful in compiling the outline. To be useful the outline should divide the thesis into a number of major points; each of the points should be further divided and subdivided until the writer can visualize the outline as a guide for research and as a skeleton for the final report. The process of subdividing should follow a logical sequence with related points grouped together. The major points should be parallel, just as the subdivisions under each heading should be parallel. The main points in the outline should support the thesis statement and should be assigned Roman numerals. The first subdivisions are given capital letters; the second, Arabic numbers; the third, lower-case letters. If it is necessary to subdivide any further than this, Arabic numbers in parentheses are used.

Example:

Thesis statement:

I. First major point
   A. First subdivision
      1. Second subdivision
      2.
         a. Third subdivision
         b.
            (1) Fourth subdivision
            (2)
   B.
II. Second major point

Since each heading or subheading in the outline denotes a division, there must be more than one part if it is to be logical. Thus, if there is a I, there must be a II; if there is an A, there must be a B, etc.

The working outline is important to the search strategy since the search should be directed to the relevant points in the outline. In the process of locating information, it is probable that other aspects of the topic not included in the working outline will be discovered and that the final outline will be changed and improved. As information is gathered the outline can be revised and new headings or subheadings added.

Example of a Topic Outline

Title: Ability of Computers to Perform Intelligent Tasks

Thesis: This paper will examine the ability of computers to perform intelligent actions which have been traditionally carried out by human beings, such as the ability to learn, to reason, to discover new meanings, to create, and to solve problems.

I. History of Research into Artificial Intelligence
    A. Charles Babbage and the attempt to develop a machine for performing mathematical functions (1812)
    B. Punch card data processors (Late 1800s)
    C. Calculating machines (Early 1900s)
    D. Advanced machines that could control other machines (1930s)
    E. Machines that could store instructions (1940s)
    F. Development of computer languages, integrated circuits, and computer chips (1950s forward)
        1. Cybernetics (comparative study of control systems)
            a. Role of feedback mechanisms
            b. Analysis of purpose
        2. Digital computers
            a. Use of symbolic systems
            b. Programmability
II. Meaning of Artificial Intelligence
    A. Ability to manipulate symbolic information
        1. Internal memory
        2. Basic programs for testing and measuring
        3. Ability to transform information in order to perform a task
    B. Problem-solving
        1. Generate and test
        2. "If-then" logic rules
        3. "Means-ends" analysis
    C. Natural language comprehension
        1. Ability to comprehend commands of natural language
        2. Ability to query
    D. Pattern recognition
        1. Ability to identify graphic patterns and images
        2. Ability to distinguish and filter out unwanted images

III. Limitations of Artificial Intelligence
    A. Limited to ability to manipulate symbolic information
    B. Unable to perform higher mental operations which involve cognitive and linguistic processes
IV. Future of Artificial Intelligence
    A. Computers capable of serving humanity by carrying out logical tasks thus releasing experts to perform other problem solving functions
    B. Computers capable of performing decision making tasks
        1. Medical applications
        2. Business applications

THE SEARCH STRATEGY

Using the thesis statement and the outline as a basis, the researcher should develop a *search strategy* or plan of research. The search strategy for the research paper involves analyzing the information needed and determining which library sources are appropriate to consult in order to get that information. It is helpful to begin by analyzing the information according to specific factors that are involved in solving the research problem.

1. *Time factor.* Is the problem of an historical nature or is it concerned with a current event? Sometimes a combination of the two is involved. For example, the research on artificial intelligence in the outline on page 304 calls for examining both the past and the present status of artificial intelligence. Therefore, the search strategy must involve using those sources which will provide both historical and current information.

2. *Scholarly or popular treatment.* The scholarly literature is written by experts or scholars in different fields. The style of writing is usually technical or complex and often requires special knowledge or background in order to be understood. While the scholarly literature may not have widespread appeal among general readers, it does have value to the researcher. Among other things, the scholarly literature is considered to be authoritative, since it is usually written by experts in the field; it is documented and therefore reliable. The bibliographies accompanying the literature are useful for further research. Popular treatment of a topic provides non-technical, easy-to-read information. It is designed to appeal to the persons who do not have specialized training in the subject. Popular treatment is desirable for brief, concise answers; often the popular literature is the only source for up-to-date information. It is also good for presenting different viewpoints as well as for contemporary opinions. An article on artificial intelligence in *Electronic Week*, a popular magazine, is quite different from one in the more scholarly journal *Human Factors*. Yet, both are of value to the researcher.

3. *General information.* General information may range from a general overview of a subject to current awareness.

4. *Specific facts.* Specific facts might include dates, historical facts, statistics, test results, etc.

5. *Geographical factors.* It is important to identify any geographical factors so that sources of information having a specific geographic orientation can be selected in the research process. For example, the researcher may want information only from a particular country or on a particular region.

6. *Primary Sources.* A first-hand or eye witness account of an event is a primary source. Newspaper stories are usually primary sources. Other examples are reports of experiments, autobiographies, letters, etc.

7. *Secondary sources.* A secondary source is one that analyzes, relates, evaluates, or criticizes based on information gathered from primary sources. Secondary sources involve the interpretation of primary sources as well as the evaluation of other secondary sources.

The informational needs must be identified and matched with the appropriate library source as part of the search strategy. Students should be familiar with the library's services and should know how its materials are organized. But more than this, they should know the characteristics of the more basic library tools so that they can know which of these to go to for specific information. The earlier chapters of this book are devoted to analyzing the major sources to consult in the library search: (1) the library catalog, (2) reference books, (3) biographical sources, (4) indexes, (5) government publications, and (6) online databases. Once some knowledge of these sources has been acquired, it is possible to determine the most appropriate tools to be consulted in order to answer a specific question. (See Figure 11.1.)

The Reference Interview

Reference librarians can provide valuable assistance with research questions if they know what information is being sought. For the researcher, the key to getting assistance is knowing which questions to ask. Following are guidelines to observe in order to get maximum help from the librarian:

1. Explain the purpose of the research.
2. Give the assignment specifications. For example, length of paper, number of sources needed, and due date.
3. Explain the level of difficulty—scholarly, technical, easy-to-understand, etc.
4. Give the time framework—current, historical.
5. Describe the kinds of sources needed—primary or secondary.
6. Ask for assistance with specific questions that may be difficult to locate—statistics, dates, little known facts.

Evaluation of Sources

As information is gathered, it is important to be critical about the sources. The information should, of course, be relevant to the outline and to the thesis. The same questions raised in planning the search strategy should be kept in mind as the search is executed. Is the information sufficiently up-to-date? Is the latest edition of a work available? Is the source reliable? Does the work reflect a particular prejudice? There are several ways to determine the reliability of a source. Some of these are listed below.

1. *Inclusion in an authoritative, selective bibliography.* Bibliographies in encyclopedia or journal articles are considered reliable sources. Guides to the literature in special subject areas and subject bibliographies are also dependable.

**RESEARCH PAPER
SEARCH STRATEGY**

Figure 11.1. Type of information and sources to consult.

Type of Information	Sources to Consult
PRELIMINARY IDEAS	ENCYCLOPEDIAS, PERIODICALS
OVERVIEW OF THE TOPIC	ENCYCLOPEDIAS, HANDBOOKS
DEFINITIONS	DICTIONARIES
PRIMARY SOURCES	INDEXES, ABSTRACTS, GOVERNMENT PUBLICATIONS
SECONDARY SOURCES	LIBRARY CATALOG, BIBLIOGRAPHIES, INDEXES AND ABSTRACTS, ONLINE DATABASES
FACTS	ALMANACS, YEARBOOKS, GOVERNMENT PUBLICATIONS
CURRENT INFORMATION	PERIODICALS, NEWSPAPERS, ONLINE DATABASES
HISTORICAL INFORMATION	LIBRARY CATALOG ENCYCLOPEDIAS
EVALUATIVE SOURCES	BOOK REVIEW INDEXES

2. *Authority of the author.* Information on the educational background, professional experience, and reputation of a writer can be located in biographical dictionaries and professional directories.

3. *Reputation of the publishing agency.* Some publishers have a solid reputation for publishing only material that they know is reliable and authoritative. On the other hand, there are many so-called "vanity presses" which publish for pay regardless of the quality of the material. In general, the presses of major universities are considered to be reliable publishers, as are the major publishing houses and scholarly societies.

4. *Use of book reviews for evaluation.* Critical evaluations of books can be found by using *Book Review Digest*, *Book Review Index*, or any of the sources to book reviews.

5. *Objectivity of the source.* One way to identify whether information is free of bias and prejudice is simply to examine the source. A publication by a political party would obviously reflect a certain bias. Governments frequently publish propaganda, while publications from a business or a commercial concern might be another form of advertising. Statistics can be manipulated so that they reflect favorably or unfavorably to suit any party with a vested interest.

TAKING NOTES

A convenient way to record information is to keep notes on index cards. The note card should identify the author's last name or short title of the source being used. The topic from the outline should also be recorded. Notes should be taken on all important facts and opinions that are relevant to the topic. When taking notes, it is best to paraphrase the words of the author although sometimes direct quotations are needed for emphasis or for authoritativeness. In either case it is important to retain the original meaning. Since material used out of context can be manipulated to distort the author's intended meaning, it is important to use the material to convey the author's intent. If statements are quoted directly, they should be copied exactly as they appear in the original and placed within quotation marks. Paraphrasing is the summarization of material so that the original author's meaning is retained, but rephrased by the researcher. In both cases the page or pages should be correctly noted on the note card.

A separate card (may be smaller) should be used to keep a complete bibliographic record of the information. It is also a good idea to include the call number on the bibliography card. The bibliographical forms are given on pages 313–326. It is helpful to know which bibliographical form the instructor requires before undertaking the actual research so that the necessary details need be copied only once. (See Figure 11.2.)

WRITING THE PAPER

Once the researcher is satisfied that sufficient information has been gathered to support all the topics in the original outline, it is time to begin on the first draft of the paper. The notes should be sorted so that they are grouped under headings to fit the topics in the outline.

The research paper, by definition, is based primarily on evidence gathered from authorities and scholars. It demands a great deal of creativity to assimilate evidence and present it so that it gives the reader a new perspective. Sufficient time should be allowed for the actual writing. It may take several drafts to achieve the well-written research paper. In writing the paper, all the elements of good writing should be employed—effective phrasing of ideas, good paragraph development, and attention to logical flow of the paragraphs into a unified paper.

should include a shortened form of the title after the author's last name. References to Henry James' *Portrait of a Lady* and his *Wings of the Dove* would be cited in subsequent references as follows:

25 James, Wings 135.
26 James, Portrait 202.

Bibliography or Works Cited

A bibliography is a descriptive list of sources of information—books, articles from periodicals, government documents, theses and dissertations, articles from reference books, and other sources of information. A bibliography may list works by one author (an *author* bibliography), or it may list references on a subject (a *subject* bibliography). A *selective* bibliography includes only some of the possible references, while a *complete* bibliography lists all the references available. Bibliographies with descriptive notes about each entry are called *annotated* bibliographies.

The preferred term for a bibliography in a research paper is "Works Cited." It includes all the sources of information used in writing the paper and is placed at the end of the paper (*MLA Handbook* 4.1). The term "Works Consulted" should be used if the list includes additional works which were not cited in the text of the paper.

The items in a bibliography may be grouped according to their form of publication. For example, books may be listed in one group and periodicals in a second group. Within each group, the items are arranged in alphabetical order.

Arrangement and Punctuation

Books in the bibliography are arranged alphabetically according to the last name of the author. If the book has more than one author, only the first name listed is inverted. If the book is listed by title rather than author, it is placed alphabetically by words in the title, excluding the initial articles "a," "an," or "the." For example, *The Guide to Good Eating* would be alphabetized by "guide." If two or more entries have the same author, the author's name is not repeated. A three space line is used to indicate the omission of the name. The first line of each entry is placed in hanging *indention*. That is, it begins about four spaces to the left of the following lines in the entry.

A period and two spaces are placed after the author's name, after the title, and after each separate element in the entry, except after the items in the *imprint* (publication information). A colon follows the place of publication; a comma comes between the publisher and the date. A period is placed at the end of the entry. The same rule is followed in citing periodical articles. A period and two spaces follow each element of the entry except in the publication information. A colon comes after the date and before the page number(s) in the entry.

Following is an example of works cited for a research paper on artificial intelligence.

WORKS CITED

"Artificial Intelligence." Encyclopaedia Britannica: Micropaedia. 1985.

Board, John E. "Can Computers Think Like People?" Electronics and Power 31 (1985): 275-76.

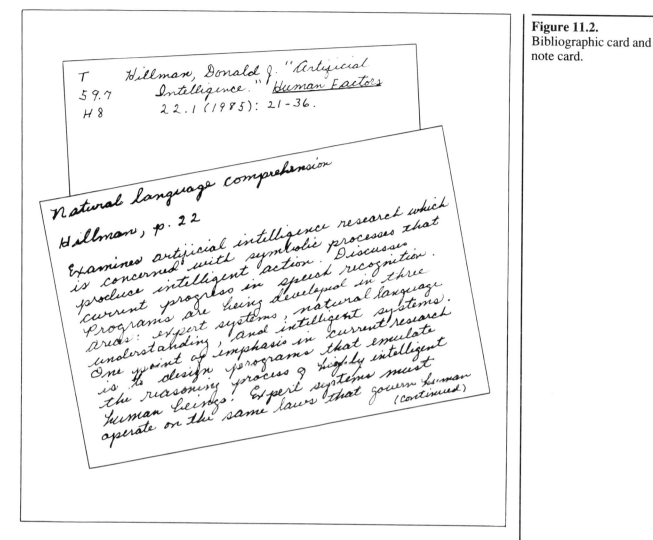

Figure 11.2.
Bibliographic card and note card.

DOCUMENTING THE RESEARCH

It is expected that a research paper will be documented since by definition it includes ideas and facts gathered from other sources. To document a research paper means to state the sources used or consulted. There are several acceptable methods of acknowledging the material used in writing a research paper.

Three of these will be discussed below:

1. Parenthetical references in the text keyed to a list of works cited
2. Full bibliographic references within the text of the paper
3. Notes

There are a number of style manuals which serve as guides for documenting research. Some scholarly disciplines recommend a style which is peculiar to that field. The style manual that is used in this text is the *MLA Handbook for Writers of Research Papers,* by Joseph Gibaldi and Walter S. Achtert (3rd ed. [New York: MLA, 1988], hereafter referred to as the *MLA Handbook*). It is widely used in the humanities.

Plagiarism

The appropriation of ideas or the copying of the language of another writer without formal acknowledgement is *plagiarism*. Plagiarism is a serious violation of legal and ethical canons; yet many students who would not dare copy another's examination paper think nothing of "borrowing" ideas and even exact language from another writer without giving credit. This is not to say that writers must document every single thing they write. Those ideas which evolved in the writer's own mind, even though they are a result of the research, do not require documentation. Nor is it necessary to document facts considered common knowledge. Ordinarily the writer should not have difficulty determining what is common knowledge. Some facts will appear over and over in the readings. Well-known facts, such as the date of America's entry into World War I, require no documentation. Little known facts, or facts about which the writer has no prior knowledge, such as details of President Wilson's peace proposals, would require documentation. If there is doubt in the writer's mind as to whether or not a fact is common knowledge, the source should be acknowledged.

Parenthetical References

The *MLA Handbook (sec.4.1)* recommends the use of parenthetical references in which citations in the text are keyed to a list of "Works Cited" as the preferred method. The "Works Cited" is a list with full bibliographic descriptions of all the sources that were used and acknowledged in the text. The source in the text is identified by a brief reference in parenthesis to the corresponding reference in the list of "Works Cited." Usually the author's last name and the page(s) cited in the text are sufficient for identification:

". . . the advancement of computer technology and the impact of the continuing information explosion are combining to hasten the transition from current data management to future knowledge management" (Kellogg 75).

If the author is mentioned in the text, it is not necessary to repeat the author's name in the citation:

Charles Kellogg believes that the time is fast approaching when computers will be transformed from data managers to knowledge managers (75).

The entry would appear in the list of ''Works Cited'' as:

Kellogg, Charles. ''From Data Management to Knowledge Management.'' Computer Jan. 1986: 75-84.

If the parenthetical reference is to a work that is listed by title in the ''Works Cited,'' the title, or a shortened form of the title, may be used. The reference "(*Digest* 137)" is sufficient to identify the title and page reference for the book cited below:

Digest of the Public Record of Communism in the United States. New York: Fund for the Republic, 1955.

Full Bibliographic References in Text

The use of a full bibliographic reference in the text to cite a source is acceptable only when one or two references are cited. The reference above to the *MLA Handbook* is an example of this form of documentation.

Notes

When notes are used for documentation, the documented material in the text of the paper is indicated by a "superscript" (a raised Arabic number) placed after the punctuation mark of material that is cited. The numbers are keyed to numbers in the notes. The first reference in the notes to the work contains full bibliographic information. Subsequent references to the same work are cited in brief. The note numbers should be consecutive throughout the paper. Notes used to document works cited in the text may appear at the bottom of the page (footnotes) or at the end of the paper (endnotes). However, notes at the end of the paper are preferred. When endnotes are used for documentation, it is not necessary to include a separate bibliography in the paper. Occasionally, however, an instructor will indicate a preference for the inclusion of a bibliography as well as notes in a research paper.

Arrangement and Punctuation of Notes

The first line of the note (footnote or endnote) is indented five spaces to the right. It begins with the raised number ("superscript") followed by a space and the author's name or first word in the title if the main entry is by title. The second line of the note begins at the left margin. The author's name is given in regular order (first name, middle name or initial, and last name). Words in the title are capitalized, except articles, prepositions, and conjunctions unless one is the first word in a title. Each word in the title is underlined. A comma follows the author's name, the title, the editor, the edition, and the series unless one of these is followed immediately by parenthesis. The facts of publication (city, publisher, date) are enclosed in parentheses. A colon follows the name of the city, and a comma comes between the publisher's name and the date. The page number follows the parenthesis mark and refers to the specific citation.

Subsequent references to the same work are cited in shortened form.

Example:

Book

[15] Barbara Tuchman, The Guns of August (New York: Macmillan, 1962) 133.
[16] Tuchman 186.

Periodical Article

[17] Jeanette F. Tudor, ''Development of Class Awareness in Children,'' Social Forces 49 (1971): 473.
[18] Tudor 479.

The use of the terms *ibid.* (meaning "in the same place"), *op. cit.* ("in the work cited") and *loc. cit.* ("in the place cited") is no longer considered good form. Current usage is to identify the work being cited with the relevant page numbers. In most cases the author's last name is sufficient to identify the work. If two or more different titles by the same author are being cited, the citation

Charniak, Eugene, and Drew McDermott. Introduction to Artificial Intelligence. Reading, MA: Addison, 1985.

Dreyfus, Hubert L., and Stuart E. Dreyfus. "Why Computers May Never Think Like People" [Excerpt from Mind over Machine]. Technology Review Jan. 1986: 42-61.

Felsen, Jerry. Decision Making under Uncertainty: An Artificial Intelligence Approach. New York: CDS, 1976.

Gardner, Howard. The Mind's New Science: A History of the Cognitive Revolution. New York: Basic, 1985.

Gervarter, William B. Intelligent Machines: An Introductory Perspective of Artificial Intelligence and Robotics. Englewood Cliffs: Prentice, 1985.

Haugeland, John. Artificial Intelligence: The Very Idea. Cambridge: MIT, 1985.

Hillis, W. Daniel. The Connection Machine. Cambridge: MIT, 1985.

Hillman, Donald J. "Artificial Intelligence." Human Factors 22.1 (1985): 21-31.

Kellogg, Charles. "From Data Management to Knowledge Management." Computer 19 (1986): 75-84.

Kopec, Danny, and Donald Michie. Mismatch Between Machine Representations and Human Concepts: Dangers and Remedies. Science and Technology Policy: FAST Series. Luxembourg: Commission of the European Communities, 1983.

Lenat, Douglas B. "Computer Software for Intelligent Systems." Scientific American 251 (1984): 204-13.

Manuel, Tom, and Michael B. Rand. "Has AI's Time Come at Last?" Electronics Week 4 Feb. 1985: 51-62.

Moyne, John A. Understanding Language: Man or Machine. New York: Plenum, 1985.

National Institutes of Health. Division of Research Resources. The Seeds of Artificial Intelligence: SUMEX-AIM. Rockville, MD: NIH, 1980.

Newell, Allen. "Artificial Intelligence." McGraw-Hill Encyclopedia of Science and Technology, 1982.

Reichman, Rachel. Getting Computers to Talk Like You and Me: Discourse Context, Focus, and Semantics: (An ATN Model). Cambridge: MIT, 1985.

Rothfeder, Jeffrey. Minds Over Matter. New York: Simon, 1985.

Shute, V. J. "Artificial Intelligence." International Encyclopedia of Education. 1985.

GENERAL RULES—NOTES AND BIBLIOGRAPHY

Regardless of the method used to document research, one needs to know certain elementary forms of documentation. While there is no one "correct" form for documentation, convention does dictate that the writer of scholarly papers follow a prescribed style--one that is consistent throughout and which communicates clearly and accurately the sources which are being documented. The forms for notes and bibliography discussed below are based on the *MLA Handbook*. Some scholarly fields may prefer a different form. The writer should consult a style manual in other disciplines if the MLA style is not appropriate. Note style and bibliography style vary only in arrangement and punctuation. The items included in each entry are essentially the same with the exception of the page reference which is omitted in a bibliographical entry for a book.

I. BOOKS

Items to include in documenting a book:

1. Author's full name. If there are more than one, but less than four authors, all of the authors' names are included. When there are four authors, it is permissible to cite all the names or to give the first one listed on the title page followed by "et al." or by "and others." If there are more than four authors, only the first one listed is cited followed by "et al." or by "and others."
2. Title of part of book if only citing one part.
3. The title of the book, as it appears on the title page.
4. Editor, translator, compiler (if any).
5. The edition if other than the first.
6. Volume if part of a multivolume set.
7. The series (if any).
8. The imprint
   a. The city of publication. If more than one place is listed on the title page, only the first one listed is used. The name of the state is included if the city is not well known.
   b. The publisher. The shortened name of the publisher is used unless there is confusion in identification. The shortened forms of publishers' names are found in the *MLA Handbook* (6.3).
   c. The date of publication. Publication date is found on the title page. If there is no publication date given, the latest copyright date is used. If neither a publication date nor a copyright date is given, the abbreviation, n.d., is used.
9. Page citation for a note entry or inclusive pages when citing a part of a book.

Examples

The examples below include first reference note form and bibliographic form for each entry.

A. Book by one author

Notes:
    [1]Ethel Hausman, The Illustrated Encyclopedia of American Wildflowers (Garden City: Garden City Pub., 1947) 28.

Bibliography:
    Hausman, Ethel. The Illustrated Encyclopedia of American Wildflowers. Garden City: Garden City Pub., 1947.

Explanation: Cite author, title, and imprint (place of publication, publisher, date). The publisher's full name is given only when there is confusion with the name of the city.

B. Book by two or more authors

Notes:
    [2]Wallace K. Ferguson and Geoffrey Bruum, A Survey of European Civilization, 2nd ed. (Boston: Houghton, 1952) 73.

Bibliography:
> Ferguson, Wallace K., and Geoffrey Bruum. A Survey of European Civilization. 2nd ed. Boston: Houghton, 1952.

Explanation: The name of the first author is inverted in the bibliographical entry. Names of other authors are given in regular order. These are given in the order in which they appear on the title page. Remainder of entry cites edition, place of publication, publisher, and edition.

B.2 Book by two or more authors with the same last name

Notes:
> [3]Will Durant and Ariel Durant, A Dual Autobiography (New York: Simon, 1977) 10.

Bibliography:
> Durant, Will, and Ariel Durant. A Dual Autobiography. New York: Simon, 1977.

Explanation: Author, title, imprint. Last name of second author is given.

B.3 Book by more than three persons

Notes:
> [4]James Davis, et al., Society and the Law: New Meanings for an Old Profession (New York: Free, 1962) 102.

Bibliography:
> Davis, James, et al. Society and the Law: New Meanings For an Old Profession. New York: Free, 1962.

Explanation: Author, title, imprint. May also use Davis, James, and others, or give all names in full.

C. Book by a corporate author

Notes:
> [5]Center for the Study of Democratic Institutions, Natural Law and Modern Society, contrib. John Cogley, et al. (Cleveland: World, 1973) 157.

Bibliography:
> Center for the Study of Democratic Institutions. Natural Law and Modern Society. Contrib. John Cogley, et al. Cleveland: World, 1973.

Explanation: Corporate author, title. contributors, imprint.

D. Book that is an edited work

Notes:
> [6]Phillip Green and Michael Walzer, eds., The Political Imagination in Literature: A Reader (New York: Free, 1969) 28.

Bibliography:
> Green, Phillip, and Michael Walzer, eds. The Political Imagination in Literature: A Reader. New York: Free, 1969.

Explanation: Editors, title, imprint.

E. A book that is part of a series

Notes:
[7]Lacy H. Hunt, <u>Dynamics of Forecasting Financial Cycles: Theory, Technique, and Implementation</u>, Contemporary Studies in Economic and Financial Analysis (Greenwich: JAI, 1976) 18.

Bibliography:
Hunt, Lacy H. <u>Dynamics of Forecasting Financial Cycles: Theory, Technique, and Implementation</u>. Contemporary Studies in Economic and Financial Analysis. Greenwich: JAI, 1976.

Explanation: Author, title of book, title of series, imprint.

F. Book that is one volume of a multivolume work, one author, each volume a different title

Notes:
[8]Dumas Malone, <u>Jefferson and the Ordeal of Liberty</u>, Vol. III of <u>Jefferson and His Time</u> 6 vols. (Boston: Little, 1962) 243.

Bibliography:
Malone, Dumas. <u>Jefferson and the Ordeal of Liberty</u>. Vol. III of <u>Jefferson and His Time</u>. 6 vols. Boston: Little, 1962.

Explanation: Author, title of Vol. III, title of set, number of volumes in set, imprint.

G. Book that is one volume of a multivolume work with one general title

Notes:
[9]Charles Warren, <u>The Supreme Court in United States History</u>, rev. ed. 2 vols. (Boston: Little, 1926) I: 231.

Bibliography:
Warren, Charles. <u>The Supreme Court in United States History</u>. Rev. ed. 2 Vols. Boston: Little, 1926.

Explanation: Author of book, title, edition, number of volumes, imprint.

H. Book that is a translation of an author's work

Notes:
[10]Friedrich Nietzsche, <u>The Birth of Tragedy and the Genealogy of Morals</u>, trans. Francis Golffing (Garden City: Doubleday, 1956) 42.

Bibliography:
Nietzsche, Frederick. <u>The Birth of Tragedy and the Genealogy of Morals</u>. Trans. Francis Golffing. Garden City: Doubleday, 1952.

Explanation: Author, title, translator, imprint.

I. Short story in a collected work (anthology)

Notes:
[11]William Faulkner, "Dry September," <u>Ten Modern Masters: An Anthology of the Short Story</u>, ed. Robert G. Davis (New York: Harcourt, 1953) 340.

Bibliography:
> Faulkner, William. "Dry September." <u>Ten Modern Masters: An Anthology of the Short Story</u>. Ed. Robert G. Davis. New York: Harcourt, 1953. 339-350.

Explanation: Author of short story, title of short story, title of book in which story appears, editor of book, imprint, pages on which story appears.

J. Essay or article in a collected work (anthology)

Notes:
> [12]James D. Barker, "Man, Mood, and the Presidency," <u>The Presidency Reappraised</u>, ed. Rexford G. Tugwell and Thomas E. Cronin (New York: Praeger, 1974) 208.

Bibliography:
> Barker, James D. "Man, Mood, and the Presidency." <u>The Presidency Reappraised</u>. Ed. Rexford G. Tugwell and Thomas E. Cronin. New York: Praeger, 1974. 205-214.

Explanation: Author of article, title of article, title of book in which article appears, editors of book, imprint, pages on which article appears in book.

II. REFERENCE BOOKS

In citing articles from encyclopedias, yearbooks, biographical dictionaries, and other well known reference books, the following items are included:
1. The author of the article, if known.
2. The title of the article as it appears in the book.
3. The title of the book in which the article appears.
4. The edition, if other than the first, and the date of publication.
5. The volume number if one of a multivolume set, unless entire set is alphabetically arranged.
6. The inclusive paging for a bibliographical entry; specific page for a note entry. If the articles are arranged in alphabetical order in the work, page numbers should be omitted.

Examples

A. Article from a multivolume general reference book

Notes:
> [13]Leroy D. Vandam, "Anesthetic," <u>Encyclopaedia Britannica: Macropaedia</u>, 1974.

Bibliography:
> Vandam, Leroy D. "Anesthetic." <u>Encyclopaedia Britannica: Macropaedia</u>. 1974.

Explanation: Author of the article, title of the article, title of the book, publication date.

B. Article from a single volume general reference book

Notes:
> [14]Romulo Betancourt, "Latin America, Its Problems and Possibilities," <u>Britannica Book of the Year</u>, *1966* (1966) 26.

Bibliography:
> Betancourt, Romulo. "Latin America, Its Problems and Possibilities." <u>Britannica Book of the Year</u>, *1966*. 1966. 19-40.

Explanation: Author of the article, title of the article, title of the book, publication date, inclusive pages.

C. Article from a multivolume subject reference book

Notes:
> [15]Eleanor Flexner, "Woman's Rights Movement," <u>Dictionary of American History</u>, ed. Joseph G.E. Hopkins and Wayne Andrews, 6 vols. (New York: Scribner's, 1961) VI. Supp. 1: 301.

Bibliography:
> Flexner, Eleanor. "Woman's Rights Movement." *Dictionary of American History.* Ed. Joseph G.E. Hopkins and Wayne Andrews. 6 vols. New York: Scribner's, 1961. VI, Supp. 1: 301-03.

Explanation: Author of the article, title of the article, title of the reference book, editors, total volumes, imprint, volume number and inclusive pages of the article. Note: If the reference book is not a familiar one or if there are other books with the same title, it is necessary to give full publication information.

D. Article from a biographical dictionary (unsigned)

Notes:
> [16]"Sellers, Peter (Richard Henry)," <u>Who's Who</u> *1976–1977,* 1976.

Bibliography:
> "Sellers, Peter (Richard Henry)." <u>Who's Who</u> *1976–1977.* 1976.

Explanation: Full name of biographee or subject of article which is used as title of article, title of biographical dictionary, and date.

E. Article from a biographical dictionary (signed)

Notes:
> [17]Arthur C. Cole, "Webster, Daniel," <u>Dictionary of American Biography</u>, 1936.

Bibliography:
> Cole, Arthur C. "Webster, Daniel." <u>Dictionary of American Biography</u>, 1936.

Explanation: Author of article, name of biographee, title of biographical dictionary, copyright date.

F. Book of quotations

Notes:
> [18]Samuel Johnson, "He who praises everybody praises nobody . . . ," <u>The Oxford Dictionary of Quotations</u>, 2nd ed. 237.

Bibliography:
> Johnson, Samuel. "He who praises everybody praises nobody. . . . " <u>The Oxford Dictionary of Quotations</u>. 2nd. ed. 237.

Explanation: Author, first line of quotation, title of book, edition, page.

III. PERIODICAL AND NEWSPAPER ARTICLES

In citing articles from periodicals the following items are included:

1. The author of the article if it is a signed article.
2. The title of the article.
3. The title of the periodical.
4. The volume number and/or issue number if it is a journal.
5. The date.
6. The inclusive pages in a bibliographical entry; the specific page reference in a note entry. If an article is not printed on consecutive pages, that is, if it begins on one page and continues on later pages, cite the beginning page followed by a "+."

Examples

A. Article from a monthly magazine (signed)

Notes:
[19]Roger Starr, "A Kind Word about Money," Harper's April 1976: 90.

Bibliography:
Starr, Roger. "A Kind Word about Money." Harper's April 1976: 79-92.

Explanation: Author of article, title of article, title of magazine, date, page(s). With a monthly magazine only the date and pages, not the volume are cited.

B. Article from a monthly magazine (unsigned)

Notes:
[20]"First National Data on Reading Speed," Intellect Oct. 1972: 9.

Bibliography:
"First National Data on Reading Speed." Intellect Oct. 1972: 9.

Explanation: Title of article, title of magazine, date, page.

C. Article from a weekly magazine (signed)

Notes:
[21]James D. Meindl, "Microelectronics and Computers in Medicine," Science 12 Feb. 1982: 793.

Bibliography:
Meindl, James D. "Microelectronics and Computers in Medicine." Science 12 Feb. 1982: 792-797.

Explanation: Author of article, title of article, title of magazine, date, page(s)

D. Article from a weekly magazine (unsigned)

Notes:
[22]"Behind the Threat of More Inflation," Business Week 18 Nov. 1972: 77.

Bibliography:

"Behind the Threat of More Inflation." <u>Business Week</u> 18 Nov. 1972: 76-78.

Explanation: Title of article, title of magazine, date, page(s).

E. Article from a journal with continuously numbered pages throughout the volume

Notes:

[23]Gerald Runkle, "Is Violence Always Wrong?" <u>Journal of Politics</u> 38 (1976): 250.

Bibliography:

Runkle, Gerald. "Is Violence Always Wrong?" <u>Journal of Politics</u> 38 (1976): 247-291.

Explanation: Author of article, title of article, title of journal, volume number, year, and page(s).

F. Article from a journal with separately numbered pages in each issue

Notes:

[24]Jay Martin, "A Watertight Watergate Future: Americans in a Post-American Age," <u>The Antioch Review</u> 2 (1975): 18.

Bibliography:

Martin, Jay. "A Watertight Watergate Future: Americans in a Post-American Age." <u>The Antioch Review</u> 33.2 (1975): 7-25.

Explanation: Author of article, title of article, title of journal, volume number, issue number, year, and pages.

G. Book review (signed)

Notes:

[25]Robert Sherrill, rev. of <u>The Time of Illusion</u>, by Jonathan Schell, <u>New York Times Book Review</u> 18 Jan. 1976: 1.

Bibliography:

Sherrill, Robert. Rev. of <u>The Time of Illusion</u>, by Jonathan Schell. <u>New York Times Book Review</u> 18 Jan. 1976: 1-2.

Explanation: Author of review, title of book, author of book, periodical in which review appears, date, page(s).

H. Book review with title (signed)

Notes:

[26]Robert Hughes, "The Sorcerer's Apprentice," rev. of <u>Journey to Ixtlan</u>, by Carlos Castaneda, <u>Time</u> 6 Nov. 1972: 101.

Bibliography:

Hughes, Robert. "The Sorcerer's Apprentice." Rev. of <u>Journey to Ixtlan</u>, by Carlos Castaneda. <u>Time</u> 6 Nov. 1972: 101.

Explanation: Author of review, title of review, title of book, author of book, periodical in which review appears, date, page.

I. Book review (unsigned)

Notes:
[27]Rev. of The Efficacy of Law, by Harry W. Jones, Choice 7 (1970): 941.

Bibliography:
Rev. of The Efficacy of Law, by Harry W. Jones. Choice 7 (1970): 941.

Explanation: Title of book, author of book, name of periodical in which review appears, volume number, date, page.

J. Newspaper article (signed)

Notes:
[28]Tom Goldstein, "New Federal Tax Law Could Foster Growth of Plans to Provide Prepaid Legal Services," New York Times 28 Sept. 1976, eastern ed.: A36.

Bibliography:
Goldstein, Tom. "New Federal Tax Law Could Foster Growth of Plans to Provide Prepaid Legal Services," New York Times 28 Sept. 1976, eastern ed.: A36.

Explanation: Author of newspaper article, summary title of article, name of newspaper, date, edition, section, page.

K. Newspaper article (unsigned)

Notes:
[29]"College Enrollment Decline Predicted for South in '80's," Morning Advocate [Baton Rouge] 28 Sept. 1976: B7.

Bibliography:
"College Enrollment Decline Predicted for South in '80's." Morning Advocate [Baton Rouge] 28 Sept. 1976: B7.

Explanation: Summary title of article, name of newspaper, city, date, section, page. Note: the name of the city is in brackets because it is not part of the title.

L. Editorial from a newspaper

Notes:
[30]"Takeovers Yes, Hold-ups No," Editorial, New York Times 28 Nov. 1986, eastern ed.: A26.

Bibliography:
"Takeovers Yes, Hold-ups No." Editorial. New York Times 28 Nov. 1986, eastern ed.: A26.

Explanation: Title of article, type of article, title of newspaper, date, edition, section, page.

IV. UNPUBLISHED THESIS

Notes:
³¹Carol A. Runnels, ''The Self Image of the Artist . . . ,'' Thesis, Louisiana State University, 1975, 10.

Bibliography:
Runnels, Carol A. ''The Self Image of the Artist. . . .'' Thesis, Louisiana State University, 1975.

Explanation: Author, title, descriptive label (thesis), degree-granting institution, year, and pages in note citation.

V. PHONOGRAPHIC RECORDINGS

Notes:
³²Elise Bell, <u>The Bronze Bow</u>, based on the book by Elizabeth George Speare, Newberry Award Records, NAR 3029, 1972.

Bibliography:
Bell, Elise. <u>The Bronze Bow</u>. Based on the book by Elizabeth George Speare. Newberry Award Records, NAR 3029, 1972.

Explanation: Performer, title of recording, source, producer of record, catalog number, date.

VI. MUSICAL SCORE

Notes:
³³Kelly Bryan, <u>March—Washington D.C.</u> (London: Novello, 1971).

Bibliography:
Bryan, Kelly. <u>March—Washington D.C.</u> London: Novello, 1971.

Explanation: Composer, title of composition, imprint.

VII. COMPUTER SOFTWARE

Notes:
³⁴<u>Dollars and Sense with Forecast</u>, computer software, Monogram, 1984, IBM PC, PCjr., XT.

Bibliography:
<u>Dollars and Sense with Forecast</u>. Computer software. Monogram, 1984. IBM PC, PCjr., XT.

Explanation: Title of program, descriptive label, distributor, year of publication, operating system for which the program is designed.

VIII. VIDEOTAPES

Notes:
³⁵<u>Our National Parks</u>, videocassette, prod. Wolfgang Bayer Productions, National Geographic Book Service, 1989, 30 min.

Bibliography
<u>Our National Parks</u>. Videocassette. Prod. Wolfgang Bayer Productions. National Geographic Book Service, 1989. 30 min.

Explanation: Title of tape, type of tape, producer, distributor, date, running time.

IX. GOVERNMENT PUBLICATIONS

Government publications vary greatly according to type and form. Consequently, citations for government publications present many problems. The information supplied on the title page or on the cover when there is no title page is not always easy to decipher. In citing government publications it is good practice to give as full information as possible in order to insure proper identification and facilitate publication location. The entries in the *Monthly Catalog of United States Government Publications* can serve as a guide for bibliographic citations, especially those since 1976 which are reproduced in card catalog format. The following general rules and examples should be helpful:

1. Author is usually a corporate author such as United States . . . . In citing documents indicate the name of the country first, unless the agency begins with *National* or *Federal*. For example:

    U.S. Office of Education

    National Aeronautics and Space Administration

    Federal Bureau of Investigation

2. Bureaus and offices are entered as subheadings under the country, not as subheadings to the department unless the name of the bureau or office is not distinctive. For example:

    U.S. Geological Survey not U.S. Interior Dept. Geological Survey.

    U.S. Geological Survey. Abstracts of North American Geology. Washington: GPO, 1970.

3. Divisions and sub-branches which are subordinate to executive departments, ministries, bureaus, and the like are entered as subheadings to those departments, ministries, bureaus, etc. For example:

    U.S. Library of Congress. General Reference and Bibliography Division. Children's Literature, a Guide to Reference Sources. Comp. Virginia Haviland. Washington: GPO, 1966.

4. Cite the name of the agency as it appears on the document:

    Dept. of Justice, not Justice Department

5. Personal authors can be used for nonadministrative publications, reports not by an official, parts of a series, single addresses, and collected editions, as well as collections of treaties of several countries compiled by an individual. The name of the issuing agency and other identifying information should follow the title since some bibliographic tools might not list the document by author. For example:

    Reid, William J., Jr., and F. P. Cuthbert, Jr. Aphids on Leafy Vegetables: How to Control Them. Agricultural Research Service, Farmers' Bulletin No. 2148. Washington: GPO, 1976.

    If the individual author is known but the agency is listed first, the individual's name is placed after the title and is preceded by a comma and the word "by."

    U.S. Consumer Product Safety Commission. Hazard Analysis of Aluminum Wiring, by Rae Newman. Washington: GPO, 1975.

6. Titles. The title of the publication follows the author's name and should be underlined. In citing a Congressional document, include such information as the number and session of Congress and the type and number of publication. This should not be underlined. Cite the

title as it appears on the title page, except in instances where the agency's name is part of the title. In that case, the two should be separated. For example: The Life-saving Benefits of the 55 Mph National Speed Limit: Report of the HTSA/FHWA Task Force.
Cite as:

> National Highway Traffic Safety Administration/Federal Highway Administration, Task Force. <u>The Life-saving Benefits of the 55 Mph National Speed Limit: A Report</u>. Washington: GPO, 1980.

7. Imprint. Since most U.S. government publications are distributed by the Government Printing Office, the imprint is usually the Government Printing Office (GPO) regardless of which agency issued the publication. Washington is the place of publication. For example:

> Washington: GPO, date.

Since the GPO is not always the publisher, the imprint should be verified in the *Monthly Catalog* or in the document itself. For example:

> U.S. Energy Research and Development Administration. <u>Development of a Modular Software System for Dynamic Simulation of Coal Conversion Plants</u>. Springfield, Va.: National Technical Information Service, 1976.

Examples

A. Agency publication

Notes:
[36]William J. Reid, Jr., and F. P. Cuthbert, Jr., <u>Aphids on Leafy Vegetables: How to Control Them</u>, Agricultural Research Service, Farmers' Bulletin no. 2148 (Washington: GPO, 1976) 15.

Bibliography:
> Reid, William J., Jr., and F. P. Cuthbert, Jr. <u>Aphids on Leafy Vegetables: How to Control Them</u>. Agricultural Research Service, Farmers' Bulletin No. 2148. Washington: GPO, 1976.

Explanation: Authors of publication, title, Government agency responsible for publication, series title and number, imprint, pages (notes).

B. Congressional hearings

Notes:
[37]U.S. Cong. Senate. Select Committee on Nutrition and Human Needs, <u>Federally Supported Food Program</u>:. . . , 95th Cong., 1st sess. (Washington: GPO, 1977) 16.

Bibliography:
> U.S. Cong. Senate. Select Committee on Nutrition and Human Needs. <u>Federally Supported Food Program</u>:. . . . 95th Cong., 1st sess. Washington: GPO, 1977.

Explanation: Senate committee as author, title, session of Congress, imprint, page (for note).

C. *Congressional bills, reports, documents*

Notes:
[38]U.S. Cong. House. Committee on the Judiciary, <u>Opposing the Granting of Permanent Residence in the United States to Certain Aliens</u>, Report to accompany H. Res. 795, 95th Cong., 1st sess., H. R. no. 691 (Washington: GPO, 1977) 3.

Bibliography:
>U.S. Cong. House. Committee on the Judiciary, <u>Opposing the Granting of Permanent Residence in the United States to Certain Aliens</u>. Report to accompany H. Res. 795. 95th Cong., 1st sess. H. R. no. 691. Washington: GPO, 1977.

Explanation: House committee as author, title, document type (Report, etc.), session of Congress, imprint, page (for note).

D. *Laws, decrees, etc.*

1. Citation to the *Statutes at Large*

Notes:
[39]PL 96-511 (Dec. 11, 1980), Paperwork Reduction Act of 1980, 94 Stat. 2812.

Bibliography:
>PL 96-511 (Dec. 11, 1980). Paperwork Reduction Act of 1980. 94 Stat. 2812.

Explanation: public law number, date approved, title of law, volume number of the *Statutes at Large*, abbreviation for *Statutes at Large*, page number.

2. Citation to the *United States Code*

Notes:
[40]20 U.S.C. 238 (1980).

Bibliography:
>20 U.S.C. 238 (1980).

Explanation: title number of code, abbreviation of *United States Code*, section number, and edition date.

E. *Court case*

Notes:
[41]Brewer v. Williams, 430 U.S. 389 (1977).

Bibliography:
>Brewer v. Williams, 430 U.S. 389 (1977).

Explanation: Name of case, volume 430 of *U.S. Reports*, page 389, date 1977.

F. Congressional Record

Notes:
^{42}Cong. Rec. 121 (1975): 40634.

Bibliography:
Cong. Rec. 121 (1975): 40634.

Explanation: *Congressional Record*, volume number, year, page number. Notice that it is not necessary to cite the subject or title of the article or its author.

ABBREVIATIONS

anon.—anonymous
bibliog.—bibliography
bibliog. f.—bibliographical footnote
bull.—bulletin
c—copyright
cf.—compare
col., cols.—column(s)
comp.—compiler, compiled by
Cong.—Congress
Cong. Rec.—Congressional Record
ed., eds.—editor(s), edition(s), edited by
e.g.—for example
enl.—enlarged
et al.—and others
f., ff.—and following
facsim.—facsimile
GPO—Government Printing Office
H. Doc.—House document
HR—House of Representatives
HR #—House bill (e.g., HR 190)
H. Rept.—House report
H. Res—House resolution
ibid.—in the same place
illus.—illustrated (by), illustrator, illustration(s)
introd.—introduction
loc. cit.—in the place cited
n. d.—no date
n. p.—no place of publication, no publisher
n. pag.—no pagination
op. cit.—in the work cited
p.—page
pp.—pages
por., pors.—portrait, portraits
pref.—preface
pseud.—pseudonym
q. v.—which see
rev.—revised by, revision, review, reviewed (by) (Review should be spelled out if there is any confusion as to meaning.)
S—Senate

S #—Senate bill (e.g., Senate 45)
S. Doc.—Senate document
S. Rept.—Senate report
S. Res—Senate resolution
[sic]—thus, so
trans. or tr.—translator, translation, translated by
vol., vols.—volume(s)

REVIEW QUESTIONS
CHAPTER 11

1. Name the steps involved in writing a research paper.

2. What are some of the things a student should take into consideration when selecting a topic for research?

3. What are the major library sources to consult when doing library research?

4. Define plagiarism.

5. What is the purpose of documentation in a research paper?

6. Name and describe three methods of documenting a research paper.

7. What is the difference between a list of "Works Cited" and a list of "Works Consulted "?

8. Name the items which are usually included in a bibliographic reference to most non-reference books.

9. How do bibliographic citations for reference books differ from those of non-reference books?

10. Name the items which are included in bibliographical references to periodical articles.

NOTES/BIBLIOGRAPHY EXERCISE

Using the information provided below, prepare a list of notes as though you were preparing notes for a research paper. Indicate after each entry the page and note numbers of the examples used in the text as models.

Note No. 1 is to a book entitled Mexican Americans, written by Joan Moore; published in 1976 by Prentice-Hall Incorporated, in Englewood Cliffs, New Jersey; the reference is to page 17.

Note No. 2, same as No. 1; the reference is to page 88.

Note No. 3 is to an article entitled Black and Hispanic socioeconomic and political competition; the article was written by Paula D. McClain and Albert K. Karnig; the title of the journal in which the article appeared is American Political Science Review; the article was published in volume 84, issue number 2, June 1990; the article is on pages 535-545; the reference is to page 540.

Note No. 4 is to an article entitled the Mexican American family; the article is in a book entitled ethnic families in America; the article was written by David Alverez and Frank D. Bean; the book was edited by Charles H. Mindel and Robert W. Habenstein; the book was published in 1976, by Elsevier in New York City; the article appears on pages 271-292; the reference is to page 271.

Note No. 5, same as No. 3, reference is to page 421.

Note No. 6 is to an unpublished master's thesis from the University of Wisconsin, written in 1981 by Carl Bowman; the title is between cultures: toward an understanding of cultural production of Chicanos; the reference is to page 30.

Note No. 7 is to an article entitled Urban Mexican Americans; written by Daniel D. Arreola, the article, which is illustrated, appears in the January-February, 1984, issue of the magazine entitled Focus; it begins on page 7 and continues on other pages later in that same issue; the reference is to page 7.

Note No. 8 is to a book review entitled a critical examination written by Philip L. Martin; the book, entitled migrant farm workers: a caste of despair, was written by Ronald L. Goldfarb; the review appears in the August 1984 issue of the Monthly Labor Review on pages 44-45; the reference is to page 44.

Note No. 9 is to an article entitled success in U.S.: stranger in land of his roots; the article is unsigned and appears in the August 22, 1983, issue of US News and World Report, on page 48; the reference is to page 48.

Note No. 10, same as No. 9.

I. Notes

II. Bibliography

Prepare a bibliography entitled the Mexican American experience from your note entries.

RESEARCH PROJECT WORKSHEET

Record information from the titles consulted for your Research Project. Items which do not apply should be labeled NA.

1. How did you locate the reference? Source used and subject heading if applicable? (For example, library catalog, *Library of Congress Subject Headings* class numbers, librarian, etc.)

2. If reference book, record subject heading used within book itself:

3. If periodical index or abstract, record name of index, volume, year, and subject heading used within index:

4. Record information necessary for bibliographic reference: (Arrange the information in correct bibliographic form on the back of the sheet.)

5. Call number of book or periodical used:

6. Evaluation of material:

7. Give the topic heading(s) from your outline for which you found infomation in this source.

8. For each topic take notes by paraphrasing the words of the author. Direct quotations may be used for emphasis or for authoritativeness. Enclose quotations in quotation marks. Record page numbers of material used.

RESEARCH PROJECT WORKSHEET

Record information from the titles consulted for your Research Project. Items which do not apply should be labeled NA.

1. How did you locate the reference? Source used and subject heading if applicable? (For example, library catalog, *Library of Congress Subject Headings* class numbers, librarian, etc.)

2. If reference book, record subject heading used within book itself:

3. If periodical index or abstract, record name of index, volume, year, and subject heading used within index:

4. Record information necessary for bibliographic reference: (Arrange the information in correct bibliographic form on the back of the sheet.)

5. Call number of book or periodical used:

6. Evaluation of material:

7. Give the topic heading(s) from your outline for which you found infomation in this source.

8. For each topic take notes by paraphrasing the words of the author. Direct quotations may be used for emphasis or for authoritativeness. Enclose quotations in quotation marks. Record page numbers of material used.

RESEARCH PROJECT WORKSHEET

Record information from the titles consulted for your Research Project. Items which do not apply should be labeled NA.

1. How did you locate the reference? Source used and subject heading if applicable? (For example, library catalog, *Library of Congress Subject Headings* class numbers, librarian, etc.)

2. If reference book, record subject heading used within book itself:

3. If periodical index or abstract, record name of index, volume, year, and subject heading used within index:

4. Record information necessary for bibliographic reference: (Arrange the information in correct bibliographic form on the back of the sheet.)

5. Call number of book or periodical used:

6. Evaluation of material:

7. Give the topic heading(s) from your outline for which you found infomation in this source.

8. For each topic take notes by paraphrasing the words of the author. Direct quotations may be used for emphasis or for authoritativeness. Enclose quotations in quotation marks. Record page numbers of material used.

RESEARCH PROJECT WORKSHEET

Record information from the titles consulted for your Research Project. Items which do not apply should be labeled NA.

1. How did you locate the reference? Source used and subject heading if applicable? (For example, library catalog, *Library of Congress Subject Headings* class numbers, librarian, etc.)

2. If reference book, record subject heading used within book itself:

3. If periodical index or abstract, record name of index, volume, year, and subject heading used within index:

4. Record information necessary for bibliographic reference: (Arrange the information in correct bibliographic form on the back of the sheet.)

5. Call number of book or periodical used:

6. Evaluation of material:

7. Give the topic heading(s) from your outline for which you found infomation in this source.

8. For each topic take notes by paraphrasing the words of the author. Direct quotations may be used for emphasis or for authoritativeness. Enclose quotations in quotation marks. Record page numbers of material used.

341

RESEARCH PROJECT WORKSHEET

Record information from the titles consulted for your Research Project. Items which do not apply should be labeled NA.

1. How did you locate the reference? Source used and subject heading if applicable? (For example, library catalog, *Library of Congress Subject Headings* class numbers, librarian, etc.)

2. If reference book, record subject heading used within book itself:

3. If periodical index or abstract, record name of index, volume, year, and subject heading used within index:

4. Record information necessary for bibliographic reference: (Arrange the information in correct bibliographic form on the back of the sheet.)

5. Call number of book or periodical used:

6. Evaluation of material:

7. Give the topic heading(s) from your outline for which you found infomation in this source.

8. For each topic take notes by paraphrasing the words of the author. Direct quotations may be used for emphasis or for authoritativeness. Enclose quotations in quotation marks. Record page numbers of material used.

343

INSTRUCTOR _____   NAME _____

HOUR & DAY _____

RESEARCH PROJECT WORKSHEET

Record information from the titles consulted for your Research Project. Items which do not apply should be labeled NA.

1. How did you locate the reference? Source used and subject heading if applicable? (For example, library catalog, *Library of Congress Subject Headings* class numbers, librarian, etc.)

2. If reference book, record subject heading used within book itself:

3. If periodical index or abstract, record name of index, volume, year, and subject heading used within index:

4. Record information necessary for bibliographic reference: (Arrange the information in correct bibliographic form on the back of the sheet.)

5. Call number of book or periodical used:

6. Evaluation of material:

7. Give the topic heading(s) from your outline for which you found infomation in this source.

8. For each topic take notes by paraphrasing the words of the author. Direct quotations may be used for emphasis or for authoritativeness. Enclose quotations in quotation marks. Record page numbers of material used.

RESEARCH PROJECT WORKSHEET

Record information from the titles consulted for your Research Project. Items which do not apply should be labeled NA.

1. How did you locate the reference? Source used and subject heading if applicable? (For example, library catalog, *Library of Congress Subject Headings* class numbers, librarian, etc.)

2. If reference book, record subject heading used within book itself:

3. If periodical index or abstract, record name of index, volume, year, and subject heading used within index:

4. Record information necessary for bibliographic reference: (Arrange the information in correct bibliographic form on the back of the sheet.)

5. Call number of book or periodical used:

6. Evaluation of material:

7. Give the topic heading(s) from your outline for which you found infomation in this source.

8. For each topic take notes by paraphrasing the words of the author. Direct quotations may be used for emphasis or for authoritativeness. Enclose quotations in quotation marks. Record page numbers of material used.

INSTRUCTOR_____   NAME_____

HOUR & DAY   _____

RESEARCH PROJECT WORKSHEET

Record information from the titles consulted for your Research Project. Items which do not apply should be labeled NA.

1. How did you locate the reference? Source used and subject heading if applicable? (For example, library catalog, *Library of Congress Subject Headings* class numbers, librarian, etc.)

2. If reference book, record subject heading used within book itself:

3. If periodical index or abstract, record name of index, volume, year, and subject heading used within index:

4. Record information necessary for bibliographic reference: (Arrange the information in correct biblio graphic form on the back of the sheet.)

5. Call number of book or periodical used:

6. Evaluation of material:

7. Give the topic heading(s) from your outline for which you found infomation in this source.

8. For each topic take notes by paraphrasing the words of the author. Direct quotations may be used for emphasis or for authoritativeness. Enclose quotations in quotation marks. Record page numbers of material used.

RESEARCH PROJECT WORKSHEET

Record information from the titles consulted for your Research Project. Items which do not apply should be labeled NA.

1. How did you locate the reference? Source used and subject heading if applicable? (For example, library catalog, *Library of Congress Subject Headings* class numbers, librarian, etc.)

2. If reference book, record subject heading used within book itself:

3. If periodical index or abstract, record name of index, volume, year, and subject heading used within index:

4. Record information necessary for bibliographic reference: (Arrange the information in correct bibliographic form on the back of the sheet.)

5. Call number of book or periodical used:

6. Evaluation of material:

7. Give the topic heading(s) from your outline for which you found infomation in this source.

8. For each topic take notes by paraphrasing the words of the author. Direct quotations may be used for emphasis or for authoritativeness. Enclose quotations in quotation marks. Record page numbers of material used.

RESEARCH PROJECT WORKSHEET

Record information from the titles consulted for your Research Project. Items which do not apply should be labeled NA.

1. How did you locate the reference? Source used and subject heading if applicable? (For example, library catalog, *Library of Congress Subject Headings* class numbers, librarian, etc.)

2. If reference book, record subject heading used within book itself:

3. If periodical index or abstract, record name of index, volume, year, and subject heading used within index:

4. Record information necessary for bibliographic reference: (Arrange the information in correct bibliographic form on the back of the sheet.)

5. Call number of book or periodical used:

6. Evaluation of material:

7. Give the topic heading(s) from your outline for which you found infomation in this source.

8. For each topic take notes by paraphrasing the words of the author. Direct quotations may be used for emphasis or for authoritativeness. Enclose quotations in quotation marks. Record page numbers of material used.

Glossary

Abstract a type of index which gives the location of an article in a periodical or a book and a brief summary of that article.

Annotated bibliography a list of works with descriptions and a brief summary or critical statement about each.

Annotation critical or explanatory note about the contents of a book or an article.

Appendix section of the book containing supplementary materials such as tables or maps.

Article a complete piece of writing that is part of a larger work.

Bibliography list of sources of information.

Blurb advertisement found on the book jacket designed to promote the sale of the book.

Book catalog list of library holdings in book form.

Book number last letter/number combination in the call number. Stands for the author of the book and sometimes the title.

CD-ROM (compact disk-read only memory) database stored on a compact disk and accessed by computer.

Call number the identification number which determines where a book or other library material is located in the library.

Card catalog library holdings recorded on 3″ × 5″ cards filed alphabetically.

Class number top part of call number which stands for subject matter of the book.

Colophon an inscription describing the type, paper, binding, or other physical components used in producing a book; also the printer's emblem or distinctive mark.

COM catalog (computer output microform) a listing in microform that is generated from computer tapes.

Commands symbols and/or terms used to retrieve computer stored information.

Copyright the legal right to control the production, use, and sale of copies of a literary, musical, or artistic work.

Contemporary belonging to the same time period in history.

Cross reference a reference from one term or word in a book or index to another word or term.

Cumulation an index which is formed as a result of the incorporation of successive parts of elements. All the material is arranged in one alphabet.

Current existing at the present time.

Database units of information which are stored in machine readable form and retrieved by use of a computer.

Dissertation research that is completed in partial fulfillment of the requirement for a doctoral degree.

Edition all copies of a book printed from a single type setting.

End-users persons who use information; used especially to refer to online searching.

Endnotes identification of sources used in a text, placed at the end of the text or, in a book, at the ends of chapters.

Footnotes identification of sources used in a text, placed at the bottom of the page.

Frontispiece illustration or portrait facing the title page of a book.

Glossary a list with definitions of technical or unusual terms used in the text.

Imprint place of publication, publisher, and either publication or copyright date.

Index alphabetical list of the subjects discussed in the book with corresponding page number; also separate publication which points to information found in other sources.

Introduction   describes the subject matter and gives a preliminary statement leading to the main contents of the book.

Italic   kind of type in which the letters usually slope to the right and which is used for emphasis.

Journal   scholarly periodical usually issued monthly or quarterly.

Keyword searching   online catalog searching using non-standardized subject headings.

MARC tapes   machine readable cataloging records on magnetic tapes produced by the Library of Congress.

Microform   printed materials which are reduced in size by photographic means and can only be read with special readers.

Notes   identification of sources used in a text, also explanatory material.

Online catalog   library catalog records in machine readable form which are accessed by use of computers.

Online search   a search that is carried out by means of a computer.

OPAC   acronym for online public access catalog.

Parenthetical references   citations placed in the text and keyed to the list of ''Works Cited.''

Preface   gives the author's purpose in writing the book and acknowledges those persons who have helped in its preparation.

Primary source   a firsthand or eyewitness account of an event.

Reprint   copies of the same edition printed at a later time.

Scope   the range of material covered in a book or article.

Secondary source   literature which analyzes, interprets, relates, or evaluates a primary source or other secondary sources.

See also reference   a listing of additional headings to consult for information.

See reference   a reference from a term that is not used to one that is used.

Serials   publications issued on a continuing basis at regularly stated intervals.

Series   publications similar in content and format.

Short-title   first part of a compound title.

Stacks   groups of shelves on which books are placed in a library.

Subtitle   second part of a compound title which explains the short-title.

Table of Contents   a list of chapters or parts of a book in numerical order with the pages on which they are located.

Thesis   a research project completed in partial fulfillment of the requirements for the master's degree.

Thesis statement   a statement of purpose in a research paper.

Title page   page in front of the book which gives the official author, title, and often the imprint.

Truncation   abbreviation of words in the commands given to search an online database.

Vendor   one who markets databases to subscribers.

Vertical file   files containing ephemeral materials such as pamphlets, pictures, and newspaper clippings.

Volume   written or printed sheets put together to form a book. One book of a series. All the issues of a periodical bound together to make a unit.

Index

Note: Only reference books and indexes that are discussed in the text are listed in this index by title. For additional titles consult the lists at the end of Chapters 6, 7, and 8.